Working with Odoo 10

Second Edition

Configure, manage, and customize Odoo to build professional-level business applications

Greg Moss

BIRMINGHAM - MUMBAI

Working with Odoo 10

Second Edition

First published: August 2015

Second edition: January 2017

Production reference: 1180117

Published by Packt Publishing Ltd.
Livery Place
35 Livery Street
Birmingham
B3 2PB, UK.

ISBN 978-1-78646-268-8

www.packtpub.com

Credits

Author

Greg Moss

Reviewer

Bruce Letterle

Commissioning Editor

Kunal Parikh

Acquisition Editor

Denim Pinto

Content Development Editor

Siddhi Chavan

Technical Editors

Prathamesh Gokarn
Sunith Shetty

Copy Editor

Safis Editing

Project Coordinator

Izzat Contractor

Proofreader

Safis Editing

Indexer

Mariammal Chettiyar

Graphics

Abhinash Sahu

Production Coordinator

Aparna Bhagat

About the Author

Greg Moss has been a Business and Information Systems Consultant for over 25 years. Starting in 1988, Greg began to work extensively in financial and accounting-related applications. He wrote his first custom billing system for a rehabilitation facility at the age of 20. He has worked extensively in the health care, point of sale, manufacturing, telecommunications, entertainment, and service industries.

Greg is a Certified Information Systems Auditor (CISA), a Certified Six Sigma Black Belt, and was the Chief Information Officer for Crownline Boats, Inc. In addition to both Music and Computer Science studies at Southern Illinois University, Greg completed a BS in Business Administration and Information Systems from Walden University. Greg also has an Information Assurance Certification from Carnegie Melon University.

In addition to Odoo, he has experience in a variety of ERP systems and was a Sage Pro partner for several years. Greg is the CEO of First Class Ventures, LLC; the owner of FirstClassComputerConsulting.com and OdooClass.com; and an Odoo Ready Partner.

In Greg's spare time he enjoys playing trumpet, saxophone, keyboard, and guitar with local bands and taking cross-country road trips with his African Grey Parrot, Bibi.

Acknowledgments

I would like to thank my wonderful wife Kelly for all her love and support; my brother Eric, for his kindness, generosity, and always being there for when someone needs him, and my Mom, a lifelong public school teacher who never hesitated to support me in anything that involved learning or creativity.

Many thanks to the great team at Silkworm for being the absolute best.

Special thanks to Diogo Duarte for his professionalism and outstanding contributions to OdooClass.com.

Also, many thanks to all the reviewers, the great people at Packt, and the Odoo community for all their support.

About the Reviewer

Bruce Letterle is a veteran of the IT and web industries, and has worked in this field since 1979. He has graduated from the University of Pittsburgh with a degree in Business Accounting. He has been very active in his church and local youth sports in the Pittsburgh area. He is the founder and managing director of Red Lab Media, a Pittsburgh based provider of web development and marketing services, and he has managed a number of computer integration and web development companies that have always been involved with open source and leading-edge technologies. He has been active with Odoo products since 2010, when they were known as OpenERP.

www.PacktPub.com

For support files and downloads related to your book, please visit www.PacktPub.com.

Did you know that Packt offers eBook versions of every book published, with PDF and ePub files available? You can upgrade to the eBook version at www.PacktPub.com and as a print book customer, you are entitled to a discount on the eBook copy. Get in touch with us at service@packtpub.com for more details.

At www.PacktPub.com, you can also read a collection of free technical articles, sign up for a range of free newsletters and receive exclusive discounts and offers on Packt books and eBooks.

https://www.packtpub.com/mapt

Get the most in-demand software skills with Mapt. Mapt gives you full access to all Packt books and video courses, as well as industry-leading tools to help you plan your personal development and advance your career.

Why subscribe?

- Fully searchable across every book published by Packt
- Copy and paste, print, and bookmark content
- On demand and accessible via a web browser

Customer Feedback

Thank you for purchasing this Packt book. We take our commitment to improving our content and products to meet your needs seriously—that's why your feedback is so valuable. Whatever your feelings about your purchase, please consider leaving a review on this book's Amazon page. Not only will this help us, more importantly it will also help others in the community to make an informed decision about the resources that they invest in to learn. You can also review for us on a regular basis by joining our reviewers' club. **If you're interested in joining, or would like to learn more about the benefits we offer, please contact us**: customerreviews@packtpub.com.

Table of Contents

Preface   1

Chapter 1: Setting Up Odoo 10   9
  Community and Enterprise Editions of Odoo   9
  Getting started with Odoo Online   10
    Taking advantage of Odoo online instant access   10
    Odoo browser requirements   10
    Odoo mobile phone and tablet support   11
    Accessing the Odoo free online trial   11
    Continuing to use the trial version of Odoo   15
    Subscribing to Odoo   15
    Using Odoo without subscription fees   17
  Getting to know the Odoo architecture   17
    Introducing the PostgreSQL database   17
    Writing code with Python   17
    Following the Model-View-Controller design   18
      Designing models   18
      Rendering views   18
      Authoring controllers   18
  Choosing your installation operating system   19
    Choosing a Microsoft Windows Odoo installation   19
      Learning Ubuntu is not required   19
      Introducing Ubuntu   19
    Choosing an Ubuntu Odoo installation   20
    Choosing another OS option for Odoo   20
  Understanding Odoo releases   20
    Upgrading Odoo   21
  Installing Odoo on Windows OS   21
    Performing an all-in-one Odoo installation on Windows   22
    Configuring Postgres on Windows   23
  Installing Odoo on Ubuntu   24
    Modifying the sources.list file   24
      Testing your Odoo installation   25
  Troubleshooting and Odoo management tips   25
    Checking your browser destination   25
    Verifying that the Odoo service is running   25

Checking for the Odoo services running in Windows 26
Checking for Odoo services running in Ubuntu 27
Starting and stopping Odoo services in Ubuntu 27
Finding the primary Odoo log file 27
Modifying the Odoo configuration file 28
Changing port numbers 28
Accessing the database management tools 28
Changing the admin password 29
Finding additional resources on installing Odoo 29
Summary 29
Chapter 2: Installing Your First Application 31
Gathering requirements 31
Implementing Odoo using a modular approach 32
Introducing Silkworm – our real-world case study 32
Creating a new database in Odoo 33
Selecting a database name 34
Loading demonstration data 34
Specifying our default language 35
Choosing an e-mail and password 35
Managing databases in Odoo 35
Installing the Sales Management module 36
Knowing the basic Odoo interface 37
Using the search box 38
Picking different views 38
Creating your first customer 39
Is this customer a company? 40
Entering data into Odoo forms 41
Editing customers sale and purchase 42
Editing customer Accounting 43
Entering a product in Odoo 44
Creating products in Odoo 45
Product Name 46
Can be Sold 46
Can be Purchased 46
Product type 46
Internal Reference 46
Sale price 47
Cost price 47
Nothing in the Sales page 47
Entering a product Invoicing page 47
Invoicing policy 48
Saving the product 48

Setting the company information	48
Saving company information	49
Entering your first sales order	50
Selecting the customer	51
Expiration date	52
Payment terms	52
Entering line items on a quotation sales order	52
Product field	53
Description	53
Delivered and Invoiced	53
Ordered Qty	53
Taxes	54
Unit price	54
Saving the quotation sales order	54
Understanding the sales order workflow	55
Send by Email	55
Print	55
Confirm Sale	55
Cancel	56
Invoicing the sale	56
What do you want to invoice?	57
Creating the invoice	57
Summary	58
Chapter 3: Exploring Customer Relationship Management in Odoo 10	59
Using CRM as a business strategy	60
Managing the customer experience	60
Treating your customer like a real person	60
Using your mission statements and company goals to drive the design of your CRM system	61
Real-world case study – improving customer experience	61
Installing the CRM application	62
Your first look at the CRM Dashboard	63
Assigning the sales representative or account manager	63
Specifying the name of the user	65
Email address	65
Access Rights	65
Sales application settings	65
User: Own Documents Only	66
User: All Documents	66
Manager	66
Language and Timezone	67
Email Messages and Notifications	67
Signature	68

Manually setting the user password	68
Assigning a salesperson to a customer	68
Understanding Your Pipeline	69
Creating a new opportunity	70
Opportunity Title	71
Customer	72
Expected revenue	72
Rating	72
Looking at opportunities in your pipeline	72
Next Activity	74
Expected Closing	74
Tags	74
Email and Phone	74
Internal Notes	74
The Contact Information page	75
Address and Contact Information	75
Mailings	75
Marketing	76
An introduction to sales stages	76
Viewing the details of an opportunity	76
Actions you can take on an opportunity	76
Using Odoo's OpenChatter feature	77
Changing the status of an opportunity	77
Managing the Opportunity	78
Following a business document	79
Modifying the stages of the sale	81
Closing the sale	82
Your opportunity converted to a quotation	83
Leads and opportunities	83
Turning on Leads in Odoo 10	84
Creating Leads in Odoo	84
Converting a lead into an opportunity	86
Using Odoo to schedule calls, meetings, and events	87
Scheduling an event	88
Adding attendees to your meeting	89
Specifying meeting details	90
Specifying tags for your meeting	90
Setting up reminders for your meeting	91
Specifying additional meeting options	91
Summary	93
Chapter 4: Purchasing with Odoo	95
Understanding the overall purchasing process	95
Setting up a vendor	96

Setting up warehouse locations   96
Generating quotations and purchase orders   96
Receiving the product   96
Settling the invoice   97
Installing the purchasing application   97
Setting up your first vendor   98
Designating vendor companies versus individuals   99
Configuring your product for procurement   100
   Supply chain information   101
      Using buy routes   101
      Using Make To Order   101
Purchasing information   101
   Product type   102
   Setting records to active   102
Setting the cost price of the product   103
Assigning vendors to the product   103
   Establishing the vendor   104
   Designating vendor product name and product code   104
   Setting minimum quantity   104
   Calculating delivery time   104
   Setting price and validity   104
Creating your first purchase quotation   105
   Adding products to your request for quotation   107
   Printing RFQs and updating status   107
   Confirming a purchase order   107
Receiving products   109
   Getting ready to receive   109
   Receiving our goods   110
Paying vendor bills   111
Summary   116
Chapter 5: Making Goods with Manufacturing Resource Planning   117
Creating manufacturing orders   117
Producing the product   118
Delivering the order   118
Defining the workflow for your business   118
A real-world example of producing a custom-printed t-shirt   118
Installing Manufacturing Resource Planning   119
   Creating your first manufacturing order   119
      What product are we going to manufacture? 121
Building your bill of materials   123
   Confirming production   125
   Checking availability   126

Producing the product	128
Analyzing stock valuation	129
Managing production by work orders	130
Creating a work center	132
Setting General Information	133
Efficiency Factor	133
Capacity	133
Overall Equipment Effectiveness (OEE) target	133
Time before and after production	134
Creating routing orders	134
Assigning the routing to a bill of materials	136
Creating a manufacturing order with routing and a work center	137
Summary	141
Chapter 6: Configuring Accounting Finance	143
Defining the chart of accounts for your business	144
Installing the Accounting and Finance application	144
Viewing the current chart of accounts	145
Getting more information on a specific account	146
Learning how transactions in Odoo get posted to accounts	147
Following transactions through the sales and accounts receivable process	150
Viewing the transactions created by validating the invoice	153
Practice posting transactions and tracking the results	157
Setting up your own accounts	157
Specifying a new account for your product category	159
Examining the available legal reports in Odoo	161
Creating journal entries	162
Summary	163
Chapter 7: Administering an Odoo Installation	165
Basic considerations for an Odoo administration	165
Have an implementation strategy	166
Development, staging, and production servers	166
Clear documentation of all Odoo configurations	166
Focusing on business continuity	167
Backing up your Odoo database	168
Restoring an Odoo database	170
Administering users in Odoo	170
Selecting a user to administer	171
Managing user preferences	172
Understanding groups in Odoo	174
Understanding group inheritance in Odoo	177

Defining menus for your group	178
Understanding Access Rights in Odoo	179
Understanding group rules in Odoo	181
Internationalization in Odoo	183
Configuring language translation	183
Using translation features to customize Odoo for your business	185
International currencies	187
Purchasing in a different currency	191
Managing supplier price lists	192
Managing sequences in Odoo	195
Multiple companies in Odoo	197
Setting up a second company in Odoo	199
Implementing a multi-company solution	200
Summary	200
Chapter 8: Implementing the Human Resources Application	203
Modular approach to Human Resources	203
Installing the Employee Directory	203
Creating a new employee	205
Department	206
Job Title	207
Manager and Coach	208
Employee personal information	208
HR Settings	209
Managing departments	210
Timesheets	210
Leave Management	213
Creating a leave request	213
Leave Type	214
Duration	215
Mode	215
Employee	215
Department	215
Submitting for approval	215
Approving leave requests	216
Recruitment Process	217
Recruiting for a new job position	218
Creating an employment application	220
Hiring employees	221
Summary	222
Chapter 9: Understanding Project Management	223
Basics of Project Management	223
Installing the Project Management application	224

Understanding the Project dashboard	225
Real-world project example for a customer	225
Creating our first project	226
Understanding project stages	228
Defining project tasks	229
Creating additional tasks	231
Completing project tasks	233
Calculating project costs and time	234
Summary	235
Chapter 10: Creating Advanced Searches and Dashboards	237
Determining the search requirements for your business	237
Creating a database with demonstration data	238
Accessing the database manager	238
Searching in Odoo	240
Using filters in list views	243
Grouping information	244
Performing a custom search	246
Specifying multiple advanced searches	248
Saving your favorite filters	248
Creating custom dashboards in Odoo 10	249
Summary	253
Chapter 11: Building a Website with Odoo	255
What is a CMS?	255
WordPress	256
Joomla	256
Drupal	256
Evoq or DotNetNuke	256
Why use Odoo Website Builder for your CMS?	257
Potential advantages to using Odoo as a CMS	257
Current limitations of using Odoo as a CMS	257
Deciding what is best for your company	258
Backing up the website you make in your Odoo database	258
Installing the Odoo Website Builder	258
Saving your web page	264
Previewing our website on a mobile device	266
Adding new pages and menus to your website	267
Adding a new page	268
Creating our frequently asked questions web page	269
Managing menus on your website	269

Adding a new menu to your website 270
Changing themes in Odoo 271
Promoting your website 272
Specifying keywords for your website 274
Creating a title and description for your website 274
Summary 276
Chapter 12: Implementing E-Commerce with Odoo 277
E-commerce and Odoo 278
Popular e-commerce platforms 278
Magento 278
Volusion 278
Shopify 278
Yahoo's Aabaco Small Business 279
Odoo as an e-commerce platform 279
Installing Odoo e-commerce 279
Basics of Odoo e-commerce 281
Setting the product price from the e-commerce page 283
Adding a picture to your product 283
Describing the product 286
Publishing your product 286
Additional configuration options for your Odoo shop 287
Modifying the order of the products on the store 288
Setting up product variants 290
Advanced e-commerce product options 293
Alternative products 293
Accessory products 294
Looking at the shopping cart 294
Seeing the draft sales order in Odoo 295
Checking out 296
Adding PayPal as a payment processor 298
Summary 300
Chapter 13: Customizing Odoo for Your Business 301
Understanding the Odoo architecture 302
Models 302
Views 302
Actions 303
Activating developer mode 303
Getting out of developer mode 304
Backing up your database 305
Restoring a database in Odoo 306

Adding a custom field to Odoo	307
Viewing the model in Odoo	308
Creating a new field in the sale order model	310
Editing the form view	312
Customizing search operations in Odoo	315
Specifying additional fields you want Odoo to use in the search	315
Editing the search view	316
Understanding actions	318
Create a new menu	320
Summary	321
Chapter 14: Modifying Documents and Reports	323
Getting the skills required to modify reports	323
What is the QWeb template framework?	324
Company report configuration	324
Problems with Wktohtmlpdf installation	325
Specifying the paper format for your reports	328
Modifying the internal report header using QWeb	328
Making our first simple change	330
Learning how Odoo organizes reports	331
Understanding the report types	333
Looking at the definition for the Sales Order form	333
Creating a new QWeb report in Odoo	338
Learning more about the power of QWeb templates	338
Using a t-if to create a dynamic QWeb template report	339
Summary	340
Chapter 15: Discovering Custom Odoo Modules	341
Exploring the Odoo application and module directory	342
Building our first Odoo module	343
Preparing your basic development environment	343
Finding your Odoo configuration file and installation	343
Specifying a custom directory to hold our Odoo modules	345
Contents of your module directory	346
Creating and editing the files	346
The __init__.py file	347
The __manifest__.py file	347
Extending an Odoo model in silkworm.py	349
Using a module to add custom fields to a model	350
Inheriting from the sales application in Odoo	350
Python conventions	351
Adding the fields to our sales order view	351
Getting ready to install our module	354

Troubleshooting your module installation	356
Using a module to add a filter to a search view	358
Adding the code to create the rush order filter	359
Creating the filter	360
Using Odoo to create websites and web services	360
Creating an XML template	362
Integrating with the Odoo API	363
Connecting to the API	363
Filtering and returning records through the API	364
Using the search/read method	364
Summary	364
Chapter 16: Comparative Analysis of Community vs Enterprise Edition	365
Getting an overview of Community and Enterprise Editions	366
Using the Odoo runbot to compare Odoo versions	367
Launching Odoo Community Edition from Odoo runbot	368
Launching Odoo 10 Enterprise from Odoo runbot	369
Examining the Odoo Enterprise interface	370
Examining Odoo 10 Enterprise Accounting	370
Looking at Odoo 10's dynamic Accounting reports	372
Using the bank integration features of Enterprise Edition	374
Sales Management enhancements	375
Automating calls with VoIP integration	375
Understanding the Subscriptions application	376
Understanding the available shipping connectors in Enterprise	378
Understanding the available manufacturing applications in Odoo	380
Product Lifecycle Management (PLM)	381
Handling maintenance requests	383
Managing production quality in Odoo	385
Summary	387
Appendix: Locating additional Odoo resources	389
Locating essential Odoo documentation	389
Visiting the official Odoo help forum	389
The Odoo Community Association (OCA)	390
Finding Odoo applications and modules	390
Getting the latest Odoo 10 release notes	390
Downloading Odoo from GitHub	390
Locating resources on Ubuntu	391
Official Ubuntu website	391
Direct download of the Ubuntu server or desktop	391
Official Ubuntu documentation	391

Getting access to additional developer documentation   391
    Getting quick access to Odoo installations using Odoo Runbot   392
Finding Postgres resources   392
    Official Postgres website   392
    Downloading Postgres   392
    Postgres documentation   393
Locating Python resources   393
    Official Python website   393
    Downloading Python   393
    Python documentation   393
Finding XML resources   394
    World Wide Web Consortium XML resource page   394
    XML tutorials and documentation   394
    Alternative Reporting solutions   394
    OCA Alternative Reporting Engine   394
    Aeroo Reports   395
    Jaspersoft reports   395
       Community edition of JasperReports Server   395
       Community edition of iReport Designer   395
    Pentaho/Kettle   395
Index   397

Preface

Working with Odoo 10, Second Edition provides a comprehensive walkthrough for installing, configuring, and implementing Odoo in real-world business environments. This book will assist you in understanding the value of Enterprise Resource Planning (ERP) systems and best practice approaches for getting a system up and running in your organization. For those that are new to ERP systems, this book will serve as an introduction so that you will be better prepared for understanding more advanced ERP concepts. If you are already experienced in ERP systems this book will give you an overview of the primary applications for Odoo and how those applications can be used in a real business environment.

Odoo is a very feature filled business application framework with literally hundreds of applications and modules available. We have done our best in this book to cover the most essential features of the Odoo applications you are most likely to use in your business. Unfortunately, there are just not enough pages to cover more advanced topics. In the `Appendix` we have included additional resources you can look to for more advanced subjects.

After the book is released, be sure to check for online updates in which we can cover more advanced subjects.

Also, PACKT offers other Odoo books that cover more advanced Odoo topics:

What this book covers

The book is divided into three sections:

1. Installation of Odoo and the basics for implementing Odoo in your business (chapters 1 through 5)
2. Introduction to accounting and finance setup and modules to help your business run more efficiently (chapters 6 through 8)
3. Advanced configurations and customization of Odoo (chapters 9 through 15)
4. Comprehensive comparison between Odoo Community and Odoo Enterprise (chapter 16)

Now let's discuss in some detail what each chapter will cover:

Chapter 1, *Setting Up Odoo 10*, gets you started right away by showing how you can use online without any setup. Just open up your browser and you are ready to get going. Next the chapter goes on to cover the different installation types and prerequisites for both Windows and Ubuntu. Instruction is provided on finding the right download package and setting up Odoo on your own server. The chapter then goes into the basics for configuring Odoo. At the end of the chapter is a useful collection of tips on how to troubleshooting your Odoo installation.

Chapter 2, *Installing Your First Application*, begins by introducing you to the real-world case study that will be used as an example throughout the book. We continue by learning how to create the company database and configure the basic company settings required to quickly get your first Odoo system up and running. The first module, Sales Management, will be installed, and we will walk through the steps of entering a customer and a product. The chapter concludes by entering a sales order and completing the sale and producing an invoice.

Chapter 3, *Exploring Customer Relationship Management in Odoo 10*, starts with a basic overview of CRM systems and their importance in today's modern business environment. After we cover the installation of the CRM module, a lead is entered for our sample company. We will demonstrate CRM workflow by turning the lead into a customer. Next, a quote is generated for our newly acquired customer, and a call is scheduled for follow-up using Odoo's meeting functionality. We also cover the Open Chatter feature that is used throughout Odoo to provide notes and messages associated with Odoo documents.

Chapter 4, *Purchasing with Odoo*, shows us how to install the purchasing module, setup suppliers, and begin purchasing and receiving products in Odoo. Later in the chapter we learn how to tie purchasing into sales orders to automatically generate draft purchase orders based on your business requirements.

Chapter 5, *Making Goods with Manufacturing Resource Planning*, begins to explore some of the primary functionality of ERP systems for manufacturing operations. You will learn how to setup your manufacturing orders and define bill of materials to specify the raw materials that will go into your final products. Manufacturing operations can then be extended with routing and work centers to provide you more control in tracking time and resources.

Chapter 6, *Configuring Accounting Finance*, discusses the Accounts Receivable and Accounts Payable basic functions. Next we will introduce the chart of accounts and discover how to set up fiscal periods. This chapter will also include the basic accounting reports.

Chapter 7, *Administering an Odoo Installation*, begins by discussing overall considerations for implementing Odoo into a business environment. This includes advice on server configurations, documenting your processes, and the importance of considering business continuity. We then go into how to manage users, groups and setup security roles to manage access to various applications within Odoo. Finally we look how to implement Internationalization for multiple languages and currencies.

Chapter 8, *Implementing the Human Resources Application*, begins by installing the basic HR modules and going over the employee directory. Other topics in the chapter will include time-sheets, recruitment process, and leave management. At the end of the chapter we look at how to hire employees using the tools in Odoo.

Chapter 9, *Understanding Project Management*, covers the features of the Project Management module in Odoo. We will create a project, see how to enter tasks and tie a project to a specific customer. Next, team members are assigned to the project, and we configure task stages. We then will go over real-world examples of using the Project Management module to more easily manage complex orders and customer needs. Finally we see how Project Management can be used along with analytic accounting provide better reporting.

Chapter 10, *Creating Advanced Searches and Dashboards*, demonstrates how to utilize the advanced search features and configure custom dashboards in Odoo. By the end of the chapter, the reader with be able to create and save custom searches to re-use later as well as add search results to dashboards.

Chapter 11, *Building a Website with Odoo*, is dedicated to exploring Odoo's powerful new website building platform. At the beginning of the chapter we look at what a Content Management System (CMS) is and some of the other popular website building platforms. We follow along with Odoo's website building tutorial and then look at the features that can be used to promote your website right from within Odoo.

Chapter 12, *Implementing E-Commerce with Odoo*, builds on the previous website chapter by adding a fully functioning online shopping cart to the website. We see how to publish products to the website and the various options to change their appearance. Midway through the chapter we cover product variants that adds additional flexibility to how you manage your products within Odoo. Finally we conclude by examining how to setup a payment processor to take payment online through PayPal.

Chapter 13, *Customizing Odoo for Your Business,* explains how to enter developer mode for making a variety of custom changes to Odoo. We will walk through how to make a backup of the Odoo database and how to restore that database using the manage database tools in Odoo. Next, we will go step-by-step on how to customize Odoo by adding fields to the database and ultimately to your forms and views.

Chapter 14, *Modifying Documents and Reports,* goes over the basic reporting options that allow you to change the footer and access the QWeb source for your internal and external reports. Next we see how to modify existing reports in Odoo.

Chapter 15, *Discovering Custom Odoo Modules,* introduces the process of developing custom solutions in Odoo. We build on what we have learned in customizing Odoo and create a module that will persist our custom field and views within our module. You will then learn how to create a simple web page that accesses the Odoo framework. Finally we go over the basics of how to utilize the Odoo API

Chapter 16, *Comparative Analysis of Community vs Enterprise Edition,* explains the primary differences between Odoo Community and Odoo Enterprise. Moving further we take a look at the powerful dynamic accounting reports as well as the bank account integration. Next, we examined the sales application and studied how Odoo Enterprise offers VoIP integration as well as a subscriptions application. Finally, we will learn about Odoo's new manufacturing applications that are only available in the Enterprise edition.

Appendix, *Locating additional Odoo resources,* includes a list of resources that can extend your knowledge in supporting an Odoo installation

What you need for this book

You should have Odoo version 10 installed on your system. It can be downloaded from the following link `https://github.com/odoo/odoo`.

Most often it is installed in VMware or on in the cloud like AWS.

1. Chapter 1, *Setting up Odoo 10,* in the book provides the basic Odoo Installation for both Windows and Ubuntu
2. Odoo now provides quality documentation on how to install Odoo on a variety of platforms: `https://www.odoo.com/documentation/10.0/setup/install.htm l`

Once Odoo is installed, no other software installation is required throughout the book.

To get the most out of this book you should understand basic business operations. For example, you should know the purpose of a sales order and a purchase order. The reader should also have basic computer skills for understanding file systems and installing software. For more advanced customization topics in the book, the reader should have a basic knowledge of databases and programming concepts.

Who this book is for

This book is for everyone who is interested in implementing an ERP system in a business organization. If you are an IT professional looking to get a functional understanding of Odoo, then this book is for you. This book is also appropriate for business and operations managers who wish to get a comprehensive understanding of Odoo and how it can be used to improve business processes.

Conventions

In this book, you will find a number of text styles that distinguish between different kinds of information. Here are some examples of these styles and an explanation of their meaning.

Code words in text, database table names, folder names, filenames, file extensions, pathnames, dummy URLs, user input, and Twitter handles are shown as follows: "We will now look at the Odoo configuration file so we can find the directory for our Odoo installation and modify the addons_path to contain our new directory."

A block of code is set as follows:

```
{
    'name': 'Screen Printing',
    'version': '1.0',
    'description': """
    This module adds functionality for screen printing companies
    """,
    'author': 'Greg Moss',
    'depends': ['base','sale'],
    'data': ['silkworm_view.xml'],
    'demo': [],
    'installable': True,
    'auto_install': False,
}
```

Any command-line input or output is written as follows:

```
sudo nano /etc/odoo/odoo.conf
```

New terms and **important words** are shown in bold. Words that you see on the screen, for example, in menus or dialog boxes, appear in the text like this: "For our example, let's go ahead and install the **CRM** application by clicking on the **CRM** button."

Warnings or important notes appear in a box like this.

Tips and tricks appear like this.

Reader feedback

Feedback from our readers is always welcome. Let us know what you think about this book-what you liked or disliked. Reader feedback is important for us as it helps us develop titles that you will really get the most out of.

To send us general feedback, simply e-mail feedback@packtpub.com, and mention the book's title in the subject of your message.

If there is a topic that you have expertise in and you are interested in either writing or contributing to a book, see our author guide at www.packtpub.com/authors.

Customer support

Now that you are the proud owner of a Packt book, we have a number of things to help you to get the most from your purchase.

Downloading the color images of this book

We also provide you with a PDF file that has color images of the screenshots/diagrams used in this book. The color images will help you better understand the changes in the output. You can download this file from `https://www.packtpub.com/sites/default/files/down loads/WorkingwithOdoo10SecondEdition_ColorImages.pdf`.

Errata

Although we have taken every care to ensure the accuracy of our content, mistakes do happen. If you find a mistake in one of our books-maybe a mistake in the text or the code-we would be grateful if you could report this to us. By doing so, you can save other readers from frustration and help us improve subsequent versions of this book. If you find any errata, please report them by visiting `http://www.packtpub.com/submit-errata`, selecting your book, clicking on the **Errata Submission Form** link, and entering the details of your errata. Once your errata are verified, your submission will be accepted and the errata will be uploaded to our website or added to any list of existing errata under the Errata section of that title.

To view the previously submitted errata, go to `https://www.packtpub.com/books/conten t/support` and enter the name of the book in the search field. The required information will appear under the **Errata** section.

Piracy

Piracy of copyrighted material on the Internet is an ongoing problem across all media. At Packt, we take the protection of our copyright and licenses very seriously. If you come across any illegal copies of our works in any form on the Internet, please provide us with the location address or website name immediately so that we can pursue a remedy.

Please contact us at `copyright@packtpub.com` with a link to the suspected pirated material.

We appreciate your help in protecting our authors and our ability to bring you valuable content.

Questions

If you have a problem with any aspect of this book, you can contact us at `questions@packtpub.com`, and we will do our best to address the problem.

1
Setting Up Odoo 10

Odoo is a powerful set of open source business applications built on the OpenObject framework. When you first install Odoo, the only functionality you will have is limited messaging options between users. From there, Odoo allows you to install the modules you need, as you need them. This flexibility makes Odoo much more accessible than many business software solutions.

In this chapter, we will get started working with Odoo by covering the installation and the basics of setting up an Odoo database.

The topics we will cover include:

- Exploring Odoo Online
- Setting up a trial company
- Installing Odoo on Windows and Ubuntu
- Troubleshooting and configuring your installation

Community and Enterprise Editions of Odoo

Beginning with Odoo 9, Odoo SA started releasing two versions of Odoo; a **Community Edition** and an **Enterprise Edition**. The Community Edition is free, open source, and primarily supported by the Odoo community. Odoo Enterprise, while also open source, requires a license based on the number of users. More recently, Odoo pricing for the Enterprise version varies depending on region.

Odoo Enterprise offers an alternative (arguably better) user interface. Additionally, there is better functionality in some applications as well as support by SA, and perhaps most critical of all, migration to the new releases of Odoo. More information on the differences between Odoo Community Edition and Odoo Enterprise Edition is available in the Odoo Enterprise Chapter 16, *Comparative Analysis of Community vs Enterprise Edition* .

This book primarily targets the Community Edition of Odoo.

Getting started with Odoo Online

Not long ago, nearly all companies kept their primary information systems in-house. This approach requires, not only a lot of capital expense in purchasing servers and software licenses, but also creates a lot of responsibility and risk in backing up data and ensuring business continuity. Today, more and more companies are choosing to host their business applications in online networks commonly called the cloud. Odoo allows you the flexibility of both options–either hosting on your own hardware, or utilizing Odoo's online software services.

Taking advantage of Odoo online instant access

The best thing about accessing Odoo online is that you can jump in and start using the software right away. You don't have to decide what operating system to use. You don't have to install any software at all. Just enter the URL into your web browser and you are ready to get started.

Another added benefit of taking this approach is, you will verify that your web browser is up-to-date and compatible with the latest version of Odoo. So even if you intend to install Odoo on your own hardware, it is still worth taking a minute to test out the online trial version of Odoo. Expect to put a great deal of time into determining which Odoo applications are right for your company.

Taking a few hours to use the Odoo online version is time well spent and you can put off installing Odoo until you are more certain it is the right software for your business.

Use the Odoo trial edition to verify browser compatibility with any older machines.

Odoo browser requirements

Odoo is designed to run on a variety of modern web browsers. Supported browsers include:

- Google Chrome (recommended)
- Firefox
- Internet Explorer
- Safari

 Macintosh users will need to make sure they are running **Mac OS X** or above. Users running older Macintosh systems are currently having difficulties running Odoo version 7. Also, in my experience, Google Chrome tends to offer the best experience in working with Odoo. Firefox is also often recommended by others in the Odoo community.

Odoo mobile phone and tablet support

Beginning with Odoo 8, Odoo includes native support for mobile phones and tablets. This has been further improved in Odoo 10. Menus are designed to flow and format properly. The new website application even includes a preview within the portal administration to emulate how the site would appear on a mobile phone. While you still suffer many of the limitations that come with a small screen size, the applications are functional and make it even easier for developers to create mobile Odoo applications.

Odoo's mobile application support covers both the Android and Apple iOS platforms. Make sure, however, that for any processes you intend to implement for your business, you test all processes thoroughly for both desktop and any mobile solutions. The smaller screen sizes might make some data unreadable or very awkward to work with.

Accessing the Odoo free online trial

Accessing the online trial version of Odoo online could not be simpler. Just open up your browser and navigate to `https://www.odoo.com/trial`.

 Please be aware that Odoo online's trial is the Enterprise Edition of Odoo. While very similar to the Community Edition, the interface will be slightly different.

You will then be prompted to choose one of Odoo's primary business applications as shown in the following screenshot:

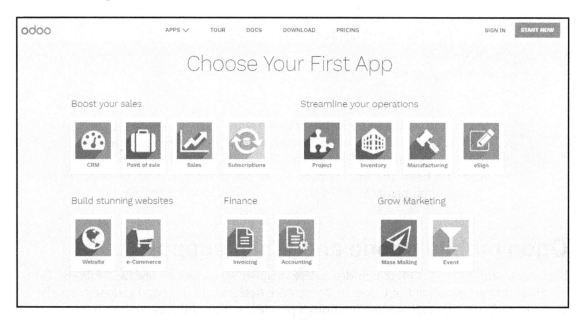

Don't worry, you can add more applications later.

Clicking on the appropriate button for the application immediately begins installing your own unique Odoo instance.

For our example, let's go ahead and install the **CRM** application by clicking on the **CRM** button:

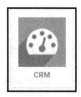

Next you will be taken to a simple sign up page:

After filling out the form, simply click **Start Now**. Be patient as it can take thirty seconds or longer for the servers to build the database and bring up the starting page. When the installation is complete, Odoo automatically signs you in so you can begin trying out the software. The goal of this approach is to get users to directly start using the software right away and avoid having to fill out lengthy forms or create logins and passwords to begin using the software.

It really is just one click and you have your own version of Odoo to play with:

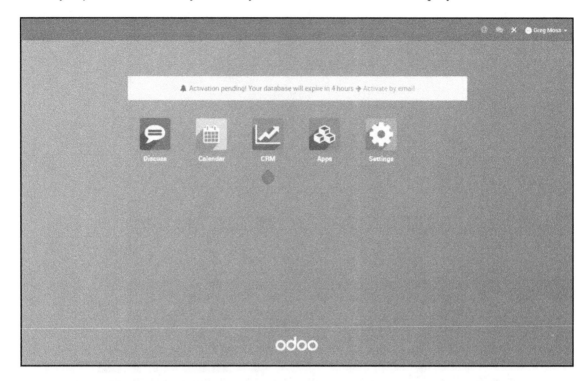

The screen now contains the Odoo dashboard for the Enterprise Edition. Please be aware that this will look a lot different to the Community Edition of Odoo even though they are very similar in terms of functionality.

We will discuss the CRM application in detail in Chapter 3, *Exploring Customer Relationship Management in Odoo 10*.

Take a few minutes to look around in Odoo to get familiar with the interface. You don't have to worry about breaking anything or doing anything wrong. If you run into problems or get confused, just close your web browser and try again.

 This is a demonstration and will only last for one four-hour session. If you close your browser, you will lose your setup and have to start over again.

Continuing to use the trial version of Odoo

At the very top of the Odoo application, just under the address bar in the browser, you will see a message that informs you of how much longer your trial version of Odoo will run before you need to register. Also, remember that it is possible to lose this instance of Odoo before the time runs out:

> 🔔 Activation pending! Your database will expire in about 4 hours → Activate by email

Clicking on the **Activate by email** link will send an e-mail to the e-mail address that you have filled out with a link to activate your Odoo database. Currently, Odoo lets you use Odoo for free as long as you only install one application.

Odoo SA has experimented quite a bit with different trial terms so do not be surprised if the trial options are slightly different by the time you are reading this.

Subscribing to Odoo

You can use one Odoo application for free without subscribing. If you wish to install more applications (as you likely will), you must subscribe to Odoo in order to keep using their enterprise cloud hosted version of the software. The first two users of Odoo are free indefinitely.

This means you can sign up and continue using Odoo with just two users without having to pay any monthly fees. For additional users, the current pricing is $25 per month, per user at the time of writing. Each application you use will also incur a monthly cost depending upon the specific application.

Below is the **Odoo Online Pricing calculator** in December 2016 in the United States:

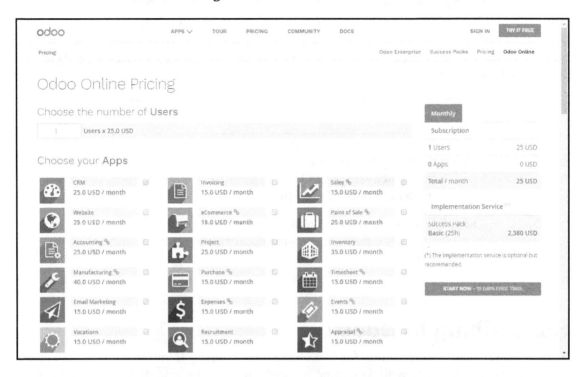

You can locate the **Odoo Online Pricing** page at: `https://www.odoo.com/pricing-online`.

Odoo Online is priced for employees that use the applications. You are not charged for customers or suppliers that access Odoo through the web portal.

Depending on your requirements, an Odoo subscription might be a good decision. Installing and maintaining an Odoo installation takes a degree of expertise and has risks for production systems. You must maintain adequate disaster recovery procedures in case of server crashes or hard drive failures. There are also complexities in applying bug fixes and migrating to newer versions of Odoo. This book will help you with many of these tasks. Yet, it can be quite convenient to have an Odoo subscription so you can focus on the functional, rather than the technical, aspects of working with Odoo.

Using Odoo without subscription fees

If you choose not to pay the subscription fee, do not fear! The remainder of this chapter will assist you with installing Odoo on your own hardware.

Getting to know the Odoo architecture

Setting up and managing an Odoo installation will require a basic understanding of the components that make up Odoo. Every business system has a set of technologies and underlying software platforms that are required for the system to function. Fortunately, unless you plan to customize Odoo, you only need to understand the very basics of the Odoo architecture to complete a successful installation.

 In this book, we provide a basic overview of the Odoo architecture. If you wish to get more detailed documentation on the Odoo architecture and technical documentation visit
https://www.odoo.com/documentation/10.0/.

Introducing the PostgreSQL database

Like most ERP systems, Odoo has specific database requirements. In this case, it is PostgreSQL. PostgreSQL is an open source, cross-platform **Object Relational Database Management System** (**ORDMS**). While not popular on the scale of Microsoft SQL Server or MySQL, PostgreSQL is an enterprise-class database server with many advanced features. In fact, PostgreSQL stacks up very well against far more expensive databases such as Microsoft SQL Server and Oracle database.

PostgreSQL runs on every major operating system. For most Odoo installations, Ubuntu is the operating system of choice. However, PostgreSQL will also run quite well under other versions of Linux, Microsoft Windows, and even Mac OS X.

You can learn more about PostgreSQL at: http://www.postgresql.org/.

Writing code with Python

The primary programming language of Odoo is Python. Like the other technologies underlying Odoo, the Python language is open source and runs on all the major contemporary operating systems. It is an extremely popular programming language which makes it very easy to find resources to help you get started.

You can learn more about the Python programming language at: `http://python.org/`.

Following the Model-View-Controller design

Odoo is built upon a **Model-View-Controller** (**MVC**) architecture. One of the primary goals of this architecture is to separate the visual display of the information from the business rules and management of the underlying data. For example, if you need to change the way data is organized in the model, it is desirable not to have to make dramatic changes to how you view the data. This is true for maintaining flexibility in viewing data. Today, it is common to have many different client applications sharing the same underlying data.

Designing models

The model essentially is the data that makes up your Odoo installation, which is stored in the PostgreSQL database. Odoo is unique, in that, database structures are typically defined by the Odoo modules at the time they are installed. The Odoo framework takes the model definitions and automatically creates the necessary table structures inside of the PostgreSQL database. Furthermore, a web interface in Odoo allows administrators to easily extend the Odoo data model in a variety of ways without having to modify the Odoo source code.

Rendering views

Each view in Odoo is defined in XML documents. The Odoo framework is responsible for rendering these view files in a web browser. Alternative views can be built to render Odoo functionality upon other platforms such as mobile devices.

Authoring controllers

The controller component of the architecture is where the business logic and workflow rules of the Odoo application are applied. The controller components in Odoo are written in Python code and stored as objects in Odoo modules.

Choosing your installation operating system

In this section, we will discuss some of the advantages and disadvantages of choosing Ubuntu or Windows for your first Odoo installation.

Choosing a Microsoft Windows Odoo installation

For the most part, Ubuntu has been the platform of choice for most Odoo installations. However, there are some reasons why you might choose to run Odoo under a Windows installation.

Some of you, after buying this book, might have already jumped ahead and installed Odoo on their Microsoft Windows computer. So, for you go-getters, that working installation of Odoo might function just fine for researching and testing its features. Often the Windows all-in-one installer provides a simple method to get Odoo up and running in a snap on your hardware. Basically, you do not have to install a new operating system.

Learning Ubuntu is not required

If you are familiar with Windows and have no Ubuntu experience, you might get going a little faster by sticking with a Windows install for your first setup. Downloading and installing modules and making changes to configuration files will be much easier if you are familiar with the operating system.

Introducing Ubuntu

While Microsoft Windows does not really need an introduction, it is probably worth giving a brief introduction to Ubuntu. In short, Ubuntu (pronounced oo-BOON-too) is a very popular open source operating system based on the Linux kernel. It has enjoyed increasing popularity because it is easy to install and very stable. Ubuntu can be installed either as a server operating system without a graphical interface or as a desktop operating system with a graphical interface that closely resembles Windows.

You can learn more about the Ubuntu operating system and why it is so popular at: http://www.ubuntu.com/.

Choosing an Ubuntu Odoo installation

It is generally accepted that Ubuntu is the recommended operating system for running a production installation of Odoo. There are several reasons why this is true:

- **Ubuntu is the primary target platform**: While Odoo is released for Windows and still well-supported, the Ubuntu installation continues to be favored. The development team for Odoo works primarily with Ubuntu for bug fixes and platform releases. It can be expected that for the most part, Odoo development will be optimized around Ubuntu, not Windows or Mac.
- **Ubuntu is open source**: Installing Odoo on any Windows operating system is going to require a license from Microsoft. While using Odoo on your Windows PC or Mac is a viable and perhaps desirable solution for testing and development, it is unlikely you will want to run Odoo on a Windows desktop system for any production environment. Why? Well, this requires Windows Server, which has much higher license costs than desktop editions. With an Ubuntu installation, you get an entirely open source and virtually cost-free solution.
- **Ubuntu has additional scalability options**: It is possible to configure a more scalable solution under Ubuntu than what you can currently configure under Microsoft Windows Server.
- **Ubuntu has strong community support for Odoo**: The fact is that a vast majority of the production installations of Odoo are running under Ubuntu. When you run into trouble or management issues with your Odoo installation, you may find it easier to get assistance if you are running an Ubuntu installation.

Choosing another OS option for Odoo

Although this book will focus on Windows and Ubuntu installations, you do have several other options. In the past, Odoo has been deployed under a variety of Linux distributions and even the Mac OS. There are also many community members actively developing client frontends for mobile platforms such as Google's Android OS.

Understanding Odoo releases

When deploying an Odoo system, it is important to understand the various Odoo versions as well as the release and upgrade policies. There is currently one major release for versions 8.0, 9.0, and 10.0 as well as a master branch, that is the latest development version, which will soon become Odoo Version 11.0. The stable versions are the standard support versions of Odoo, and typically, the ones you should choose to install for most situations. The master version is the development version and will often contain bugs and unfinished features. This is primarily downloaded by developers or those who wish to get a look at the latest features.

Upgrading Odoo

The goal of the Odoo development team is to release two stable version upgrades each year. Odoo further labels some stable versions as **Long Term Support** (**LTS**) versions. These releases are supported by Odoo for those that have an Odoo Enterprise support contract. For any production environment, it is smart to choose an LTS version. Most importantly, installing an LTS release of Odoo will make bug fixes and patches much easier to implement.

 At the time of writing this, the most recent stable LTS version is version 10.0.

Installing Odoo on Windows OS

We begin our installation by locating the packages that are currently available to install. You can find the current list at: `http://nightly.odoo.com/`.

Odoo Nightly builds

Builds

Every night, a new set of packages is generated for the branches listed below. This set consists of **deb** and **rpm** packages for Debian and RedHat distributions, an **exe** package for Windows and a **source** package.

10 (stable) - Community Edition
Odoo 10 was released in October 2016 and is supported until Odoo 13 - the recommended version.

9 (stable) - Community Edition
Odoo 9 was released in October 2015 and is supported until Odoo 12.

8 (stable)
OpenERP 8 was released in September 2014 and is supported until Odoo 11.

master (dev) - Community Edition
This branch contains experimental features - for testing only.

Check out our installation and deployment guides.

The preceding screenshot is the **Odoo Nightly builds** page that is the jumping off point for downloading the source files for installation.

The examples and case studies in this book use Odoo 10.0. This means you should select the 10.0 (stable) version of Odoo to download. You can navigate directly to the Odoo 10.0 downloads here: `http://nightly.odoo.com/10.0/nightly/`.

Index of /10.0/nightly/

../		
deb/	19-Dec-2016 02:19	-
exe/	19-Dec-2016 02:47	-
rpm/	19-Dec-2016 02:28	-
src/	19-Dec-2016 02:14	-

It is entirely possible that Odoo will change the URL as new versions are released. To best follow the examples in this book, download a 10.x installation of Odoo.

Windows installations use the EXE packages. Click on the `exe` directory to get the list of downloads that are available.

Naturally, the specific download packages are going to change on a nightly basis.

The latest version of the stable LTS release will contain the most current Odoo build with bug fixes included and will appear at the bottom of the list. By the way, the upload dates you'll see are in **Coordinated Universal Time (UTC)** and therefore, might be many hours ahead of your time zone, especially if you live in the Western Hemisphere.

Click the latest EXE file to download the latest build to your computer.

Performing an all-in-one Odoo installation on Windows

Installing Odoo using the all-in-one package is very simple. After the package has finished downloading, double-click on the `exe` file to begin the installation wizard.

The first screen will prompt you to select the language for your install.

After you have selected the language and clicked on **OK**, the wizard will continue with the installation. From here, everything will continue like a normal Windows installation.

 I highly recommend that you choose the **Custom install**, so you can select the directory for installation. The default directory name contains the lengthy build number making it rather difficult to work with in the command prompt.

Configuring Postgres on Windows

During the install, you will be asked to provide information for the PostgreSQL connection.

It is recommended that you change the username and password for security purposes. The default username/password is shown in the preceding screenshot. These values will be written into the Odoo configuration file. The username and password provided will be the administration credentials for the PostgreSQL database, so be sure to remember them.

After the wizard is complete, if you leave **Start Odoo** checked and then click on **Finish**, Odoo should open up in your default browser.

If Odoo fails to launch, you can look at the Troubleshooting Odoo Installations section later in this chapter for solutions to some of the problems commonly encountered during installation.

Installing Odoo on Ubuntu

This book will walk you through the installation procedure for Odoo on Ubuntu using the latest all-in-one nightly package. Depending on your Ubuntu installation and how you want to work with Odoo, there are alternative installation methods.

At the time of writing, Odoo is most commonly installed on Ubuntu version 16.04.

Modifying the sources.list file

Installing Odoo in Ubuntu is easy when you use the **Debian** repository. In order to perform these operations you may have to be the root user. If you have an account that has the permissions to do so you can temporarily change to the root user by entering `sudo -s`.

For better security and to guarantee you are installing the correct package, Odoo now signs their distributions. The following command adds the correct key to your Ubuntu installation so that it will recognize the Odoo package:

```
wget -O - https://nightly.odoo.com/odoo.key | apt-key add -
```

Next we want to add the distribution to the `/etc/apt/sources.list` file with the following command line: `echo "deb http://nightly.odoo.com/10.0/nightly/deb/ ./" >> /etc/apt/sources.list.d/odoo.list`. This installs the package.

You can start the installation process by entering these commands into a terminal window:

```
sudo apt-get update
sudo apt-get install odoo
```

The Odoo packages will be first downloaded and then installed. This is an all-in-one installation and should set up all the necessary packages, PostgreSQL, and library dependencies required to run Odoo.

By default the deb installation will place the source in the following directory:

```
/usr/lib/python2.7/dist-packages/odoo
```

Testing your Odoo installation

Point your browser to `http://localhost:8069` and you should see the Odoo database creation page appear.

Troubleshooting and Odoo management tips

As far as ERP installations go, Odoo is typically very easy to install. Unfortunately, it is possible for an installation to fail for a variety of reasons. In this next section, we will discuss some of the most common installation issues and provide some troubleshooting tips for diagnosis problems with an Odoo installation.

Checking your browser destination

If you have followed the default installation, then your Odoo installation should be accessing Odoo at `http://localhost:8069`.

Make sure the URL is exactly as you see it above. If you did change the port number during installation, make sure you change the port in the URL.

Verifying that the Odoo service is running

If you are unable to pull up Odoo in the browser, it might be good to verify that the Odoo services are running.

Checking for the Odoo services running in Windows

Pull up the task manager and go to the **Services** tab, then look for `odoo-server-10.0`. The status should be running, as shown in the following screenshot:

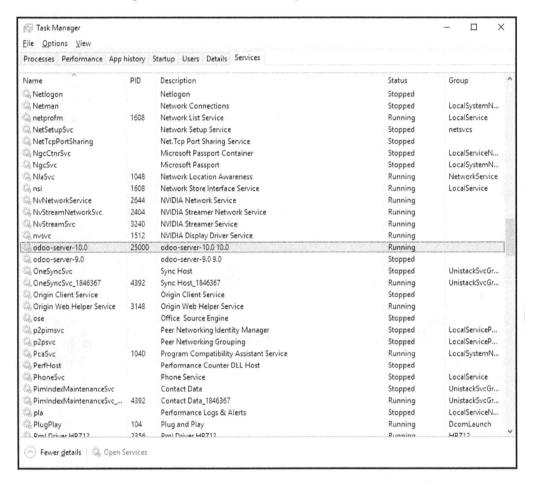

Here is an example of the `odoo-server-9.0` service successfully running on Windows.

Additional Odoo troubleshooting steps for Windows can be found at:
`https://doc.Odoo.com/install/windows/server/complementary_install_information/`.

Checking for Odoo services running in Ubuntu

In Ubuntu, you can locate the Odoo services by running the following command in a terminal window:

```
ps aux | grep Odoo
```

You will then see the Odoo service listed if it is running:

```
root@ubuntu:~# ps aux | grep odoo
odoo      14341  1.0 11.1 925300 111756 ?       Sl   11:40   0:02 /usr/bin/python /usr/bin/o
doo --config /etc/odoo/odoo.conf --logfile /var/log/odoo/odoo-server.log
postgres  14489  0.0  1.1 308992 11016 ?        Ss   11:42   0:00 postgres: odoo postgres [l
ocal] idle
root      14539  0.0  0.1  21292  1008 pts/17   S+   11:45   0:00 grep --color=auto odoo
root@ubuntu:~#
```

Starting and stopping Odoo services in Ubuntu

When managing an Odoo server, one of the most common tasks you will find yourself performing is starting and stopping the Odoo services. Odoo allows you to start and stop the services with a command switch.

To start the services use following commands:

```
sudo /etc/init.d/odoo start
```

To stop the services use following commands:

```
sudo /etc/init.d/odoo stop
```

Finding the primary Odoo log file

Odoo writes many messages, warnings, and error messages to a log. Often when troubleshooting problems, this log file is valuable in determining what action you should take. In a default installation, the log file is located at `/var/log/odoo/odoo-server.log`. The log is especially valuable to locate problems you may have when installing new modules.

Modifying the Odoo configuration file

The Odoo framework allows you to specify a configuration file for your installation. By default, this file is located at /etc/odoo/odoo.conf.

Using this file, you can change many of the attributes of Odoo.

Changing port numbers

By default, Odoo runs on port 8069. For many installations, the default port will work fine. There are situations, however, where it can be useful to change this default port. One common scenario would be the need to run more than one version of Odoo. Multiple installations cannot run on port 8069, so you will need to modify the port. Sometimes there are security reasons behind changing ports as many hackers are aware of the default ports people use.

Fortunately, changing the default port number is easy.

Simply enter the following code:

```
Port=[port]
```

For example, Port=8059 will change the default port for the web client to port 8059.

Accessing the database management tools

Odoo offers database management tools that can be accessed easily through your web browser. This makes it easy to create, back up, and even delete databases all through a web interface. While there are sometimes links available on the login page that will take you to these tools, it is possible that when installing some applications such as the website builder, you will not find a link easily.

To access the database management tools, use the following path:

```
[ServerAddress]:[port]/web/database/manager
```

Changing the admin password

As mentioned earlier, by default, Odoo sets the password for these operations to `admin`. To secure your server, it is necessary to change this password in your configuration file:

```
Admin_password=[your password]
```

Also, be careful while starting up your Odoo server from the command line without specifying an alternative password or the path to the configuration file. If you do, you leave the instance open with the default password.

Finding additional resources on installing Odoo

Installing and configuring Odoo can quickly become a very complex task that is outside the scope of this book. In the appendix of this book, you will find links to additional resources that can assist you with installing Odoo.

Summary

In this chapter, we saw how easy it was to get started using Odoo online. We discussed how to set up a trial company and the basics for creating a database and installing your first module. If you choose not to use the online services, you likely found the topics on installing Odoo on Windows or Ubuntu helpful. Finally, we discussed various methods of troubleshooting and configuring Odoo.

In the next chapter, we will begin to jump into our first real business applications in Odoo. You will get introduced to our real-world case study and set up the basic configuration for the company. We will walk you through setting up your first product and, finally, creating and printing your first sales order.

2
Installing Your First Application

We have learned about the various applications that Odoo has to offer and how you can install Odoo on your own system. Before the release of Odoo 8, most users were focused on ERP and financial-related applications. Now, Odoo 10 has added several important applications that allow companies to use Odoo in much greater scope than ever before. For example, the website builder can be installed to quickly launch a simple website for your business. A task that typically would have been accomplished with a content management system such as WordPress.

Despite all the increasing options available in Odoo, the overall process is the same. We begin by looking at the overall business requirements and decide on the first set of applications that we wish to implement. After understanding our basic objectives, we will create an Odoo database and configure the required company information.

Next, we begin exploring the Odoo interface for creating and viewing information. We will see just how easy Odoo is to use by completing an entire sales order workflow. We will finish up the chapter by reviewing some of the more advanced sales order configuration options.

Topics that we will cover include:

- Adding a password-protected database to our installation
- Installing and configuring the Sales Management module
- Using interface features to view, edit, and find information
- Entering a new customer
- Adding our first product to sell
- Writing an order and confirming it for invoicing

Gathering requirements

Setting up an Odoo system is no easy task. Many companies get into trouble believing that they can just install the software and throw in some data. Inevitably, the scope of the project grows and what was supposed to be a simple system ends up a confusing mess. Fortunately, Odoo's modular design will allow you to take a systematic approach to implementing Odoo for your business.

Implementing Odoo using a modular approach

The bare bones installation of Odoo simply provides you with a limited messaging system. To manage your Odoo implementation, you must begin with the planning of the modules with which you will work first. Odoo allows you to install just what you need now and then install additional Odoo modules as you better define your requirements. It can be valuable to take this approach when you are considering how you will implement Odoo for your own business.

Don't try and install all the modules and get everything running all at once. Instead, break down the implementation into smaller phases.

Introducing Silkworm – our real-world case study

To best understand how to work with Odoo, we will build our exercises around a real-world case study. **Silkworm** is a mid-sized screen printer that manufactures and sells t-shirts as well as a variety of printing printing. Using Odoo's modular design, we will begin by implementing the **Sales Order** module to set up the selling of basic products. In this specific case, we will be selling t-shirts. As we proceed through this book, we will continue to expand the system by installing additional modules.

When implementing Odoo for your organization, you will also want to create a basic requirements document. This information is important for configuration of the company settings in Odoo, and should be considered essential documentation when implementing an ERP system.

Creating a new database in Odoo

If you have installed Odoo on your own server you will need to first create a database. As you add additional applications to Odoo, the necessary tables and fields will be added to the database you specify.

Odoo Online:

If you are using Odoo Online, you will not have access to create a new database and instead will use Odoo's one click application installer to manage your Odoo installation.

If you have just installed a fresh copy of Odoo, you will be prompted automatically to create a new Odoo database:

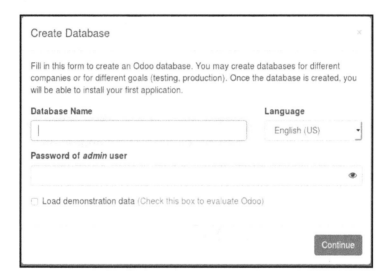

In the preceding screenshot, you can see the Odoo form to **Create Database**.

Odoo provides basic instructions for creating your database. Let us quickly review the fields and how they are used.

Selecting a database name

When selecting a database name, choose a name that describes the system and that will make clear the purpose of the database. There are a few rules for creating an Odoo database:

- Your database name cannot contain spaces and must start with a number or letter
- Also you will need to avoid commas, periods, and quotes
- Underscores and hyphens are allowed if they are not the first character in the name

It can also be a good idea to specify in the name if the database is for development, testing, or production purposes.

For the purposes of our real-world case study, we will use the database name:

`SILKWORM-DEV`

We have chosen the `-DEV` suffix as we will consider this a development database that will not be used for production or even for testing.

 Take the time to consider what you will name your databases. It can be useful to have standard prefixes or suffixes depending on the purpose of your database. For example, you may use `-PROD` for your production database or `-TEST` for the database that you are using for testing.

Loading demonstration data

Notice the box labelled **Check this box to evaluate Odoo**. If you mark this checkbox when you create a database, Odoo will preload your tables with a host of sample data for each module that is installed. This may include fake customers, suppliers, sales orders, invoices, inbox messages, stock moves, and products. The purpose of the demonstration data is to allow you to run modules through their paces without having to key in a ton of test data.

For the purposes of our real-world case study in this book, do not load demonstration data.

Specifying our default language

Odoo offers a variety of language translation features with support for more than 20 languages. All of the examples in this book will use the English (US) language option. Be aware that depending on the language you select in Odoo, you may need to have that language also installed in your base operating system.

Choosing an e-mail and password

Unlike previous versions of Odoo in which the database was created with an administrator account named admin, Odoo 10 uses the email address you provide as your administrator account. This is also known as the superuser account.

The password you choose during the creation of the database will be the password for this admin account.

Choose any password you wish and click on **Create Database** to create the SILKWORM-DEV database.

Managing databases in Odoo

The database management interface allows you to perform basic database management tasks such as backing up or restoring a database. Often with Odoo, it is possible to manage your databases without ever having to go directly into the Postgres database server. It is also possible to set up multiple databases under the same installation of Odoo. For instance, you may want in the future to install another database that does load demonstration data and may be used to install modules simply for testing purposes.

If you have trouble getting to the interface to manage databases, you can access the database management interface directly by going to the /web/database/manager path.

[35]

Installing the Sales Management module

After clicking on **Create Database**, it can take a little time depending on your system before you are shown a page that lists the available applications:

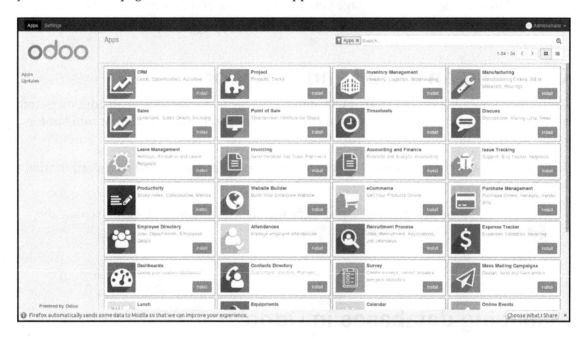

This screen lets you select from a list of the most common Odoo modules to install.

There is very little you can do with just an Odoo database with no modules installed. Now we will install the **Sales Management** module so we can begin setting up our business selling t-shirts:

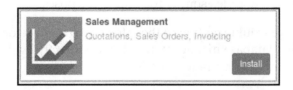

Click on the **Install** button to install the **Sales Management** module.

During installation of modules and other long operations, you will often see a **Loading** icon at the top center of your screen. Unlike previous versions of Odoo that prompted for accounting and other setup information, Odoo now completes the installation unattended.

Knowing the basic Odoo interface

After the installation of the sales order application, Odoo 10 now takes you to the Discuss menu where your inbox and other communication activities are located. You will also notice that Odoo provides small purple tear drops that provide helpful tips:

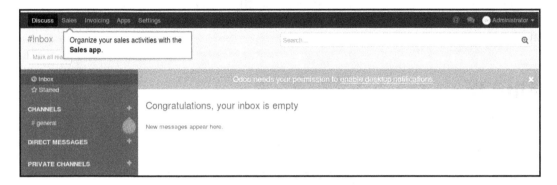

As you can see, the application menus are across the top of the interface. Click on the Sales menu to bring up the sales application. This takes you directly to the **Sales** dashboard. As we have just installed the application, there is very little to see in the dashboard, but we can see the available menu options along the left edge of the interface.

The menus along the top allow you to change between the major applications and settings within Odoo, while the menus down the left side outline all your available choices. In the following screenshot, we are in the main **Sales** menu:

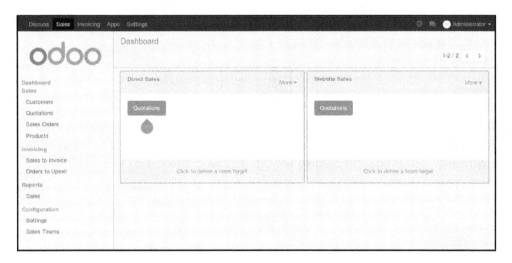

In the dashboard, each sales team is represented with their own panel. In this case we can see the **Direct Sales** and **Website Sales** team are set up by default.

Let's look at one of the main master files that we will be using in many Odoo applications, the **Customers**. Click the **Customers** menu on the left.

Let's take a moment to look at the screen elements that will appear consistently throughout Odoo. In the top left of the main form, you can clearly see that we are in the **Customers** section.

Using the search box

In the top right corner of our form we have a search box:

The search box allows you to quickly search for records in the Odoo application. If you are in the **Customers** section, naturally the search will be looking for customer records. Likewise, if you are looking at the product view, the search box will allow you to search the product records that you have entered into the system.

Picking different views

Odoo also offers a standard interface to switch between **Kanban** view and list view. In some forms you will have additional options such as the Graph view. You can see the icon selections under the search box in the right corner of the form:

The currently selected view is highlighted in dark. If you move the mouse over the icon you will get a tool-tip that shows you the description of the view. As we have no records in our system currently, let us add a record so we can further explore the Odoo interface.

Creating your first customer

Helpful instructions prompt you to begin entering your first customer into Odoo by clicking the **Create** button:

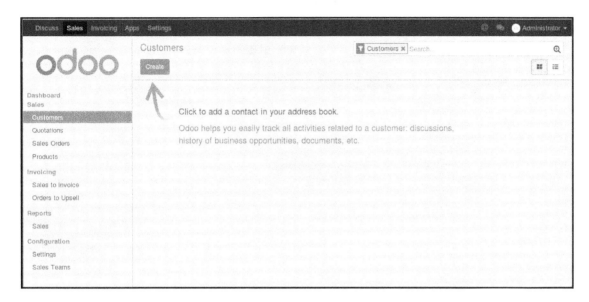

This is the Odoo **Customers** form. Clicking **Create** will generate a customer record.

Silkworm sells t-shirts to both businesses and retail customers. For this example, we will use a fictional customer named `Mike Smith` who wishes to purchase several t-shirts. Odoo offers flexibility in collecting customer information, and by default, most fields are not required. If you see a field that is purple, that is a required field. In Odoo 10, the only required field for customers is the name.

The rest of the fields are optional. Later we will learn how you can configure Odoo to make additional fields required.

In this example, we have filled out some of the basic fields for our fictional customer, Mike Smith:

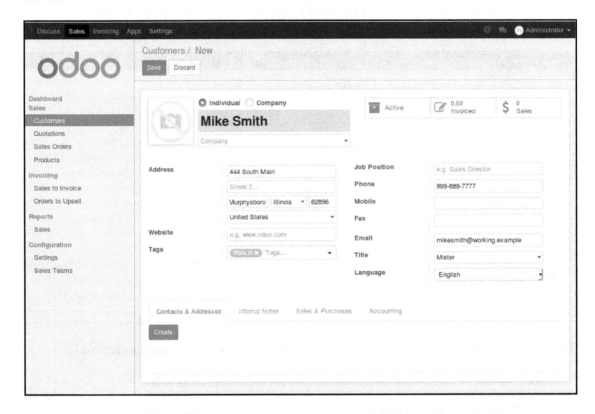

Is this customer a company?

At the very top of the form is a radio selection option to inform Odoo if this customer is an individual or a company. For our example, we are using a walk-in retail customer. If you were doing a business-to-business type operation, then often your customers would select the **Company** option.

In previous versions of Odoo, you were not allowed to have multiple contacts if you had the individual option selected. In Odoo 10, you can create contacts for individuals as well as companies.

Entering data into Odoo forms

Odoo utilizes a consistent interface to enter data throughout the application. Once you have learned how to enter data into one form, you should have no problem entering data into other forms in Odoo.

Required fields will always be in purple. If you see a purple field, you must fill in that data or you will not be able to save the record. You can move between fields by using your mouse or the *Tab* key. *Shift+Tab* will take you back to the previous field. Unlike some systems, you cannot move between fields in Odoo by using the arrow keys.

In many forms, you will have to select lists that allow you to choose from a list to populate the field. You can use your keyboard to type and limit the items that are displayed in a select list. By using the *Tab* key on your keyboard to find the appropriate item in the list, it is possible to enter data into a form with limited use of the mouse.

In the version of Odoo 10 installed for this chapter, it is necessary to first go down and choose the country before the states list can be populated. If you try to enter the state first the list will be empty if there is no country selected.

Many select lists have two options at the bottom that will allow you to use additional search options or to create an item that is not in the list:

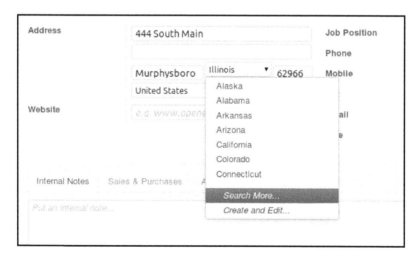

In this example, we see a list of states with the option for additional searching or to create a new state that is not in the list.

Odoo has the ability to work with customers in a variety of languages. For our example, we will leave this as English. If, however, you were working with a company that prefers their documents in other languages, you could specify that language and Odoo will manage the translation.

Use the **Internal Notes** area to enter any additional notes that you wish to keep on the customer.

Editing customers sale and purchase

The bottom area of the customer screen is divided into a series of tabs or page's that assist in organizing customer information. In the **Sales & Purchases** page, we can assign such options as a salesperson and other sales related options:

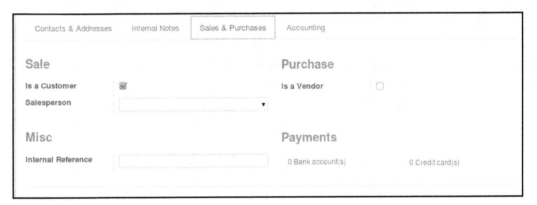

The available options in the customer **Sales & Purchases** page are:

Is a Customer: This is the customer checkbox known in Odoo as a boolean field. It can be marked checked or unchecked. Odoo has a unique method of storing data related to people in the system. All individuals are stored in the same table (res_partner) regardless of whether if they are a customer or supplier. The customer flag tells Odoo that this is in fact a customer record. This field must be checked for Odoo to recognize Mike Smith as a customer.

Salesperson: The salesperson field allows you to select who the direct salesperson will be for this customer. While the field is not required, it is often populated if you are integrating your sales management system with the **Customer Relationship Management (CRM)** module. We will use this field in the chapter on CRM; for now we can leave the field blank.

Internal Reference: Often when implementing Odoo, a company already has an existing customer numbering system in place. The reference field is the perfect field to populate with an existing customer number. Otherwise this field can be left blank or used for another purpose. For our example, we are going to leave this field blank.

Is a Vendor: Because Odoo stores customer and vendor data in the same table, it is possible to be both a customer and a supplier. In this example, we will keep Mike Smith as a customer only.

Odoo uses a common database to store customer and supplier records. This makes it easier to manage data as customers, and suppliers are designated by simple checkboxes in the **Sales & Purchases** page on the customer screen.

Editing customer Accounting

In previous versions of Odoo, the **Accounting** page was quite intimidating to new users. Thankfully, in Odoo 10 the accounting page is much simpler and simply allows you to specify terms and fiscal information:

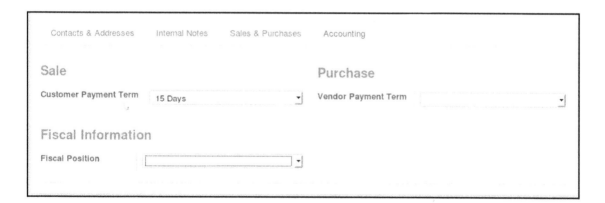

Here are the available options in the customer accounting page:

Customer Payment Term: It is common in many businesses for different customers to have different payment terms. Perhaps for a lifelong customer, you would extend 30 or even 60 day net terms for them to pay their invoice. For a new customer, you may require immediate payment. Additional terms can be configured in Odoo depending on your needs. The default payment terms included are:

- **Immediate Payment**
- **15 Days**
- **30 Net Days**

For our example, we will set the payment term to 15 Days.

Vendor Payment Term: Much like the **Customer Payment Term**, this field will determine the payment terms for the supplier. Because a partner can be both a customer and supplier, we have separate terms for each.

Degree of debtor trust: This field allows you to assign how much trust you have in a given customer to pay their debts. The default selections are:

- **Normal debtor**
- **Good debtor**
- **Bad debtor**

Fiscal Position: The **Fiscal Position** field is sometimes also known as the tax status and in some systems is represented simply as taxable. Odoo 10 now provides a robust fiscal position framework that allows you to set up rules for your customers and vendors for almost any scenario. Fortunately, for simple installations you can avoid this field entirely.

Remember to click on the **Save** button to add your new customer record to the database.

Entering a product in Odoo

Now that we have a customer, it is time we enter some products to sell to our new customer. For our example, we are going to enter a medium white cotton t-shirt. Click on the **Products** item in the menu on the left:

Creating products in Odoo

Create a new product by clicking the **Create** button.

The following screenshot is for the **General Information** page of the product form for entering a product record into Odoo:

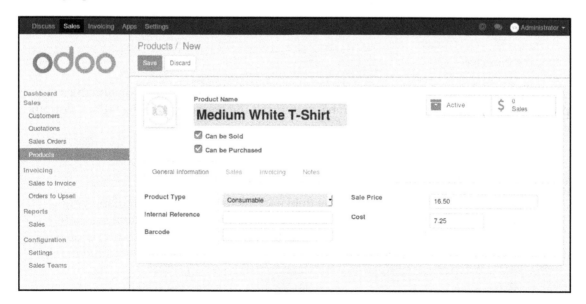

Product Name

The **Product Name** is what will be displayed on the sales orders, invoices, and in all other screens that refer to this specific product. For our example, we are selling a `Medium White T-Shirt`.

Can be Sold

Much like the customer active flag, you can use **Can be Sold** to remove products from showing up on product lists by unchecking **Can be Sold**. For our example, we want to sell this t-shirt to `Mike Smith` so we will leave the option checked.

Can be Purchased

Even though we have not yet installed the purchasing system, Odoo 10 lets you specify whether if a product can be purchased. We will accept the default that we in addition to selling this t-shirt, we can purchase them as well. This will play an important function when we get to the chapter that discusses the Odoo purchasing application.

Product type

Product type is the first option in the **Information** page on the product screen. There are two available product types:

- **Consumable**

- **Service**

Service product types will not create procurements in purchase orders. Consumables are products that you actually sell and can be configured to generate purchase orders. For our example, we will set the product type to Consumable.

Internal Reference

For the most part, Odoo utilizes the **Name** field and the description when displaying product information. It is very common that a company has a coding system for their products. The **Internal Reference** field is useful to enter an alternative product code or number for the product. In this example, we will leave the internal reference field blank.

Sale price

This field sets the sales price of the item as it will appear on the sales order. For our example, we are setting the sales price of the t-shirt to $16.50.

Cost price

This field sets the cost of the item that can be utilized for simple profit margin calculations. So we have a value in here, we will set a cost of $7.25 for the t-shirt.

Nothing in the Sales page

Installing the **Sales** application creates a **Sales** page of the product form. By default, however, this page is completely empty. As we install more applications and change configuration settings, this page will be populated with appropriate information. This is a common occurrence in Odoo. As you configure your applications, make sure to check back in forms as you will likely have additional options.

Entering a product Invoicing page

By default Odoo has setup a tax of 15% for both our customer taxes and our vendor taxes. However, there will be times when you have a product that has a specific tax. In the United States, one example is that cigarettes often have a more substantial tax than other items such as food. Odoo allows you to specify additional tax options for a given product in the accounting page. Taxes can be specified for both the customer and the supplier separately.

The following screenshot is of the **Accounting** page located in the product form:

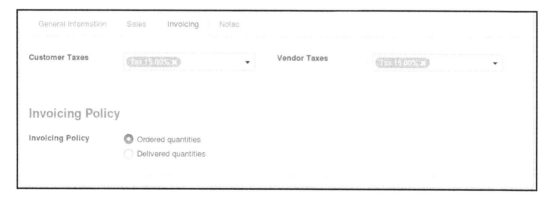

You will also notice that Odoo allows you to have multiple taxes for the same product. This would allow you to have a base tax that would apply to all products and then simply add an additional tax, or even a tax credit, depending on that specific product.

Invoicing policy

By default, Odoo configures invoicing so that the line items of the invoice will be created based on the ordered quantities from the sales order. This means that even if none of the items have shipped, the customer will still be invoiced. Alternatively, you can change the invoicing policy so that the customer is invoiced on the delivered items. If you have items on a sales order that have not shipped yet, the customer will not be invoiced for those items.

Saving the product

Clicking the **Save** button stores the product record in Odoo. If you click on **Discard**, you will get prompted with a warning message that you will lose your changes.

Setting the company information

We have entered both a customer and a product. However, before we create a sales order, we still have some work to do in setting up our company. Currently, Odoo does not even know the name of our company and has, by default, used **YourCompany** as the name.

It takes a few steps, but we can locate the company information by choosing **Settings** from the top menu and then choosing **General Settings** from the sub-menu on the left. In the form that comes up you will find a link at the far right labeled **Configure your company data**.

Click the link and you are presented with the settings for your company.

The following screenshot shows company record filled with the data for our sample case study:

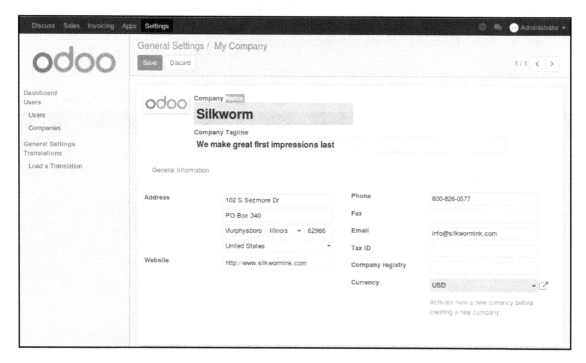

Here, we have supplied the company name along with address, e-mail, phone, website, and the company slogan. It is also possible to click the photo icon at the top left to assign a logo to the company.

Saving company information

Click **Save** to update the company information. We are now ready to enter our first sales order.

Entering your first sales order

Now for the moment we have all been waiting for. We finally get to sell our products by entering a sales order. To get to the **Sales Order** screen, click **Sales** in the top menu and then choose **Sales Orders** from the sub-menu on the left.

The following screenshot shows existing sales orders and allows users to create a new sales order:

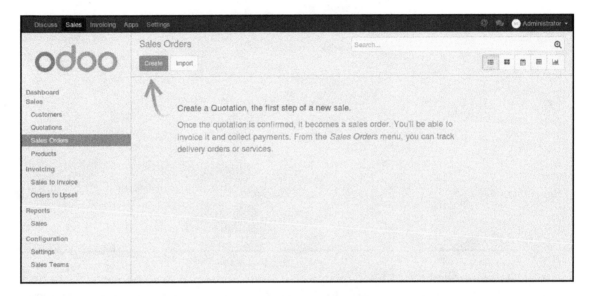

Click on the **Create** button to create a new sales order. Every brand new sales order begins as a quotation and stays in that state until you confirm the sale. Only after confirming the quotation will your sale be referred to as a **Sales Orders**.

The following screenshot is a new sales order form with the cursor set on the **Customer** field:

Selecting the customer

When you create a new quotation sales order, you are prompted to first select the customer from the select list. As you add customers you will have the option to search and locate customers for the sales order. For now, we will select the customer we entered in earlier in the chapter, Mike Smith.

You will not be able to begin entering line items until you have specified the customer for the sales order.

Expiration date

By default, there is no expiration date for the quote. However, if you would like to specify a date in which the quote will no longer be valid you can specify it here:

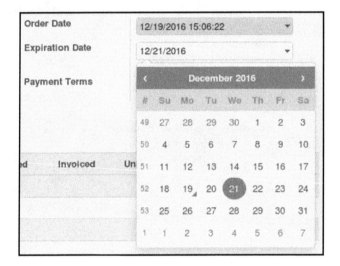

Payment terms

Odoo will automatically bring in the payment terms for the customer you select. On the sales order you have the option to override the customer's payment terms for the specific sales order.

Entering line items on a quotation sales order

Now we are ready to begin specifying the product we wish to sell. Click on **Add an item** in the line item area to add a line to the grid. The first field will be **Product**. Select **Medium White T-shirt** from the list box.

Your line item fields should populate and look like this:

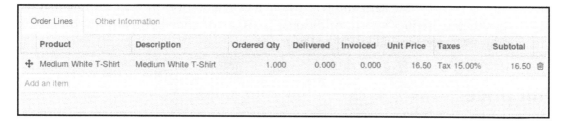

Order Lines	Other Information						
Product	Description	Ordered Qty	Delivered	Invoiced	Unit Price	Taxes	Subtotal
✛ Medium White T-Shirt	Medium White T-Shirt	1.000	0.000	0.000	16.50	Tax 15.00%	16.50 🗑
Add an item							

Product field

Each line item starts out by selecting the product. You can add products on-the-fly by choosing **Create and Edit** from the bottom of the list. Once there are more products in the list, you can also bring up a product search window using the **search more...** option. After you select the product field, Odoo retrieves the tax and pricing information from the server to display in the line item.

In Odoo 10 the total is automatically updated as you add new line items. Odoo provides an update link next to the **Total** on the form. You should consider hitting this if you have any doubt as to the accuracy of the total.

Description

Odoo will pull over the description from the product record to populate the **Description** field on the line item. It is possible to override the description on the quotation sales order. For this example, we will leave the description as it pulled over from the product record.

Delivered and Invoiced

As we are just entering the sales order, both of these will be zero. They will be updated automatically as your process delivery orders and creates invoices.

Ordered Qty

Product quantity will be 1 as default. Naturally, you will change this field to the quantity of products you have sold. We will just leave the quantity as 1 for this example.

Taxes

Odoo supports taxes by line item and will automatically pull over the 15% tax rate that we have defined in the product record. Additional taxes can be added or removed from the line item. For this example, we will leave the tax at 15%.

Unit price

Odoo pulls the sale price from the product record to populate the unit price in the line item. It is possible to override the price in the line item. For this example, we will leave the unit price at $16.50.

Be careful of changing prices in the line items of Odoo. It is possible that if you click back on the product field or tab through other fields in the line item, the unit price will flip back the price in the product record. If you are changing prices in the line items, make sure to double-check your unit prices before you confirm your sales order.

Saving the quotation sales order

Click **Save** to save the quotation. The form will refresh, displaying the full customer address as well as updating the tax and final total of the quotation sales order.

The following screenshot is of our first quotation in Odoo:

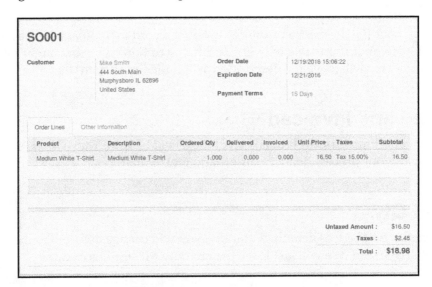

Understanding the sales order workflow

Although we started out entering a sales order, the current state of this order is a **Quotation**. Odoo 10 displays the current state of transactions in the top right corner of the form:

This indicator makes it very easy to see the current stage of a transaction throughout the Odoo workflow. In this example, we can see that this is currently a Draft quotation. We can also see that the quotation would first need to be sent and/or be confirmed as a sales order, before finally the quotation can be considered Done.

The available actions you can take on this quotation are displayed at the top left corner of the form.

The following screenshot is of available actions for an Odoo quotation:

Send by Email

Clicking the **Send by Email** button will send a copy of the quotation to the e-mail address in the customer's file. Setting up your e-mail configuration will be a topic for another chapter.

Print

Even in the digital age it is still very common to need a printed copy of a quotation or sales order. Clicking the **Print** button will generate a PDF document containing your quotation.

Confirm Sale

The **Confirm Sale** button will convert the quotation into a sales order and push the transaction further down the sales workflow.

Cancel

Clicking the **Cancel** button will prompt you to cancel this quotation. The quotation is not deleted and can still be viewed. Cancelling the quotation ends the sales order workflow, and the quotation will only be kept in the system for archive purposes.

Click on the **Confirm Sale** button to convert this quotation into a sales order. You will see the status change for the sales order from **Quotation** to **Sales Order**.

Invoicing the sale

Depending on the workflow of the business, a lot of different things can happen after you have confirmed a sales order. In manufacturing companies, you may need to both purchase products and create a manufacturing order to produce the final product before you invoice the customer. In our example, we are going to go ahead and invoice the customer for the t-shirt they have ordered. Click the **Create Invoice** button to generate an invoice for the sales order.

An Odoo **Invoice Order** wizard pops up to walk you through the invoice creation process.

The following screenshot is of the **Invoice Order** wizard:

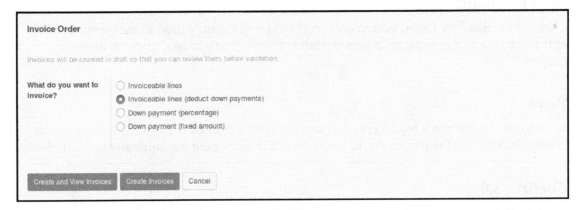

What do you want to invoice?

Odoo provides a variety of options for invoicing the entire sales order, or instead invoicing based on other methods. The available choices are:

- **Invoiceable lines (deduct down payments)**: Choose this option if you both want to invoice the lines and deduct any down payments you have received. This is the default option. Using the invoiceable lines without deducting down payments will simply ignore any of those payments when producing the invoice.
- **Down payment (percentage)**: You will be prompted to enter the percentage amount of the down payment.
- **Down payment (fixed amount)**: You will be prompted to enter a fixed amount of the down payment.

Creating the invoice

For our example, we will be using the default option. As we have no down payments, Odoo will process the sales order the same as if you chose the first option, **Invoiceable lines**. Click **Create Invoice** to generate the invoice. Initially, the invoice is created in a **Draft** state. Clicking **Validate** will confirm the invoice and post the transaction.

If you have followed along and everything works as it should, then you will see an invoice similar to the following screenshot:

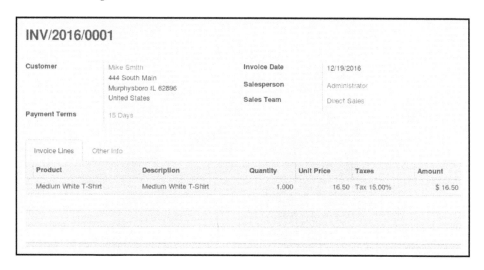

At this time, it is worth noting Odoo's use of an interface feature called breadcrumb. These links, which appear on form views just below the topmost menu, allow you to traverse from your invoice back to the relevant sales order from which it derived. Use of these links is the preferred method of backtracking to prior screens, as opposed to using your browser's back button.

Summary

In this chapter, we started by creating an Odoo database. We then installed the **Sales Order Management** module and created our first customer. With our customer created, we turned our attention to setting up a product in Odoo and entering our basic company information. Next, we created a quotation and followed the workflow all the way through to confirming the sales order and generating an invoice.

In the next chapter, we'll look at our sales strategy and what we want to achieve via CRM software.

3
Exploring Customer Relationship Management in Odoo 10

Until recently, most business and financial systems had product-focused designs, while records and fields maintained basic customer information, processes, and reporting typically revolved around product-related transactions. In the past, businesses were centered on specific products, but now the focus has shifted to center the business on the customer. A **Customer Relationship Management** (**CRM**) system provides the tools and reporting necessary to manage customer information and interactions.

In this chapter, we will cover the following:

- Looking at what it takes to implement a CRM system as part of an overall business strategy
- Install the CRM application and set up salespersons that can be assigned to our customers
- Learn how to create and manage Leads
- Create opportunities and schedule events in Odoo
- Discover the Odoo Open Chatter feature

Using CRM as a business strategy

Before jumping into the specific CRM features of Odoo, it is valuable to briefly discuss the importance of a comprehensive approach to implementing a CRM system into your business. The fact is that successfully implementing a CRM system requires much more planning than just installing software and asking employees to fill in the data. CRM software systems are only a technical tool in assisting your sales and marketing department in acquiring and keeping customers. Certainly the software will play an important role, but to obtain real benefits from a CRM system you must do the hard research to understand your customer and exactly how you wish to shape their customer experience.

It is critical that the sales people share account knowledge and completely understand the features and capabilities of the system. They often have existing tools that they have relied on for many years. Without clear objectives and goals for the entire sales team, it is likely that they will not use the tool. A plan must be implemented to spend time training and encouraging the sharing of knowledge to successfully implement a CRM system.

Managing the customer experience

Today, customers face a wide range of choices when it comes to purchasing products and services. At the most fundamental level, customers often build great loyalty to brands in which they have a positive customer experience. Companies such as Apple and Harley Davidson are successful largely because of fierce brand loyalty based on positive customer experiences. Making the most of a CRM system requires you to put yourself in the role of your customer and develop a consistent strategy to improve their overall customer experience.

Treating your customer like a real person

As computers became more common, it wasn't long before people began to feel like they were treated like a number by many companies. In many ways, CRM systems turn the tables around. Instead of treating customers like cattle, a smart account manager using a CRM system can greatly personalize the customer experience. You treat your customer like an individual, and they will reward you with their loyalty.

Because you are looking to create a very personalized customer experience, it is important to thoroughly look at your customer's interactions with the company when designing your own CRM system. A company who sells high-end security systems to government institutions will need to provide drastically different customer experiences than a company that is marketing a pool maintenance service.

Using your mission statements and company goals to drive the design of your CRM system

A good CRM system will build around the core goals and mission of your company. If your company does not have customer-focused goals or mission statements, then you should address that before beginning to design a CRM system. Most critically, there needs to be focus on concerns and interactions that have a direct impact on customer experience. A good CRM system will not just manage the sales process, but the entire customer experience and interactions before and after the sale.

Real-world case study – improving customer experience

Now we will take a detailed real-world look at how a CRM system can be implemented to improve customer experience. We begin by looking at the company slogan:

"We make great first impressions last".

Here we have a slogan that most certainly speaks to the value of customer experience. To make that great first impression and keep it, there are several critical service expectations:

- Orders must be accurate and easy for customers to place
- Orders must be delivered on time
- Quality must be excellent

While listing these customer service goals may seem obvious, explicitly naming your objectives is important when building a CRM system. There is a natural tendency when building a CRM system to focus almost exclusively on customer acquisition and pre-sale activities. We must take care to remember that a CRM system must also support processes that manage the entire customer experience. These are the kind of scenarios that you want to consider when building your own CRM system:

- How are problem orders handled?
- How is the customer contacted if there is a product back order?
- If the customer calls, can the service representative easily provide delivery tracking information?

Installing the CRM application

If you have not installed the CRM module, login as the administrator and then click on the **Apps** menu. In a few seconds the list of available apps will appear. The CRM will likely be in the top left corner in the **Apps** dashboard:

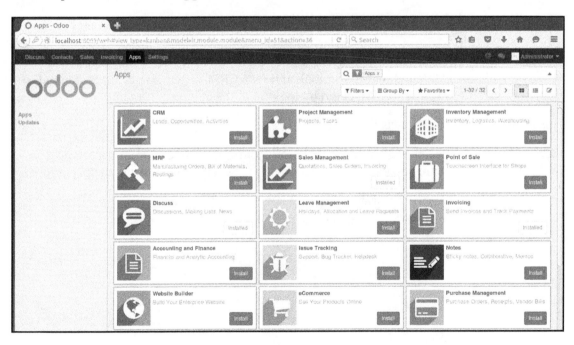

Click on Install to set up the CRM application.

Your first look at the CRM Dashboard

Like with the installation of the **Sales** application, Odoo takes you to the Discuss menu. Click on **Sales** to see the new changes after installing the CRM application. New to Odoo 10 is an improved CRM **Dashboard** that provides you with a friendly welcome message when you first install the application. You can use the dashboard to get an overview of your sales pipelines and get easy access to the most common actions within CRM:

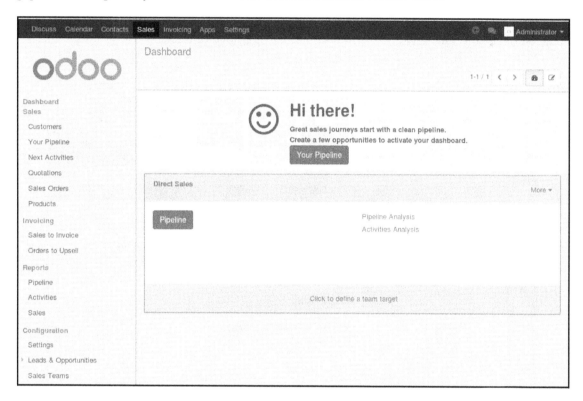

Assigning the sales representative or account manager

In Odoo 10, like in most CRM systems, the sales representative, or account manager plays an important role. Typically, this is the person who will ultimately be responsible for the customer account and a satisfactory customer experience.

While most often a company will use real people as their salespeople, it is certainly possible to instead have a salesperson record refer to a group, or even a sub-contracted support service.

We will begin by creating a salesperson who will handle standard customer accounts. Note that a sales representative is also a user in the Odoo system.

Create a new salesperson by going to the **Settings** menu, selecting **Users**, and then clicking the **Create** button. The new user form will appear. We have filled in the form with values for a fictional salesperson, `Terry Zeigler`.

The following screenshot is of the user's **Access Rights** tab:

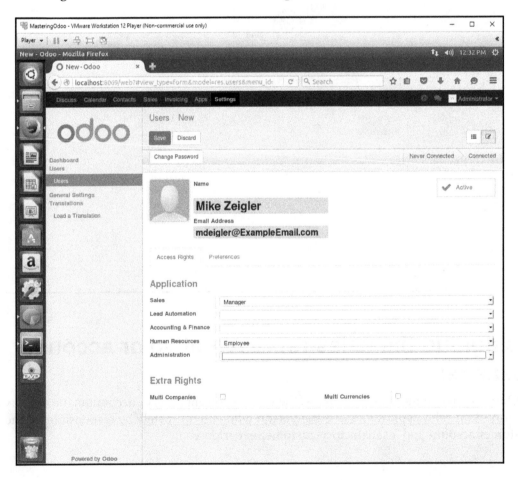

Specifying the name of the user

You specify the username just like you assigned the name of your customer in the preceding chapter. Unlike some systems that provide separate first name and last name fields, with Odoo you specify the full name within a single field.

Email address

Beginning in Odoo 9, the user and login form prompts for e-mail as opposed to user name. This practice has continued in Odoo version 10 as well. It is still possible to use a user name instead of e-mail address, but given the strong encouragement to use e-mail address in Odoo 9, and Odoo 10, it is possible that in future versions of Odoo the requirement to provide an e-mail address may be more strictly enforced.

Access Rights

The **Access Rights** tab lets you control which applications the user will be able to access. By default, Odoo will specify `Mr.Ziegler` as an employee so we will accept that default.

Depending on the applications you may have already installed or dependencies Odoo may add in various releases, it is possible that you will have other Access Rights listed.

Sales application settings

When setting up your sales people in Odoo 10, you have three different options on how much access an individual user has to the sales system. The following screenshot shows the available options:

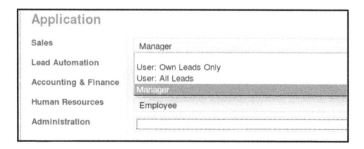

User: Own Documents Only

This is the most restrictive access to the sales application. The user with this access level is only allowed to see the documents they have entered themselves or which have been assigned to them. They will not be able to see the **Leads** assigned to other salespeople in the sales application.

User: All Documents

With this setting, the user will have access to all documents within the sales application.

Manager

The **Manager** setting is the highest access level in the Odoo sales system. With this access level, the user can see all **Leads** as well as access the configuration options of the sales application. The **Manager** setting also allows the user to access statistical reports.

We will leave the **Access Rights** options unchecked. These are used when working with multiple companies or with multiple currencies:

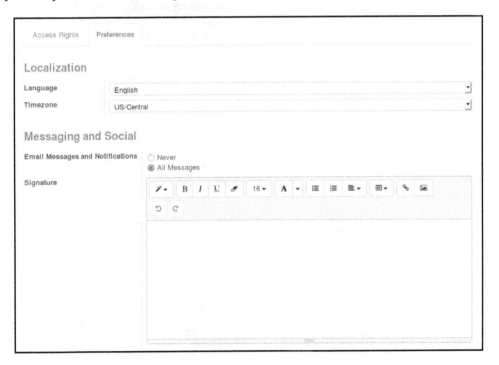

The **Preferences** tab consists of the following options:

Language and Timezone

Odoo allows you to select the language for each user. Currently, Odoo supports more than 20 language translations. Specifying the **Timezone** field allows Odoo to coordinate the display of date and time on messages.

 Leaving **Timezone** blank for a user will sometimes lead to unpredictable behavior in the Odoo software. Make sure you specify a timezone when creating a user record. Better yet, check the customization chapter on how you can make **Timezone** a required field!

Email Messages and Notifications

In Odoo 7, messaging became a central component of the Odoo system. In version 10, the support has been improved and it is now even easier to communicate important sales information between colleagues. Therefore, determining the appropriate handling of e-mail, and circumstances in which a user will receive e-mail is very important. The **Email Messages and Notifications** option lets you determine when you will receive e-mail messages from notifications that come to your Odoo inbox.

For our example, we have chosen **All Messages** e-mails. This is now the new default setting in Odoo 10. However, since we have not yet configured an e-mail server, or if you have not configured an e-mail server yourself, no e-mails will be sent or received at this stage.

Let's review the user options that will be available in communicating by e-mail.

Selecting the **Never** option suppresses all e-mail messaging for the user. Naturally, this is the setting you will wish to use if you do not have an e-mail server configured. This is also a useful option for users that simply want to use the built-in inbox inside Odoo to retrieve their messages.

Selecting the **All Messages** (discussions, e-mails, followed system notifications) option sends an e-mail notification for any action that would create an entry in your Odoo inbox. Unlike the other options, this action can include system notifications or, other automated communications.

Signature

The **Signature** section allows you to customize the signature that will automatically be appended to Odoo-generated messages and e-mails.

Manually setting the user password

You may have noticed that there is no visible password field in the user record. That is because the default method is to e-mail the user an account verification they can use to set their password. However, if you do not have an e-mail server configured, there is an alternative method for setting the user password.

After saving the user record, use the **Change Password** button at the top of the form:

A form will then appear allowing you to set the password for the user.

Now in Odoo 10, there is a far more visible button available at the top left of the form. Just click the **Change Password** button.

Assigning a salesperson to a customer

Now that we have set up our salesperson, it is time to assign the salesperson their first customer. Previously, no salesperson was assigned to our one and only customer, Mike Smith. So let's go to the **Sales** menu and then click on Mike Smith to pull up his customer record and assign him Mr.Ziegler as his salesperson. The following screenshot is of the customer screen opened to assign a salesperson:

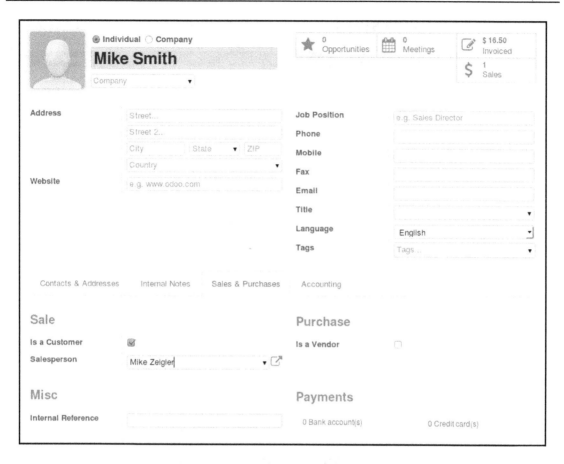

Here we have set the sales person to `Terry Zeigler`. By assigning your customers a salesperson, you can then better organize your customers for reports and additional statistical analysis.

Understanding Your Pipeline

Prior to Odoo 10, the CRM application primarily was a simple collection of leads and opportunities. While Odoo still uses both leads and opportunities as part of the CRM application, the concept of a Pipeline now takes center stage. You use the Pipeline to organize your opportunities by what stage they are within your sales process.

Click on **Your Pipeline** in the **Sales** menu to see the overall layout of the **Pipeline** screen:

In the preceding **Pipeline** forms, one of the first things to notice is that there are default filters applied to the view. Up in the search box you will see that there is a filter to limit the records in this view to the **Direct Sales** team as well as a **My Opportunities** filter. This effectively limits the records so you only see your opportunities from your primary sales team. Removing the **My Opportunities** filter will allow you to see opportunities from other salespeople in your organization.

Creating a new opportunity

In Odoo 10, a potential sale is defined by creating a new opportunity. An opportunity allows you to begin collecting information about the scope and potential outcomes for a sale. These opportunities can be created from new **Leads**, or an opportunity can originate from an existing customer.

For our real-world example, let's assume that Mike Smith has called and was so happy with his first order that he now wants to discuss using Silkworm for his local sports team. After a short conversation we decide to create an opportunity by clicking the **Create** button.

You can also use the + buttons within any of the pipeline stages to create an opportunity that is set to that stage in the pipeline.

In Odoo 10, the CRM application greatly simplified the form for entering a new Opportunity. Instead of bringing up the entire opportunity form with all the fields you get a simple form that collects only the most important information. The following screenshot shows the new **Opportunity** form:

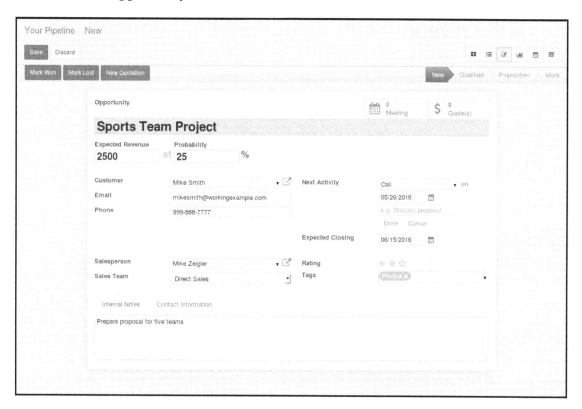

Opportunity Title

The title of your opportunity can be anything you wish. It is naturally important to choose a subject that makes it easy to identify the opportunity in a list. This is the only field required to create an opportunity in Odoo 10.

Customer

This field is automatically populated if you create an opportunity from the customer form. You can, however, assign a different customer if you like. This is not a required field, so if you have an opportunity that you do not wish to associate with a customer, that is perfectly fine. For example, you may leave this field blank if you are attending a trade show and expect to have revenue, but do not yet have any specific customers to attribute to the opportunity.

Expected revenue

Here, you specify the amount of revenue you can expect from the opportunity if you are successful. Inside the full opportunity form there is a field in which you can specify the percentage likelihood that an opportunity will result in a sale. These values are useful in many statistical reports although they are not required to create an opportunity.

Increasingly more reports look to expected revenue and percentage of opportunity completions. Therefore, depending on your reporting requirements you may wish to encourage sales people to set target goals for each opportunity to better track conversion.

Rating

Some opportunities are more important than others. You can choose none, one, two, or three stars to designate the relative importance of this opportunity.

Looking at opportunities in your pipeline

When you navigate to the Sales menu and choose **Your Pipeline**, you will see your opportunities displayed in the **Kanban** view. Here we see our brand new $2,500 opportunity along with the customer and the next action we need to take and when we need to take it.

The following is a screenshot of the Kanban view of the pipeline:

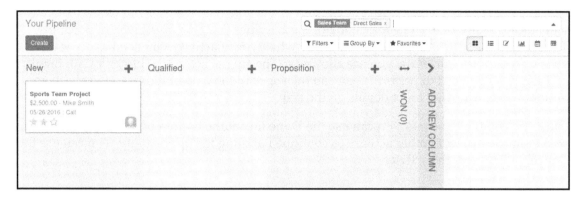

Clicking the small arrow on the Kanban card will bring up a small menu allowing you to perform actions related to the opportunity.

Let's edit the opportunity by double clicking on it and choosing the **Edit** button:

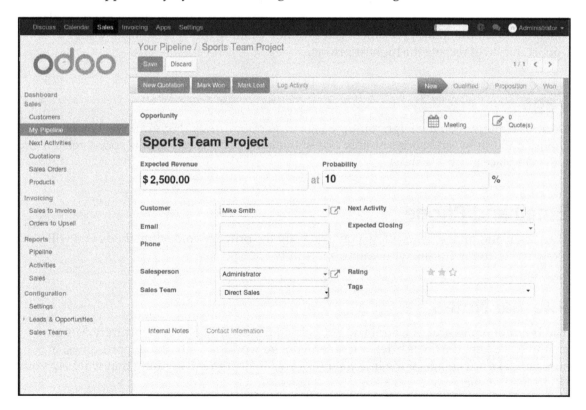

Next Activity

Previously in Odoo 9, you really only tracked one action at a time. Now in Odoo 10, Odoo will automatically keep an historical log of the activities you take on a given opportunity. The **Next Activity** field allows you to specify what type of activity you need to do next on your opportunity. Currently, you are allowed to specify the activity as either a **Call**, **Email**, or **Task** that you need to perform. You can then specify the date of the task along with an optional note providing more details on the task.

Once you complete the task you can use the **Done** link at the bottom of the **Next Activity** area to finish and set another activity to continue handling the opportunity. You can use the **Cancel** link to clear the activity.

Expected Closing

When managing your opportunities, it is important to establish a goal for when you wish to close the sale. Providing an expected closing date is handy for managing opportunities and running reports, and identifying which opportunities are due to be closed. The priority setting ranges from lowest to highest, with three settings between. In defining your CRM system, you should identify business rules for determining under what conditions an opportunity will receive the highest priority.

Tags

Odoo also allows you to assign multiple tags to an opportunity. For example, you could choose trade show, and sports as tags to designate the opportunity that is sports-related and will take place at a trade show.

Email and Phone

The e-mail and phone fields allow you to specify the primary contact methods you will likely use to communicate with your opportunity.

Internal Notes

The **Internal Notes** area is where you provide all the details on the opportunity. For our example, we kept the notes brief, but when you are working with real opportunities, make sure you take advantage of the internal notes area to document anything that will help you in closing the sale.

The Contact Information page

When you create an opportunity from either a customer or a lead, the information is automatically brought over into the **Lead** page tab in the **Opportunity**. The following screenshot is of the **Lead** tab of **Opportunity form**:

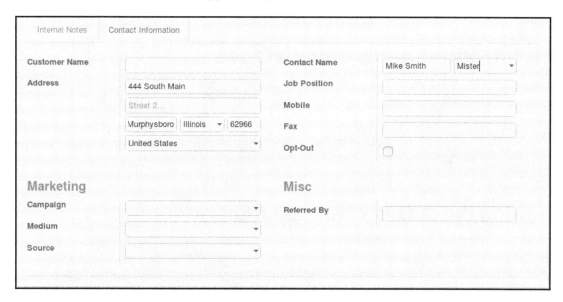

Address and Contact Information

The top half of the **Contact Information** page contains the standard address and other contact information. This information is automatically populated if you choose a customer, but can be overwritten for the opportunity if you desire. The **Function** field could be used to provide a bit of detail on the event that triggered the opportunity.

Odoo does not provide separate fields for first and last names, like many other accounting systems. Consider this as you plan how to organize customers in your system.

Mailings

The **Opt-Out** checkbox prevents the lead or customer associated with this opportunity from receiving mass mailings.

Marketing

Also new in Odoo 10 is the ability to assign campaigns to an opportunity as well as set the medium (that is, phone, email, television), and source of the campaign.

Save the **Opportunity** by clicking the **Save** button at the top of the form.

An introduction to sales stages

At the top of the Kanban view you can see the default stages that are provided by an Odoo CRM installation. In this case, we see **New**, **Qualified**, **Proposition**, and **Won**.

As an opportunity moves between stages, the Kanban view will update to show you where each opportunity currently stands. We can see this here because, this **Sports Team Project** has just been entered in the **New** column.

Viewing the details of an opportunity

If you click the three lines at the top right of the `Sports Team Project` opportunity in the Kanban view, which appears when you move your mouse over it, you will see a pop-up menu with your available options. The following screenshot shows the available actions on an opportunity:

Actions you can take on an opportunity

Selecting the **Edit** option takes you to the opportunity record and into edit mode for you to change any of the information. In addition, you can delete the record or archive the record so it will no longer appear in your pipeline by default.

The color palette at the bottom lets you color code your opportunities in the Kanban view. The small stars on the opportunity card allows you to highlight opportunities for special consideration. You can also easily drag and drop the opportunity into other columns as you work through the various stages of the sale.

Using Odoo's OpenChatter feature

One of the biggest enhancements brought about in Odoo 7 and expanded on in later versions of Odoo was the new **OpenChatter** feature that provides social networking style communication to business documents and transactions.

As we work our brand new opportunity, we will utilize the OpenChatter feature to demonstrate how to communicate details between team members and generate log entries to document our progress.

The best thing about the OpenChatter feature is that it is available for nearly all business documents in Odoo. It also allows you to see a running set of logs of the transactions or operations that have affected the document. This means everything that applies here to the CRM application can also be used to communicate in sales, purchasing, or in communicating about a specific customer or vendor.

Changing the status of an opportunity

For our example, let us assume that we have prepared our proposal and made the presentation. Bring up the opportunity by using the right-click **Menu** in the Kanban view or going into the **list** view and clicking the opportunity in the list.

It is time to update the status of our opportunity by clicking the **Proposition** arrow at the top of the form:

Notice that you do not have to edit the record to change the status of the opportunity. At the bottom of the opportunity, you will now see a logged note generated by Odoo that documents the changing of the opportunity from a new opportunity to a proposition. The following screenshot is of OpenChatter displaying a changed stage for the opportunity:

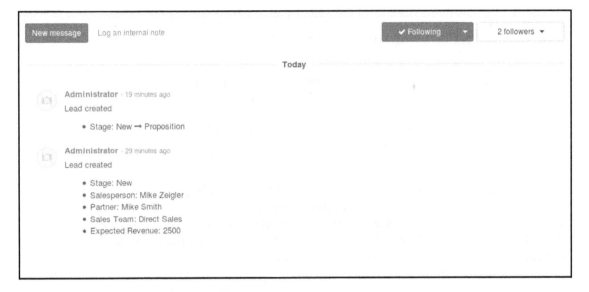

Notice how Odoo is logging the events automatically as they take place.

Managing the Opportunity

With the proposal presented, let us take down some details from what we have learned that may help us later when we come back to this opportunity. One method of collecting this information could be to add the details to the **Internal Notes** field in the opportunity form. There is value, however, in using the OpenChatter feature in Odoo to document our new details.

Most importantly, using OpenChatter to log notes gives you a running transcript with date and time stamps automatically generated. With the **Generic Notes** field, it can be very difficult to manage multiple entries. Another major advantage is that the OpenChatter feature can automatically send messages to team member's inboxes updating them on the progress. *Let us see it in action!*

Click the **Log an Internal note** link to attach a note to our opportunity. The following screenshot is for creating a note:

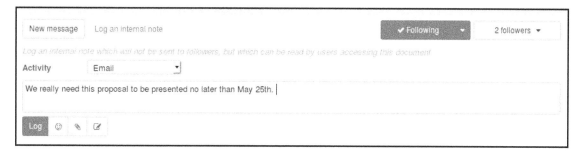

The activity option is unique to the CRM application and will not appear in most documents. You can use the small icons at the bottom to add a smiley, attach a document, or open up a full featured editor if you are creating a long note.

 The full featured editor also allows you to save templates of messages/notes you may use frequently. Depending on your specific business requirements this could be a great time saver.

When you create a note, it is attached to the business document, but no message will be sent to followers. You can even attach a document to the note by using the **Attach a File** feature. After clicking the **Log** button, the note is saved and becomes part of the OpenChatter log for that document.

Following a business document

Odoo brings social networking concepts into your business communication. Fundamental to this implementation is that you can get automatic updates on a business document by following the document. Then, whenever there is a note, action, or a message created that is related to a document you follow, you will receive a message in your Odoo inbox. In the bottom right-hand corner of the form, you are presented with the options for when you are notified and for adding or removing followers from the document.

The following screenshot is of the OpenChatter follow options:

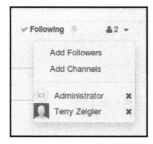

In this case, we can see that both **Terry Zeigler** and **Administrator** are set as followers for this opportunity. The **Following** checkbox at the top indicates that I am following this document. Using the **Add Followers** link you can add additional users to follow the document.

The followers who are notified are viewed by clicking the arrow to the right of the **Following** button. This brings up a list of the actions that will generate notifications to the followers:

The checkbox next to **Discussions** indicates that I should be notified of any discussions related to this document. However, I would not be notified, for example, if the stage changed.

When you send a message, by default the customer will become a follower of the document. Then whenever the document status changes, the customer will receive an email. Test out all your processes before integrating with an email server. For additional resources on community modules that help manage the chatter features, please see the `Appendix`.

Modifying the stages of the sale

We have seen that Odoo provides a default set of sales stages. Many times, however, you will want to customize the stages to best deliver an outstanding customer experience. Moving an opportunity through stages should trigger actions that create a relationship with the customer and demonstrate your understanding of their needs. A customer in the qualification stage of a sale will have much more different needs and much more different expectations than a customer in the negotiation phase.

For our case study, there are sometimes printing jobs that are technically complex to accomplish. With different jerseys for a variety of teams, the final details need to go through a final technical review and approval process before the order can be entered and verified.

From a business perspective, the goal is not just to document the stage of the sales cycle; the primary goal is to use this information to drive customer interactions and improve the overall customer experience.

To add a stage to the sales process, bring up **Your Pipeline**, and then click on the **ADD NEW COLUMN** area in the right of the form to bring up a little popup to enter the name for the new stage:

After you have added the column to the sales process, you can use your mouse to drag and drop the columns into the order that you wish them to appear. We are now ready to begin the technical approval stage for this opportunity.

Drag and drop the **Sports Team Project** opportunity over to the **Technical Approval** column in the Kanban view. The following screenshot is of the opportunities Kanban view after adding the technical approval stage:

We now see the **Technical Approval** column in our **Kanban** view and have moved over the opportunity. You will also notice that any time you change the stage of an opportunity that there will be an entry that will be created in the OpenChatter section at the bottom of the form. In addition to the ability to drag and drop an opportunity into a new stage, you can also change the stage of an opportunity by going into the form view.

Closing the sale

After a lot of hard work we have finally won the opportunity, and it is time to turn this opportunity into a quotation. At this point, Odoo makes it easy to take that opportunity and turn it into an actual quotation.

Open up the opportunity and click the **New Quotation** tab at the top of the opportunity form:

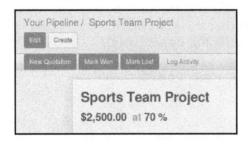

Unlike Odoo 8, which prompts for more information, in Odoo 10 you get taken to a new quote with the customer information already filled in:

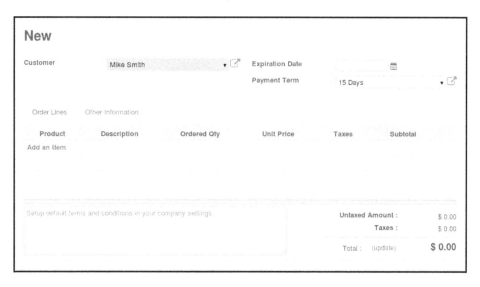

Your opportunity converted to a quotation

The workflow in Odoo handles moving over all the required information from your opportunity to your quotation document. At this point, you are ready to begin adding line items and creating a quotation just like we did in Chapter 2, *Installing Your First Application*.

Please note that, because you created a new quotation from an opportunity, Odoo still leaves the opportunity open. Therefore, you must go back into **Your Pipeline** and mark the opportunity as won if you are truly done with the opportunity.

Leads and opportunities

Odoo provides two primary documents for managing interactions with your customers or potential customers. You can think of the **Leads** as less critical, and perhaps less likely to turn into a real sales situation than an opportunity. A good example of **Leads** would be that you get a few dozen business cards from people you met at a conference. You could add each of them as a **Leads** for further follow up. An example of an opportunity would be if you met someone at a conference and had a detailed conversation on how your company provides appropriate services.

Many people get confused between when to use **Leads** and when to use opportunities. The best way to remember is that **Leads** are intangible and are essentially potential contacts. Opportunities should be more clearly defined, have some sort of expected income of successful, and provide significant project details and scope compared to a simple lead.

Turning on Leads in Odoo 10

When you first install the Odoo CRM application, **Leads** are turned off by default. You can enable **Leads** by first choosing**Settings** under the **Configuration** section in the **Sales** menu. In the settings form under the **Leads** you can turn on **Leads** by selecting the second option and then clicking **Apply**:

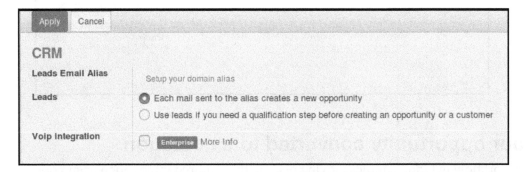

Once you have applied the changes to the settings, Odoo will refresh and add a **Leads** option to your sales menu.

Creating Leads in Odoo

It can often take quite a bit of work to uncover an opportunity. In Odoo, you create **Leads** when you need a qualification step before creating an opportunity or a customer. For example, you may receive a business card or an unqualified lead from your website. Another common situation is that **Leads** are purchased perhaps from a mailing list and then imported into Odoo.

Let's create a new lead for a potential customer we met at a local event.

Under the **Sales** menu, click **Leads** and then the **Create** button to open a new lead. The following screenshot is of the form used for creating a new lead:

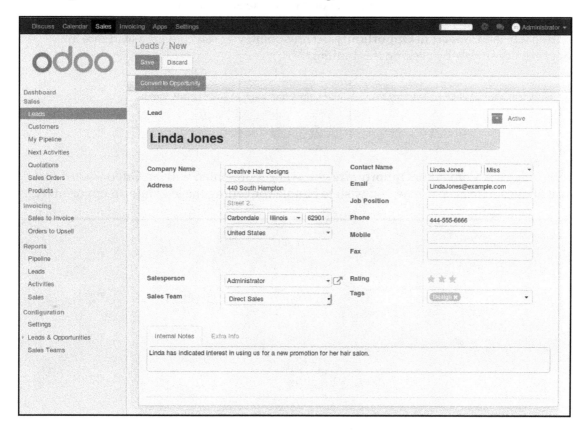

As you can see, the form is very similar to the standard customer screen. There is a good reason for this, as Odoo uses a standard structure to hold address information for **Leads**, customers, suppliers, and users/employees. In our example, we have filled out the basic contact and address information as well as assigned our sales representative to this lead.

Converting a lead into an opportunity

Leads will stay **Leads** indefinitely until you take some action to either turn them into opportunities or mark them as lost/dead. You will notice at the top left of your form is a button labeled **Convert to Opportunity**. At any point, you can convert a lead into an opportunity simply by clicking this button:

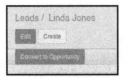

Once you click **Convert to Opportunity** you will get presented with an Odoo wizard that will allow you to choose how you wish to handle converting the lead into an opportunity:

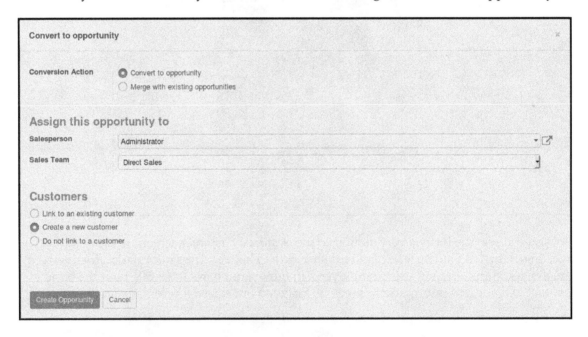

Each of the options presented are pretty well self-explanatory. The conversion action determines whether you will create a new opportunity or merge this lead with an existing opportunity. You get the option of assigning the opportunity to a specific sales person.

Finally, you get to tell Odoo if you wish to create a new customer for this opportunity or if instead you wish to assign this opportunity to an existing customer.

Using Odoo to schedule calls, meetings, and events

Often when working with leads and opportunities you will find it beneficial to schedule meetings and calls. Odoo provides a built-in meeting scheduler that you can use specifically to manage your schedule and relate those events to customers within Odoo. Odoo considers it so useful that they have a dedicated menu for it. Let's take a look at how we can schedule an event in Odoo. Meeting scheduling is handled in the messaging menu of Odoo. Begin by choosing **Calendar** from the main menu.

Odoo will then display your personal calendar:

Odoo will bring up the current week. Arrows at the top left of the form allow you to quickly navigate to the previous and next month, respectively. To the right of the title is the option to look at the calendar by week or by day. This can be particularly valuable to see more information when you have many meetings scheduled.

On the far right you have a small calendar for the next month. This small calendar is interactive and you can use it to quickly jump to that month and even a specific day.

Scheduling an event

Scheduling an event is very easy. Simply click on the day you wish to schedule an event. You will then be prompted to give a name to the event and to either create or edit the event:

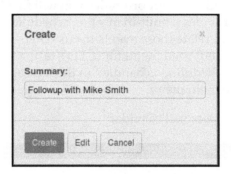

After entering the event summary, you will have two options. You can directly create the event, or you can choose **Edit** to provide additional details about the event.

Depending on how you want to organize and manage your meetings, it may work for you just fine to create the event; provided the event summary is enough information for you to take the action you require. Typically, however, it will be a better practice to edit this event and provide some more details.

Click **Edit** to create an event and automatically bring it up for editing:

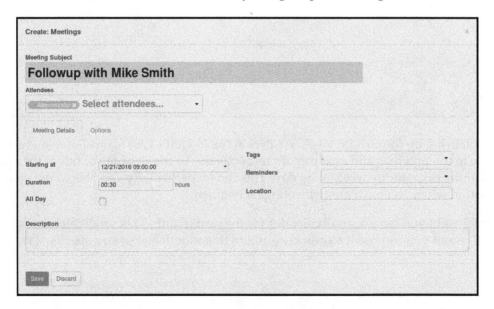

Odoo will automatically bring over the event summary that you filled in after clicking on the day. Notice, however, that instead of **Event Summary** the title is now **Meeting Subject.** Perhaps Odoo will modify this in the future for greater consistency.

Adding attendees to your meeting

By default, you are the only person attending this meeting. When you are meeting with a client, customer, or vendor it is largely up to you whether you wish to add the attendee here in the list. For our purpose, we will add `Mike Smith` to the list of attendees. Odoo will automatically search in real time as you type out the name:

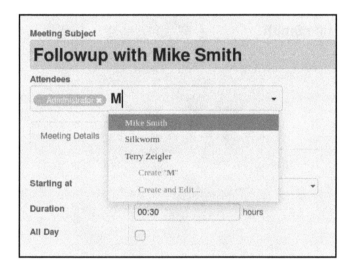

Odoo will then add the attendee to the attendees list. For internal communications, this can be used to make sure all of the necessary team members are notified of the meeting if they are also using the Odoo schedules.

Odoo will provide you with a warning if you add an attendee who does not have an email address. In this case, Odoo will still add the attendee, but naturally any automated notifications cannot be delivered to the attendee.

Specifying meeting details

Odoo's meeting scheduler offers quite a few different options that assist you in customizing the meeting. One of the first things to notice is that by default, Odoo schedules the meeting for the full day. If your meeting does not have a specific time you can check the **All Day** option. After you have checked the option, the **Duration** field disappears and is replaced with an **Ending at** field to specify the ending day for the event. This allows you to specify events that may span several days:

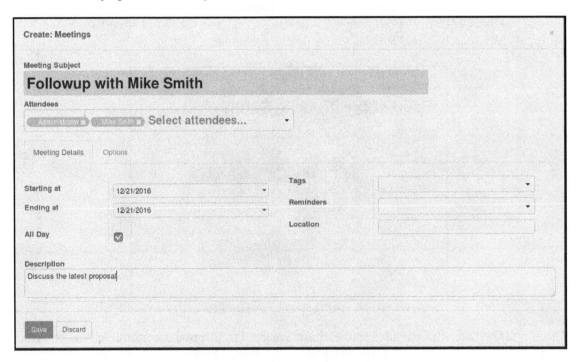

Specifying tags for your meeting

Odoo provides a set of default meeting tags that quickly tell you the overall scope of the meeting. You can specify multiple tags as well as create new tags to organize your meeting schedules:

Setting up reminders for your meeting

Often you may like to have a reminder or notice a little bit before your meeting. Setting reminders can possibly help prevent you from missing an important meeting. Odoo offers two kinds of basic reminders, notifications and e-mail reminders.

Notifications will prompt you visually on screen in the top right corner of your window when the reminder times comes. Email reminders will send you an e-mail:

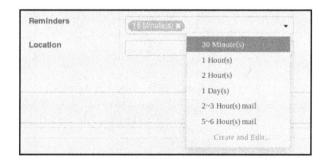

In addition to tags and reminders you also have the option to specify the location of the meeting. This location is a simple text field and is just some extra information that you can use to keep your team members informed.

Specifying additional meeting options

Under the options page, Odoo allows you to specify several additional options for meetings. One of the most powerful features is the ability to configure reoccurring meetings. When you select the reoccurring option, additional options will become available in which you can select the interval.

Depending on the interval you select, the form will refresh with the appropriate options for that interval. In the following screenshot, we have selected a weekly interval. Odoo then allows us to select which day(s) of the week the meeting will repeat:

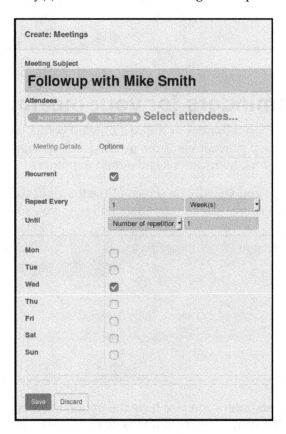

In addition to selecting the specific days, you can also specify how long until the reoccurring meeting will end. The preceding example demonstrates how you can specify a meeting to end based on the number of repetitions. If you choose, you can select an end date to stop the reoccurring meeting.

Summary

In this chapter, we started by discussing the role of a CRM system in a modern day business. We installed the CRM module, created salespeople, and proceeded to develop a system to manage the sales process. In our example, we walked an opportunity through the various stages in the sales process. Finally, we saw how to modify stages in the sales cycle and turn the opportunity directly into a quotation.

In the next chapter, we will turn our attention to purchasing products and setting up the MRP application to handle production operations.

4
Purchasing with Odoo

In this chapter, we start getting into what could be considered the core functionality of most ERP systems. We will begin by setting up a vendor and then purchasing raw material components. After the products arrive, we then receive the products into inventory and pay the invoice to complete the purchasing cycle.

Topics we will cover in this chapter include:

- Examining a typical purchasing process for a business
- Setting up your vendors and warehouse locations
- Entering a quote and turning it into a purchase order
- Receiving products from your vendors
- Paying invoices

Understanding the overall purchasing process

Let us begin by taking a 30,000-foot view of the purchasing process. Putting together a purchasing system requires several steps, and initially it can be confusing for people new to ERP systems. But when you break the steps down and look at them individually, the process becomes much easier to understand.

Setting up a vendor

When you set up a vendor, you are determining the individuals or companies that are providing you with products. Sometimes vendors are also referred to as suppliers. In Odoo, it is perfectly possible to create a product and sell it without implementing a purchasing system. However, to begin using your system for purchasing, you will need to configure the vendors.

The steps you take with setting up a vendor are much the same as setting up a customer. In fact, now is as good a time as any to tell you that Odoo maintains core customer, employee, and vendor records all in the same model (or table) named `res.partner`. Odoo distinguishes between customers, vendors, and those who are both with the use of the **Is a Customer** and **Is a Vendors** checkboxes.

Setting up warehouse locations

Once you have decided to start using Odoo to purchase your products, you will need to set up locations to receive them. In a simple operation, you may only have one location, but other companies may have literally hundreds of warehouse locations. In Odoo, each location can maintain its own address, and it is possible to create nested sub-locations for better management and reporting of inventory.

Generating quotations and purchase orders

To acquire the raw product, you will need to create **Request for Quotations** and/or purchase orders to send to your vendors. In purchasing, these are the documents you create that tell the vendors which products you require, the quantity in which you require them, and what you expect to pay for those products. Often this process is referred to as procurement. Depending on the industry and the specific location of the company, it is possible that there might be a variety of methods to manage quotations and approvals when purchasing products.

Receiving the product

In a simple purchasing workflow, once your purchase order has been received by the vendor, you will be waiting for them to fulfill the order. At some point, you will receive the product. Depending on your industry, this could be the same day or can even stretch to months. When the delivery is complete, you receive the products and they will move into the location you select.

Now that the product has been received, you are ready to create a manufacture order. But first, let's pay the vendor for what we ordered.

Settling the invoice

Once you have received the product, it is just a matter of time before you must pay for it. Invoicing can happen at the time you order the product, before the product is shipped to you, or after you have received the product. Regardless of when you get an invoice, you can be sure that if you are receiving products, you will eventually be invoiced for them.

When an invoice is received, it is essential to compare it to the purchase order for accuracy. Any discrepancies between the purchase order and invoice must be resolved before the invoice is paid. Essentially, this is your way of ensuring that you are only paying for the products you have authorized for purchase. Finally, it is good practice to match the receiving or delivery order to the purchase order and invoice as well. This *three-way match* ensures that you got exactly what you ordered and that invoice reflects exactly what you are required to pay.

Installing the purchasing application

Odoo is a modular set of applications in which you only install the applications you need. Therefore, we must install the purchase management application to continue. By this point, you should be familiar with the process of installing a new application to Odoo. Following is a screenshot of the **Purchase Management** application in **Apps** list:

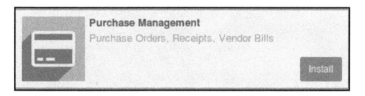

When you install the purchasing application, you will get two new menus:

- Purchases
- Inventory

It is possible that these menus may already exist or that purchasing may already be installed if you have installed another module such as e-commerce, that requires **Purchase Management** as a dependency.

The **Purchases** menu is where you can create quotations and purchase orders for the products you purchase from your vendors. In the **Inventory** menu, you can manage physical inventories. If you take a few moments to look through the menus you will notice you can access some of the same features from both menus. For example, you can get to the **Products** view from either menu.

Setting up your first vendor

To begin setting up our first vendor, you will select **Purchases** | **Vendors** and click on **Create**:

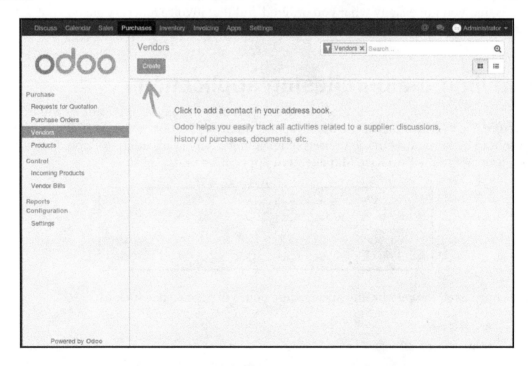

This is the **Vendors** listing, but as it is empty, you will see instructions on how you can add a new vendor. Odoo also lists a few of the features that you can expect from vendor management such as tracking discussions, history of purchases, and documents associated with a vendor.

After clicking **Create**, Odoo will bring up the vendor form for you to fill out:

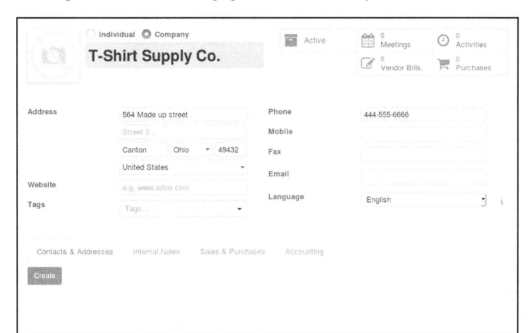

This form is very much like the customer form because it is based on the same basic structure. In fact, it is perfectly acceptable for a customer to also be a vendor. When you create a new vendor record, a vendor checkbox is automatically marked for you under the **Sales & Purchases** page on the form. Sometimes this can get a little confusing for people new to Odoo. This chapter will start to make the relationships between companies, contacts, customers, and vendors in Odoo clearer.

Designating vendor companies versus individuals

Much like when you set up a customer, the **Company** and **Individual** options at the very top of the form are where you inform Odoo of the relationship you have with this vendor. Typically, you will be purchasing products from a company.

For our example, we will choose the **Company** option.

Once you've filled in the vendor name, address, and other contact information, as well as the required accounting information, click **Save** at the top of the form.

Configuring your product for procurement

When we set up our first product, we were only concerned with selling the product to a customer. We essentially named the product and set the price at which we wish to sell it. To purchase the product from our vendor, we must provide a little more information. To do this, we will edit the product and change the information under the procurement tab.

Go to **Purchases | Products**, then click on the option for `Medium White T-Shirt` to bring up the product form. Then click **Edit** to enter the edit mode.

Following is a screenshot of the **Inventory** section of the product form:

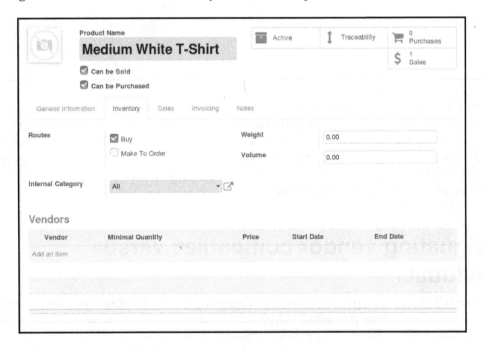

At the top of the form, check **Can be Purchased** so that the purchasing systems know to include this product in the list of products when you make a purchase order.

Supply chain information

In Odoo 10, you have far more options to manage your purchasing supply chain, using routes. Fortunately, by default, Odoo sets up two of the most common routes. These routes are **Buy** and **Make to Order**. For purchasing, we must check the **Buy** checkbox so that Odoo can properly route the products we purchase from our vendor to our internal warehouse location.

Using buy routes

When you configure a buy route, you can purchase products in one of two ways. One of the ways to purchase this product would be to create a purchase order and add the product to the purchase order manually. This is the typical manual purchasing system where a purchase agent perhaps uses other events outside Odoo or examines reports in Odoo to create purchase orders.

In addition to creating manual purchase orders, you can also create re-ordering rules that will automatically create draft purchase orders when the stock of the product dips below a set minimum. This method works well on products that are ordered frequently and frees up your purchasing managers from having to manually create purchase orders for some or even most of your inventory.

Using Make To Order

When you configure a Make to Order route, you are telling Odoo that you wish for draft purchase orders to be created when a sales order includes that specific product, regardless of the stock you have on hand. For example, even if you had 2,000 of a product in stock and a customer orders ten of that product, Odoo will create a draft purchase order for 10 units if you have the **Make To Order** route checked.

Often a business would use the make to order option when they do not need to keep stock on a product and instead will either manufacture or purchase the product for reselling once a sales order is confirmed. It is certainly possible to use a combination of buy and make to order with re-ordering limits to set up a system in which you always keep a minimum quantity in stock, but a draft purchase order is created for sales orders which include that product. Remember, draft orders can always be cancelled, so depending on the processes in your purchasing department, it may be desirable for them to get make to order purchase drafts even if they wish to maintain their own minimum and maximum limits within Odoo.

Purchasing information

In addition to the changes under the **Procurement** tab, there are also a few changes we need to make under the **General Information** page on the product form:

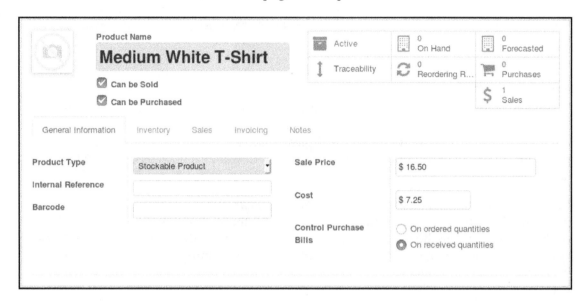

Product type

When you configure purchasing, you will want to pay special attention to product type. For this example, we have chosen **Stockable Product** because we wish to manage the inventory of the product and perhaps sell directly out to the customer. Alternatively, you can choose a consumable product type. This would be a good choice for products you don't wish to manage in inventory and just plan to purchase and use, such as office supplies or coffee filters for the break room.

Setting records to active

Like most records in Odoo, you can set a product to **Inactive** so that it will no longer be available when creating new sales orders or purchase orders. You can do this from the **General Information** tab on the product page.

Once you have any transactions associated with a product, you will not be allowed to delete that product from the system. Instead, set **active** to **false** so that the product will no longer appear in the active lists. To view these inactive records, you can use the advanced search feature to create a filter to show records where the active flag is false.

Setting the cost price of the product

Often, you will wish to assign a cost to the product. This will be the cost that will appear on your purchase quotations, though it can be overwritten at any time to reflect a vendor's new pricing. If your vendor happens to give you a one-time discount, you will want to reflect that change on the actual purchase order, rather than here in the base product record. For our example, we have set the cost price of the shirt to 7.25.

Assigning vendors to the product

At the bottom of the **Inventory** tab is the option to add vendors. It is very common that a company may have multiple vendors which offer the same product.

Click on **Add an Item** in the vendor grid to add the vendor to the product:

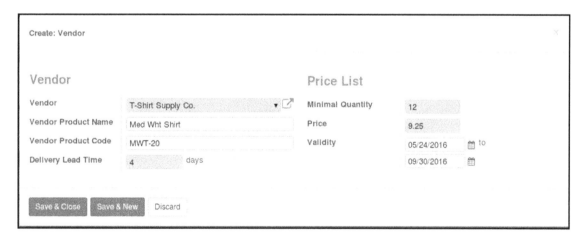

Establishing the vendor

You have the choice in the drop-down list to search for vendors as well as to create and edit a new vendor on the fly. To the far right of the drop-down, you can use the small icon to edit the current vendor. In the pop-down we have selected **T-Shirt Supply Co**. as the company to provide our blank `Medium White T-shirts`.

Designating vendor product name and product code

Because a vendor may use different product codes or product names than your company does to describe a given product, here you have the option to specify how the vendor identifies the product. This information will be displayed on the purchase quotations and purchase orders you create to make sure you get the right product from the vendor.

Setting minimum quantity

Vendors will often have a minimum order quantity for a product. Sometimes, vendors may actually sell you a lower quantity but the cost per unit is dramatically higher. Setting a minimal quantity in this form allows you to prevent those problems by forcing purchase quantities to be at least the minimal quantity value. For our example, we will set the minimal quantity to `12`.

Calculating delivery time

Depending on the vendor, a product may take less or more time to obtain. Often this can make a difference when you are putting together a time-sensitive purchase quotation. A product may be cheaper, but if the delay is too long and puts the delivery time in jeopardy, you may need to buy the product at a higher price from another vendor who can deliver the product faster. Setting the delivery time in days for the vendor to deliver the product provides your purchasing agents with the information they require to make decisions based on price and availability. For our example, we have set the delivery time to `4 days`.

Setting price and validity

Now in Odoo 10 you can also specify the price for the item from that specific vendor. This simplifies managing your vendor pricing. When you select the given item for a specific vendor, you will get the price you have specified here. Optionally, you can specify validity dates so you can proactively manage products when suppliers bring on new products or perhaps discontinue a product.

Creating your first purchase quotation

Now that we have our vendor entered and the product associated with the vendor, we are ready to create our first **Request for Quotation** (**RFQ**). This is typically the document you will create when requesting pricing from a vendor (sometimes called a vendor) prior to actually ordering the product. For our example, we are going to create a **RFQ** for Medium White T-Shirts.

Go to **Purchases | Requests for Quotation** and click on **Create** to make a new **RFQ**:

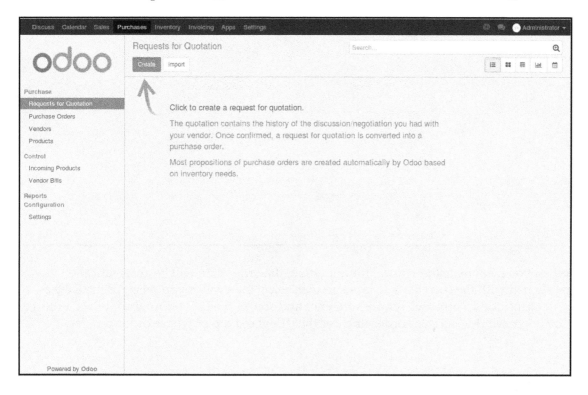

After you click on **Create**, the **RFQ** will appear for you to enter the required information:

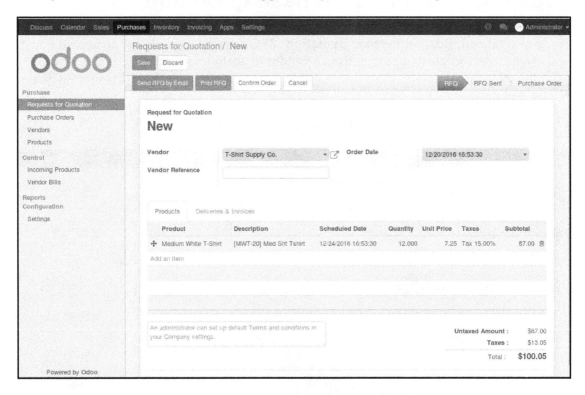

When you first create the request for quotation, the order date will be automatically populated with the current date. You can then select the vendor you wish for the **RFQ** as well as include an optional vendor reference and source document. An example of a source document would be a sales order number that triggered the purchase order process.

Adding products to your request for quotation

After you click **Add an Item** you can select the product from the drop-down list on the far left. The description will automatically be filled in. The scheduled date will be determined based on the delivery delay from the vendor. We also find the minimum order quantity from the vendor has been pulled to the **RFQ**. Finally, the unit cost is populated from the unit price on the **Procurements** tab of the product.

Printing RFQs and updating status

For now, we will skip the **Deliveries & Invoices** and go right to printing our **RFQ**. By default, Odoo will print to a PDF file. This file can easily be attached to e-mails. Once you have configured an e-mail server, you can configure Odoo to automatically send the purchase order by e-mail.

The status is then updated to show that the **RFQ** has been sent:

Confirming a purchase order

Once you have a final quotation, you are ready to confirm the purchase order. It is very important to understand that once you have confirmed, it becomes a purchase order and it can no longer be modified. Once you are sure you wish to finalize the purchase order, click the **Confirm Order** button. Any modifications that need to be made at this stage would require you to duplicate and cancel the original order. This is necessary so that Odoo can maintain an audit trail.

If you happen to receive an error message reading **No Expense Account** when you attempt to confirm the order, check your settings for your chart of accounts. You must have an expense account designated for the products contained on the PO.

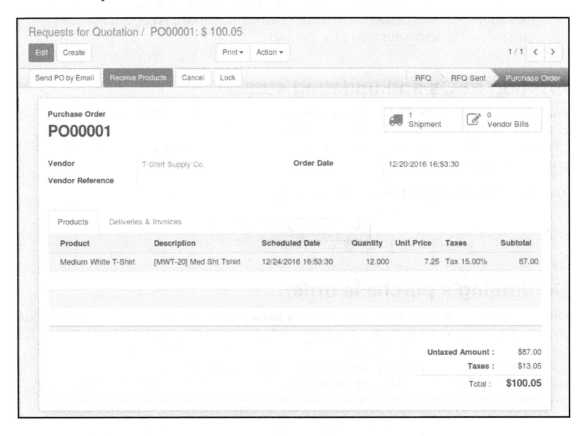

The preceding screenshots shows the RFQ form. Once you have confirmed, the form will refresh to show the new status of the purchase order. At this point, you are waiting on the vendor to deliver the products and send you an invoice. The status is updated to **Purchase Order** and is now just one step from the **Done** condition.

After clicking **Confirm**, you will notice in the upper-right corner that we can see there is one incoming shipment. Each of these is an active button that you can click to see the corresponding shipments or invoices associated with this purchase order.

Receiving products

If everything goes as planned, the products we have ordered will be arriving within four days or less. Once the products have arrived, we must receive our products into inventory.

Click **Receive Products** to bring up the **Receiving** form:

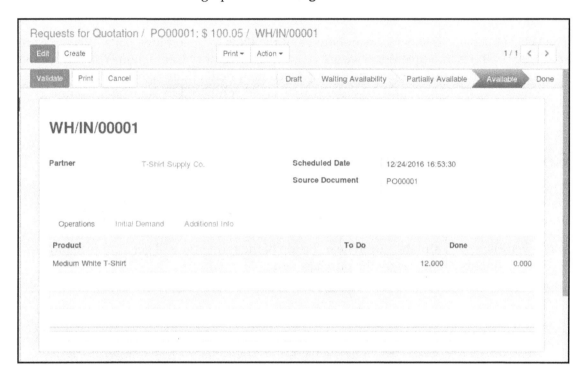

Getting ready to receive

At this point we have not actually received the product yet. This is just showing us the details on the product that we are ready to receive. The **WH/IN/00001** is sequentially assigned for each transaction.

Please be aware that it is possible the transaction name **WH/IN/000001** may be different in your installation as Odoo changes the sequences that are defined in a default installation from time to time. These names can be user-configured by going to **Settings | Sequences & Identifiers | Sequences**. You could even change the default prefix from **PO** to whatever you desire, as long as it does not conflict with the prefix of another module.

The **WH** in the name is short for warehouse and the **IN** is for incoming goods. When we are receiving products into inventory, we are creating an inventory transaction. You can see the associated purchase order under the **Source Document** field on the right side of the form. We can also see the actual time the order was received compared to the scheduled time of the order. In this case, we can see we received the order in plenty of time.

Receiving our goods

By editing the transfer and changing the value in the **Done** column, you can specify an alternate quantity if what you have received does not match the quantity on the purchase order. For this example, we will assume that the entire product arrived as expected.

When you click the **Validate** button near the top of the form you will get a confirmation to receive the quantity that was on the purchase order:

Once you click **Apply**, the quantity in the **Done** column matches the **To do** quantity; the product is now in inventory. Since all of the products on this purchase order have been received, the purchase order status at the top right is set to **Done**. Finally, you will notice the **Reverse** button that is available for instances in which you need to manage product returns:

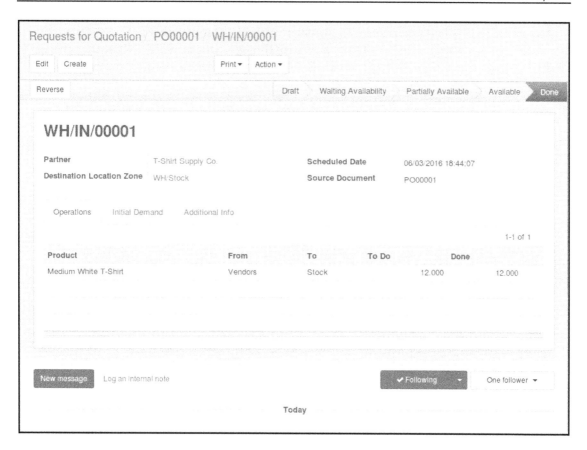

If you would like to verify that your goods have been received into inventory, look up the Medium White T-Shirt under **Products** and click on the **Inventory** tab. You should notice its quantity on hand increased by 12 units. Odoo automatically adjusts stock levels as products are received into your company's inventory. Likewise, stock levels are decremented if products are returned to their vendor.

Paying vendor bills

Once you have received your product, sooner or later you should receive a bill. This is often called a supplier or vendor invoice. It is of course possible to receive a bill before you receive products. Each business will have to decide the exact workflow for when they pay bills and under what conditions.

Unlike in Odoo 8, when you confirm a purchase order in Odoo 10 there is no visible record of a draft invoice or bill. This was likely a control that was put in place so that the receiving of the bill from the vendor would be required and help prevent someone from simply validating the purchase order and creating and sending out a bill.

To create a vendor bill, go to the **Invoicing** menu and select **Purchases | Vendor Bills**:

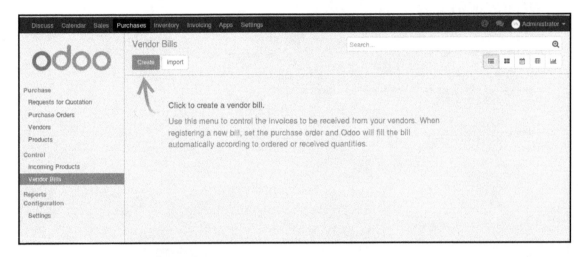

Click **Create** to bring up the **Vendor Bills** form.

In the workflow, the user should now have the vendor bill in front of them that they need to pay. Use the **Vendor** drop-down menu to select the vendor.

Next, use the **Add Purchase Order** drop-down menu to select the purchase order **PO00001 : $ 100.05** as the one we wish to pay:

At this point, you will see all the necessary information from the purchase order including the product, description amount, and tax:

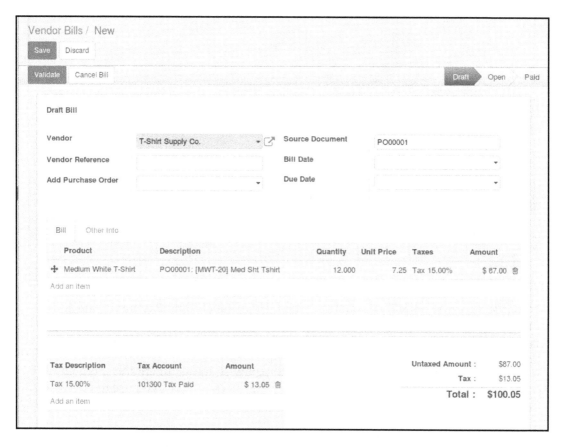

From here you can click **Validate** to create the bill. This will then leave the bill with the status **Open**, until you register a payment or ask for a refund.

So let's pay this bill. Click on **Validate** on **Register Payment** page as shown:

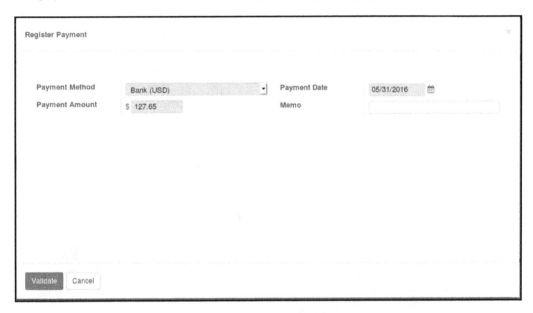

Most of the information will automatically be filled out including **Payment Date** and **Payment Amount**. You can change these if necessary. The one piece of information you must provide is the **Payment Method**. For our example, we have chosen **Bank (USD)**.

The **Memo** can be used to create whatever note you wish to document this payment. For example, you can use the **Memo** field to specify the check number you use to pay your vendor.

 When implementing a purchase order system, it is critical to train users thoroughly on how transactions are tied together. While many forms allow you to click on a link to view a related record, fields such as **Payment Ref** store the data just as text. Train and encourage users to quickly use copy and paste rather than re-entering data into search fields.

Odoo will allow you to configure multiple payment methods. For now, choose **Bank** and click **Validate** to complete the transaction.

You have now completed the entire purchasing cycle from purchasing, to receiving, to finally paying for the product:

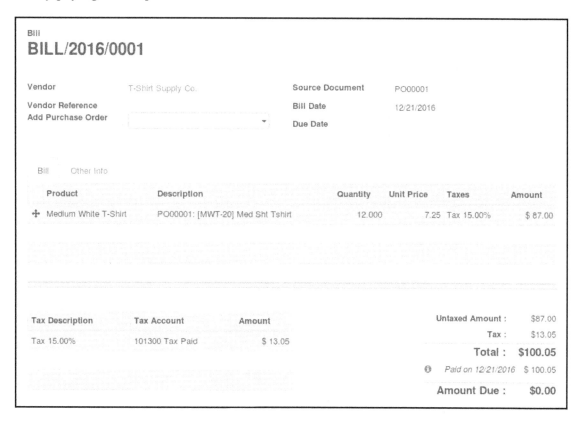

In the prior screenshot, you can see the final paid invoice for our purchased products. Notice at the bottom-right of the form it shows that we have a balance of zero. Now we can also see a summary of the payment as well by hovering over the little information icon above the amount due.

Summary

In this chapter, we installed the purchasing application and set up a vendor to purchase products. Next, we successfully purchased products and received those products into inventory. After our products were received into inventory, we proceeded to pay the invoice to complete the payment cycle.

In the next chapter, we will take the raw materials we have just received into inventory and use them to manufacture and deliver a finished product. We will create manufacturing orders to define the steps of the production process and allocate the required resources. Coordinating all of your resources, including machinery and manpower, can be a daunting and time-consuming task, but we are learning how Odoo makes this significantly more manageable.

5
Making Goods with Manufacturing Resource Planning

In this chapter, we will cover how you can use Odoo to manage the process of manufacturing products. Once you have received the required raw products in your inventory, you can begin manufacturing the end product. Part of the functionality of an ERP system is to assist you in scheduling these orders based on available resources. One of the resources is, of course, the raw product. Other resources could include available labor or the availability of a particular machine. Essentially, the goal is to schedule the manufacturing order at a time that all resources are available and produce the product for an on-time delivery.

In this chapter, we will cover the following topics:

- Setting up the manufacturing process
- Defining our bill of materials
- Manufacturing our final product
- Analyzing the inventory report

Creating manufacturing orders

Manufacturing orders define the product you wish to build, the resources required, and when you wish to produce the product. They also designate when you wish to produce the product. In addition, they can contain information about work orders and routings that are related to that manufacturing order.

Producing the product

When it is time to actually produce the product, you then inform Odoo of each of the products produced and your manufacturing order changes to a status of **Complete**. In a typical workflow, your raw materials are moved out of the inventory, and your finished product is added into your inventory.

Delivering the order

After a product has been produced and has been put into the inventory, it can be packaged and delivered to the customer. Depending on the specific manufacturing environment, a product may not even sit in a physical inventory location at all and instead may be shipped almost immediately to the customer. Meanwhile in another industry, you may have a product that is produced and then sits in a warehouse for months before delivery. Of course it is always possible that something gets produced and gets left in dead stock. In this case, you would never have a delivery order and instead use a process to determine how to manage that dead inventory.

Defining the workflow for your business

Much like configuring the CRM application, oftentimes the most complex part of setting up a purchasing and manufacturing system is not the ERP software itself. Instead the real challenge is to understand the business requirements and how the current processes can best be implemented. If you have never set up a purchasing and manufacturing system before, it is highly recommended that you supplement your knowledge with additional source material on the subject. Please refer to the appendix for references to additional resources on ERP and manufacturing.

A real-world example of producing a custom-printed t-shirt

In Odoo, you manufacture products by creating manufacturing orders. For our example, we will be printing T-shirts that have a custom designed logo. The basic manufacturing process itself involves using a screen to apply ink to each of the T-shirts. For now, we don't need to know all the details of this process to begin using Odoo to help schedule and track the manufacturing of the product.

The basic steps in the process are simple:

1. Define a bill of materials that determine what items are needed to produce the final product
2. Use a manufacturing order to print a design on the blank T-shirts
3. Deliver the printed T-shirts to a customer

Installing Manufacturing Resource Planning

We must now install the **Manufacturing Resource Planning (MRP)** application so that we can begin configuring our T-shirt production. By now you should begin to understand the modular nature of Odoo. Install the **MRP** applications just like you did with the other Odoo applications:

Choose **Apps** and install the **Manufacturing** application:

Clicking the **Install** button installs the **MRP** application.

Creating your first manufacturing order

The flexibility of Odoo provides a variety of approaches that you can take in setting up your system. Manufacturing can also become a complex topic and is one of the more challenging aspects of setting up any ERP system. For our first manufacturing order, we will ignore many advanced options.

Keep it simple at first. There are many options and it will take time to understand them all. If you are new to manufacturing systems, it will take you longer to implement Odoo, and you should consider hiring professional consultants to assist you.

To create your first manufacturing order, go to the **Manufacturing** menu, choose **Manufacturing Orders**, and then click **Create**:

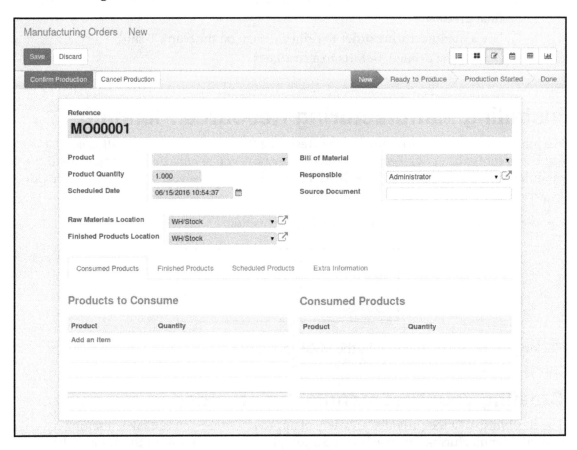

This is the manufacturing order as it appears just after you have hit **Create**.

Take a minute to look through the various tabs and get an idea of the information that is collected for a manufacturing order. Don't worry if you don't understand all the options yet. We will begin with a simple product and look at some of the most important aspects of creating a manufacturing order. Later, we will explore some of the more complex manufacturing scenarios.

What product are we going to manufacture?

The only product we have entered into Odoo so far is the medium white T-shirt, which is blank. Nothing is printed on the T-shirt when it is received from the supplier. Now, we want to create a manufacturing order that will produce a new product in which we print on the T-shirt a design of the customer's choice.

For our operations, we can still use the medium white T-shirt. But now instead of selling the blank T-shirt directly to our customer, it will be used as a raw material for our manufacturing order.

Let's first configure the final product that is to be created during the manufacturing process, that is, the complete T-shirt with the final design that will ship to the customer. For our example, it will be a **Class of 2016 T-shirt**.

Odoo allows you the ability in most forms where it is appropriate to create a product on the fly. Let's create a product by clicking the drop-down arrow under the **Product** tab and choosing **Create and Edit...**:

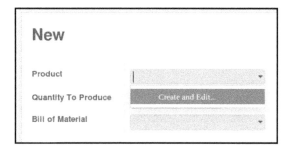

Using the quick **Create and Edit...**, you can add your finished products directly when creating a manufacturing order. In some workflows where you may use a separate system for handling sales orders, this option can be a fast way to create the required finished products to push into the inventory.

Next, you will fill out the product form with the fields required for a finished product:

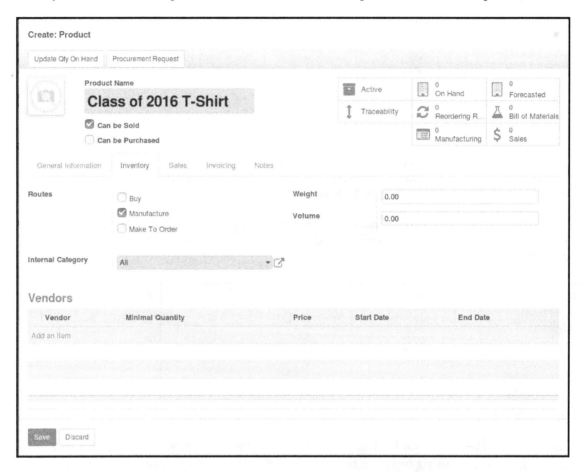

The **General Information** and **Inventory** tab should look familiar by now. Starting in Odoo 9, Odoo provides routes that allow a lot of flexibility in defining complex workflows and supply management operations. Fortunately, the more common routes are already configured and we can check **Manufacture** to let Odoo manufacturing know that this product is part of the manufacturing workflow. Only products that have the supply method of **Manufacture** can be selected as a product on a manufacture order.

Please also notice at the top of the form that the **Can be Purchased** box is unchecked. This will keep this product from appearing in the product list on a purchase order. Since we cannot purchase this product directly from a supplier, we don't want it appearing in our product list when working within purchasing.

Building your bill of materials

A **Bill of materials** (**BOM**) is essentially a list of products that are required to produce another product. You can think of it like the list of ingredients for a recipe. Odoo needs to know what materials are required for us to produce this `Class of 2016 T-shirt` product.

In complex products, a bill of materials can be nested. For example, it may take many products to make a sub-product and then several sub-products to make a final product.

 Don't let nested BOM intimidate you. Once you understand how a simple BOM is processed you will more easily see how you can group parts together. Think about grouping more complex BOM by assembly and work centers. This makes it easier to see your inventory in real time as BOM can be processed at each stage of your operations, properly using up materials and creating finished sub-assemblies.

For our first bill of materials example, we will be keeping the bill of materials simple. We are just going to require the white T-shirt. The rest of the operation, printing the actual T-shirt, will be incorporated into the manufacturing order. In other words, if there are enough white T-shirts, this manufacturing order can be processed, and we can produce the final product. For now, the inks and screens will not be managed in the manufacturing process. This is an example of starting simple and adding more complexity as we build up the system.

A smart button in the top-right of the form shows you a count of the bill of materials attached to this product:

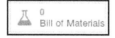

Clicking this button will bring up the bill of materials listing for that product:

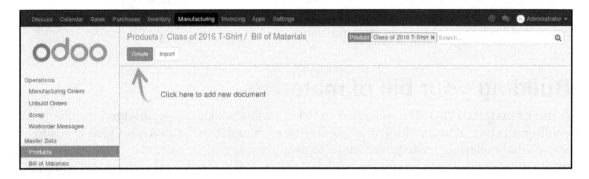

Naturally, this is a blank list, as we have not yet defined any bill of materials for this product. Notice in the top right corner, the product filter that is restricting this list view to only display the **Bill of Materials** that are for the `Class of 2016 T-shirt`.

Clicking **Create** will now bring up a blank **Bill of Materials** form with the `Class of 2016 T-shirt` automatically pre-populated as the finished product to build:

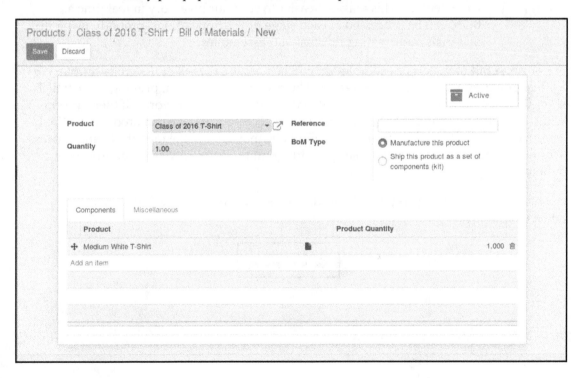

Many of the fields will be automatically filled out as Odoo knows we are creating a bill of materials for our `Class of 2016 T-Shirt` product. In this example, we have added the **Medium White T-Shirt** to the bill of materials. When we manufacture one `Class of 2016 T-Shirt`, we will require one medium white T-shirt.

Many times, if not most of the time, a bill of materials will contain multiple items. Regardless of the number of items in the bill of materials, the way it is processed is exactly the same.

It is possible that your manufacturing order or bill of materials screen may look slightly different than the ones you see here. One reason is that, depending on the modules that are installed and what options are selected, the forms may have different content. Another common reason is that Odoo is currently getting frequent updates that can change the appearance of a given form.

Confirming production

Once you click **Confirm Production**, you are ready to manufacture the product. Odoo will provide reasonable defaults, which you can override as required. When production is confirmed, that does not mean that production has actually taken place. Confirming production has only informed the system that production is ready to proceed. You can tell we are ready to begin manufacturing because the **Produce** button is available.

Here is what our `Class of 2016 T-Shirt` **Manufacturing Order** looks like now:

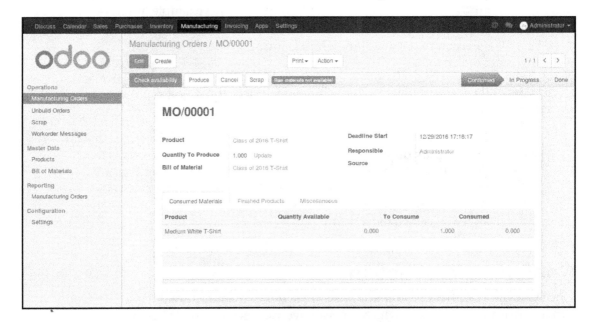

This is the manufacturing form showing the products waiting to be consumed to produce the order. In this case, it is our `Medium White T-Shirt`. You will also notice that this item is in red, and at the top of the form you can see the warning **Raw materials not available!**. This informs us that we must check the availability of our raw goods before we can begin manufacturing this product.

Checking availability

Odoo manufacturing links into the inventory automatically and it will use available stock to complete the order. As we have already purchased `Medium White T-Shirts` in the previous chapter, clicking the **Check availability** button will hide the button and remove the red highlight on the **Medium White T-Shirt** as well as remove the material warning message.

Please be aware that at this stage, if you don't have an available quantity, Odoo will continue to display the **Check availability** button and the warning message until the product is acquired and put into the inventory. Each time you click **Check Availability**, Odoo will look into the inventory to see if we have the necessary products so we are ready to produce. Alternatively, you can click **Produce** to identify to Odoo manufacturing that you are in fact ready to produce this product even if the inventory within the system does not meet the necessary requirements. Note that doing this will give you negative inventory quantities in your warehouse.

After the raw product has been acquired and we are ready to produce our final product, the form will be updated and the state changed:

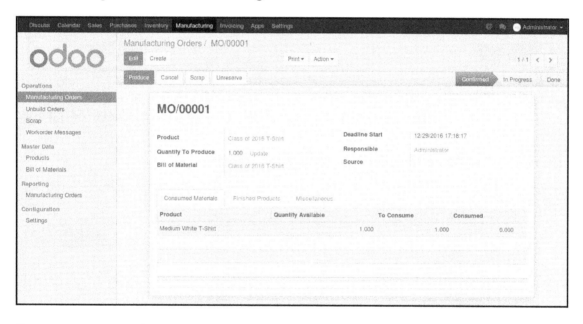

Here, we can see in the grid the quantity of `Medium White T-Shirt` available, the amount we will consume in the manufacturing order, and finally the total that will be consumed once the order is complete.

Producing the product

After you click the **Produce** button, you will be prompted to confirm that the product has been produced:

In Odoo 10, the production wizard has been simplified to ask only for the quantity of the number of finished goods you wish to produce. For our example, we will leave the quantity set to **1.000** unit.

Click the **Record Production** button to produce the product:

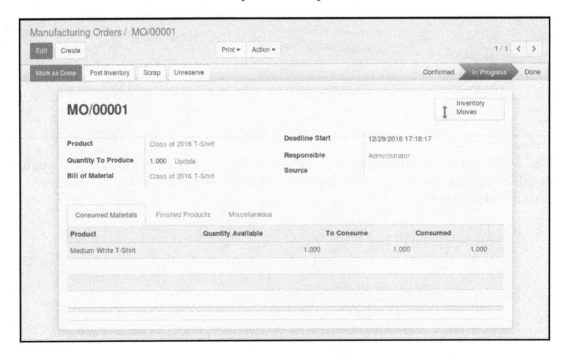

The product has then been produced and is ready to be posted into inventory. If at this stage you go and look at the product record you will not see any Class of 2016 T-Shirt on hand. At this stage you can click the **Mark as Done** button and Odoo will both post the inventory and mark the manufacturing order as done. Alternatively, you could click the **Post Inventory** button to add the Class of 2016 T-Shirt to inventory and then use a separate step to click the **Mark as Done** button to move the order to the done state.

Congratulations, you have just used Odoo to manufacture your first product!

Analyzing stock valuation

In our example, we have taken a raw material and increased its value by producing a finished product. One of the easiest ways to see the effect of our manufacturing order is to look at the inventory valuation report, which can be found at **Inventory | Inventory Valuation**.

Here you will see that we now have one **Class of 2016 T-Shirt** and 11 **Medium White T-shirts**. The inventory is accurately reflecting the purchases made by us as well as the products consumed and produced by our manufacturing order:

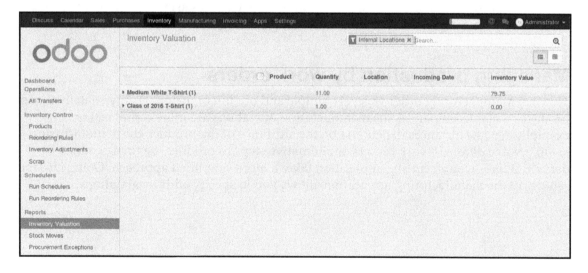

With this view, everything is collapsed and as a result, many of the columns are empty. For example in this view, you don't see anything under **Location** or **Incoming Date** because the data is rolled up. You can use the small triangles on the far left of the grid to drill down into the data and see more details on how the stock value is derived. Here is the same data, but expanded out so you can see the details:

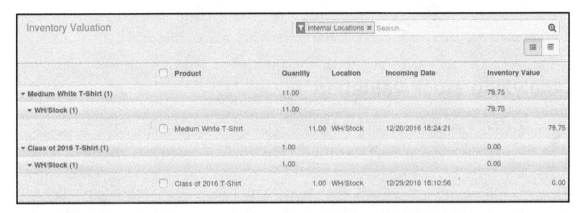

In the more detailed listing, you will see how you can get a great deal of information on the operations by looking at the stock move column. Here we can see exactly where the product came from, where it went, and how it affects the product quantity for that location.

Managing production by work orders

This first manufacturing order was very simple and our bill of materials only contained one product. In many companies, the manufacturing operations are more complex. For example, in some instances depending on the attributes of the product, the manufacturing could involve different work centers or alternative steps to produce the final product. By default, Odoo's manufacturing application takes a more simplified approach. Going into the settings of the manufacturing application allows you to specify additional options.

Simply go to the **Manufacturing** | **Settings** menu and select under the **Configuration** section on the left. Here under **Routing & Planning** you can check **Manage production by work orders**. Once this option is checked, you will have the ability to manage more complex manufacturing processes inside Odoo:

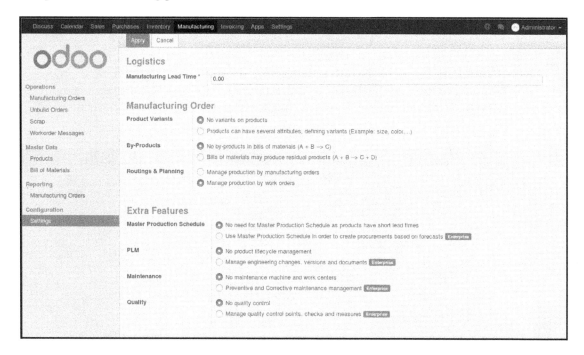

After you apply the changes, the menus will refresh, and new options will be added to the manufacturing application.

 Sometimes when adding new functionality to Odoo, such as applications or modifying settings, it can be helpful to do a **shift-refresh** on your browser to make sure Odoo is refreshed with the latest options.

Creating a work center

In our previous simplified manufacturing order, we specified the raw product required in a bill of materials and then turned that into a finished product. Now we will expand this example to specify the human labor that goes into printing our `Class of 2016 T-Shirt`. In Odoo, we define the parameters in a work center.

For the purpose of our example, we will create a work center called `Printing` that is responsible for taking the blank T-shirt and applying the design to create the final product. We begin by going to the manufacturing application and under the **Master Data** menu choosing the **Work Centers** option. Then we click **Create** to set up a new work center record:

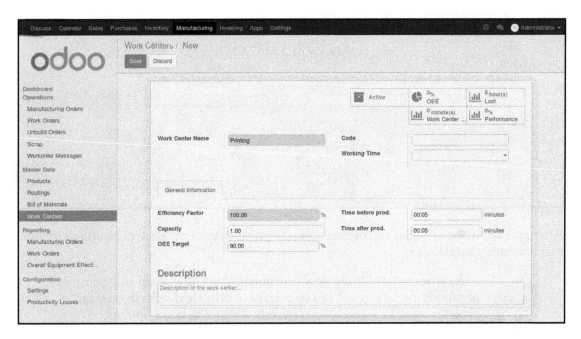

In our example, we have named the work center **Printing**. In a full implementation, it would be common to have different work centers based around the work performed.

Setting General Information

When defining a work center, it is possible to define **General Information** that will allow you to estimate the cost and time required to produce your products. In our example, we are going to configure this work center so that we can estimate the time required to produce a T-shirt.

Efficiency Factor

The **Efficiency Factor** is a metric of how efficient this work center is at completing tasks. Often, the **Efficiency Factor** is most valuable in allowing you to tweak your work center capacity without modifying many of the other variables. If, for example, you have an efficiency factor of 200.00 (or 200 percent) then the work center will complete twice as many tasks. For our example, we are leaving the efficiency factor as the default of 1.00 or 100%.

Capacity

The **Capacity** allows you to determine how many tasks the work center can do in parallel. For example, if you had a work center that could be configured with three workers and all three workers can complete a cycle at the same time, you could set the capacity per cycle to three. When a manufacturing order is then routed to the work center, the work center can complete three tasks at the same time. For our example, we will assume one worker, and therefore one capacity per cycle.

Overall Equipment Effectiveness (OEE) target

In Odoo 10 the manufacturing application now places far more emphasis on tracking and reporting. A central metric to the information provided is **Overall Equipment Effectiveness (OEE)**. This is essentially a calculation that determines what percentage of your manufacturing time is used in actual production. The closer this is to 100%, the more efficient use you are making of your resources. By setting a work center goal you can determine how well your work center is meeting expectations.

Time before and after production

Many work center operations will have time required for set up and tear down times outside of the time consumed by actually producing the product. This is certainly true for our example. It takes time for someone to prepare a printing press with inks before the first T-shirt can be printed. For our example, we have estimated five minutes of set up time. Likewise, when we are done producing the last product in our work order it takes time to clean up and prepare for the next job. In this example, we have estimated five minutes of time at the end of production for clean-up operations.

Creating routing orders

After defining a work center, you need to define a way to specify under which conditions you should use the work center. This is accomplished by defining routings. For our example, we are going to keep it simple and use routing to send our manufacture order to the printing work center for the finished product to be produced. In a real-world example, the job may use routings to go through many work center operations before the final product is produced.

To create a routing order, go to the **Manufacturing** application and choose **Routings** under the **Configuration** submenu. Click **Create** to bring up the new routing form:

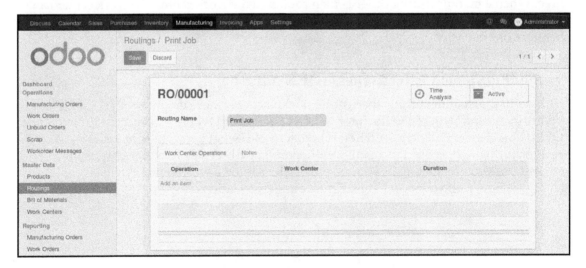

In our example, we have named the routing **Print Job** and specified the

Next, we will define our work station operation by clicking **Add an Item** and bringing up the **Operation** form:

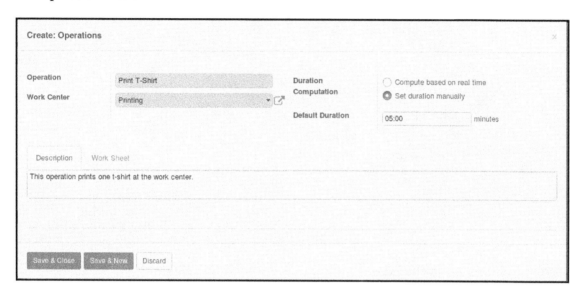

When defining our operation, we can name it whatever we wish, but in this case I picked **Print T-Shirt**. This indicates that this operation is more specific than the simple **Print Job** we are assigning to the routing order.

For complex routings, you can specify the sequence of the operations. We could, for example, have a **Design** operation and a **Build Screen** operation before the print job operation. Then we could specify a **Quality Assurance** operation and a **Packing** operation after the **Print Job**. You would handle all of these in exactly the same way you set up the printing work center and created the required operations to produce the product. By starting simply and adding additional operations and complexity over time, you can often get up and running much more quickly than trying to track every little task right from the beginning.

Once you have set up your operation, your routing should resemble the following form:

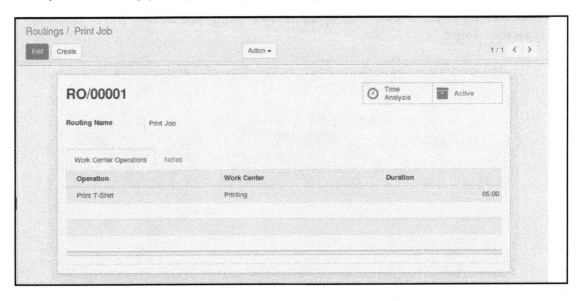

Here we can see the finished routing along with the operation details.

Assigning the routing to a bill of materials

Now that we have created a routing we need to tell the bill of materials to use our newly defined routing. In previous versions of Odoo it was possible to assign a routing right on the work order. In Odoo 10, if you don't set up the routing on the bill of materials it will not be available to you when you create a manufacturing order.

Pull up the BOM for our `Class of 2016 T-shirt` and set the routing to the `Print Job` we just created:

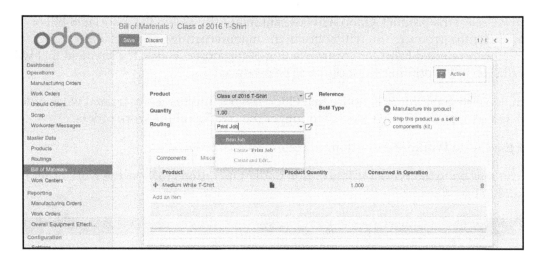

Creating a manufacturing order with routing and a work center

Now that we have defined our work center and our routing operation, we can create a manufacturing order that will utilize our new production steps. In this example, we are going to produce 15 Class of 2016 T-Shirts:

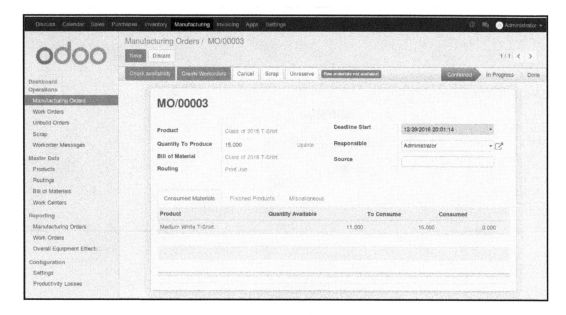

When we select the product, Odoo will now automatically assign the associated bill of materials for the product. You will notice in the manufacturing order that Odoo automatically selected **Print Job** for the routing of this order. This is the key field that will send this job to the printing work center to be produced.

When you click **Save** you will notice that Odoo has not automatically created work orders. There is a separate button in Odoo 10 to trigger the creation of the work orders.

Click the **Create Workorders** button to create the work order.

You can now go to the **Work Orders** option under **Operations** to view the work order in the default Kanban view:

Clicking on the `Class of 2016 T-Shirt` will then bring up the work order for you to review:

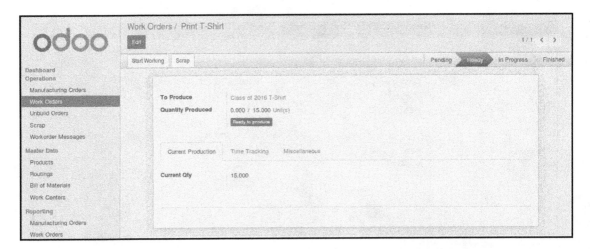

As you can see from the label, we have a **Ready to produce** label and so we can now click the **Start Working** button at the top of the form.

At this point Odoo considers this to be a real-time tracking system. That means that when your worker begins the job that is when they should click the button. When the workers has completed the job, they should click the **Done** button. By implementing tablets or other workstations capable of running Odoo, you can create a manufacturing environment that automatically tracks the time of your operations.

If you click on the **Time Tracking** tab, you can see details on the current operations as well as a timer that displays the updated duration of the operation in real-time:

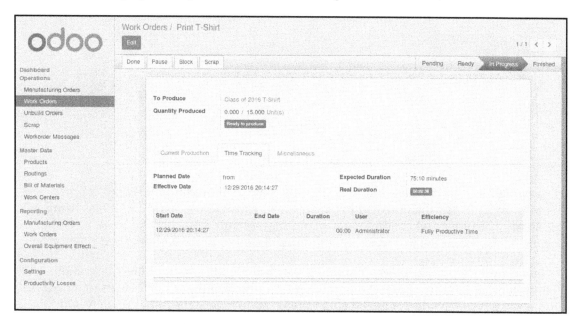

Now that you have had a chance to see the operation running, let's go ahead and click **Done** so we can see the results of our work in Odoo.

Odoo now refreshes the screen and moves the state of the workstation operation to Done. There is one thing that needs to be mentioned. Workcenters can perform their operation to completion regardless of the quantities in their inventory. This means that you would most likely have an internal process in which the worker would first check the availability on the manufacturing order before the worker even bothers to pull up the work order.

Let us now go and look at the manufacturing order:

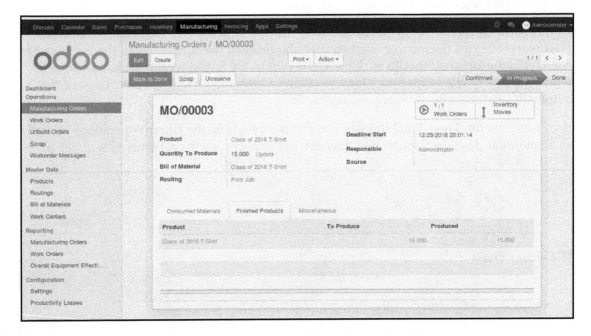

Here we can see that, because that was the only work order required to complete the manufacturing order, the **Finished Products** tab already shows the 15 T-shirts as being produced. The order will continue to stay **In Progress** until you click the **Mark as Done** button. At that point the manufacturing order will simply drop out of the list.

If you now go to your **Inventory Valuation** you will see the results of these operations. Remember that while we did not have enough inventory of the white T-shirts that because we started the work order, Odoo let us go ahead and produce them. Fortunately, Odoo keeps complete track of everything revealing that if in fact the worker was able to produce 15 T-shirts that the inventory must have been incorrect. We therefore see a negative number of `Medium White T-Shirts` in our inventory as well as the 16 `Class of 2016 T-shirts` produced from the two manufacturing orders in this chapter:

Summary

In this chapter, we installed the MRP application to begin setting up our manufacturing process. A bill of materials was created to define what products would be consumed when our product was manufactured. We manufactured our final product and looked at the inventory analysis report to verify our results. We then turned on the work center feature so we could explore how to set up work centers and routings to get more control over our manufacturing operations.

In the next chapter, we will take a closer look at accounting and other reporting options. Setting up your chart of accounts is an important step that we'll cover, as well as reviewing journal entries, creating invoices, and receiving payments. We will also be defining sales taxes and managing fiscal periods. Yes, there is a lot more to cover!

6
Configuring Accounting Finance

One of the nice things about Odoo is you can get up and running fairly quickly without having to spend a lot of time setting up complicated accounting and finance options. Odoo does a reasonable job of creating a basic chart of account structures as a starting point and allowing you to get familiar with Odoo. When setting up a production system for your company, however, you will want to take time to properly define your accounting requirements.

In this chapter, we will learn how to configure accounting in Odoo, which includes the following:

- Installing the Accounting and Finance application
- Examining the chart of accounts
- Learning how the other applications create transactions in accounting
- Adding new custom accounts
- Configuring fiscal years and periods
- A quick overview of the available accounting reports
- Creating journal entries

Defining the chart of accounts for your business

The backbone of an accounting system setup is the chart of accounts. Wikipedia defines a chart of accounts like so:

A **Chart of Accounts** is a created list of the accounts used by a business entity to define each class of items for which money or the equivalent is spent or received. It is used to organize the finances of the entity and to segregate expenditures, revenue, assets and liabilities in order to give interested parties a better understanding of the financial health of the entity.

It is very likely that if you are setting up Odoo for an existing business, you will be asked to configure the chart of accounts in Odoo to match the account structure the business is already using. Even if you are not tied to any existing chart of accounts, it is inevitable that you will need to have a firm understanding of how the accounting functionality in Odoo works if you are going to have a successful implementation.

If you are completely unfamiliar with accounting, then this chapter may prove somewhat challenging. It is important to get familiar with accounting basics if you want to succeed in implementing any ERP system. In the `Appendix`, you can find resources that can help you get started in learning basic accounting.

Installing the Accounting and Finance application

Odoo configures a basic accounting structure when you install base modules such as **Sales and Purchasing**. To access all of the accounting configuration options, you must install the **Accounting and Finance** module. If this application is not already installed in your configuration, go to settings and click on **Apps** to pull up the available applications. Find **Accounting and Finance** and click on **Install** to install the module:

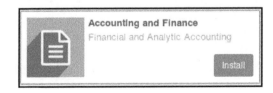

After you have installed the **Accounting and Finance** module, your menu structure at the top of Odoo will change. Before installing the application, you probably had an **Invoicing** menu that contained the necessary options for the **Sales and Purchasing** applications. Once the **Accounting and Finance** module is installed, the **Invoicing** menu is replaced with an **Accounting** menu and is populated with several more options.

Viewing the current chart of accounts

We will begin by learning how to view the current **Chart of Accounts** in Odoo.

Go to the **Accounting** menu and choose **Chart of Accounts** under the **Adviser** sub-menu. Immediately, you will see the chart of accounts sorted by the **Code** column:

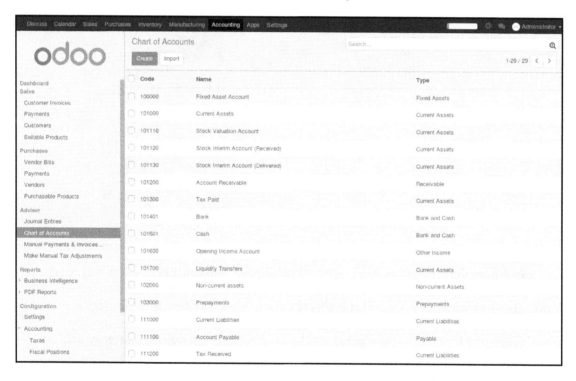

In the preceding screenshot, we see the currently configured **Chart of Accounts**, including the **Code**, **Name**, and **Type** of account. Unlike previous versions of Odoo, Odoo 9 no longer has hierarchical (otherwise known as nested) accounts. This simplifies the management of your chart of accounts while still providing you with the ability to have accounting reports that meet the needs of your business.

Getting more information on a specific account

In Odoo 9, the type of account is used by the various reports to determine if that account should be included, and if so, where on the report to include that account. Clicking on one of the accounts will bring up the account along with an example report structure so you can see just how that account type will be represented.

Click on the **Account Payable** account in the **Chart of Accounts** list view:

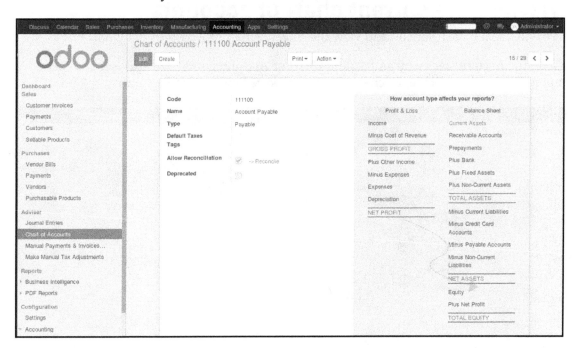

You can see on the far right of the preceding screenshot that payables are on balance sheet reports and that they are subtracted from total assets to give you your net assets. Understanding how the account type affects your reports is critical to setting up a successful business system. Odoo simply makes this a little easier to understand by providing a quick reference. The panel on the right will not change no matter which account you will choose.

Learning how transactions in Odoo get posted to accounts

All transactions that take place in Odoo create **Journal Entries** that either credit or debit a specific account. Each journal entry must balance. This means that the debits must equal the credits. Odoo makes it very easy to examine your **Journal Entries** so you can see exactly where each transaction is posted.

To view the **Journal Entries**, go the **Accounting** menu, and under the **Adviser** sub-menu, click **Journal Entries**. By default, Odoo applies a filter restricting the journal entries to only **Miscellaneous Operations**. Clear this filter to see all the journal entries:

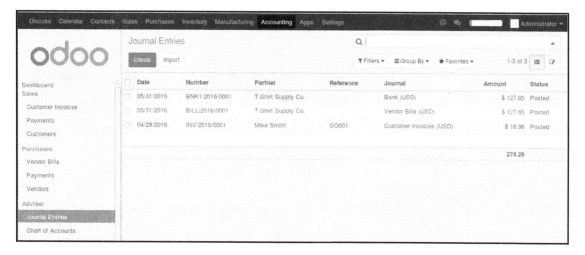

In the preceding screenshot of the listing, you can see three journal entries.

If you do not see any journal entries in your list, make sure you have cleared the **Miscellaneous Operations** filter. Odoo applies it by default.

You can see that in the journal listing you get a summary including the amount and the status, indicating if the journal entry is posted or unposted. You can also see that in the invoice journal entry that we have a reference provided to the original sales order.

Notice that the journal entry summary does not contain any references to specific accounts in **Accounting and Finance**. To see these details, we must click on a specific journal entry. Click on the last journal entry, the invoice for $18.98 assigned to our customer/partner Mike Smith.

You will now see the details of the transaction and each account that was involved:

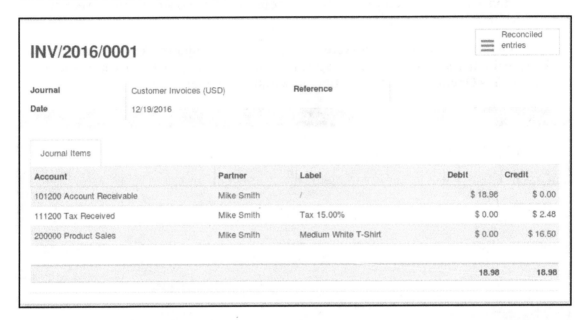

When we open the account, we see all the postings to the specific accounts that were involved. In the first row, we can see that **Accounts Receivable** was debited $18.98 for the invoiced t-shirt order. Next, in the second row, Odoo has posted a credit of $2.48 sales tax on the order. This goes into 111200 Tax Received. Finally, in the third row we see that a $16.50 credit was posted to 200000 Product Sales for the actual t-shirts themselves. Notice how the **Debit** column matches the **Credit** column. **Debits** and credits must always be equal in a journal entry.

Under each of these items is more detail on the transaction. Click on the first posting to
`101200 Account Receivable` to pull up more details on that posting:

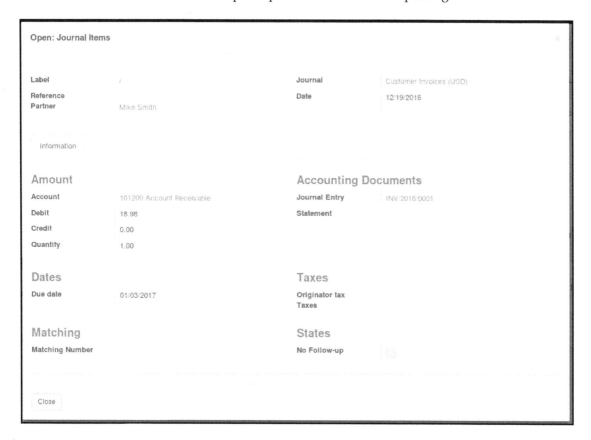

In preceding screenshot you can use the links to quickly find the partner, account, journal,
and journal entry related to the posting.

If this is still a little confusing, don't worry. We are now going to follow through a set of
transactions from the **Accounts Receivable** side so you can better understand how Odoo
handles accounting transactions.

Following transactions through the sales and accounts receivable process

In the previous example, we were looking at the chart of accounts and determining what transactions created the entries. Next, we will sell an item to a customer and see exactly how that transaction affects the accounting entries in the journal.

Let's begin by creating a new sales order.

Go to **Sales** and click on **Sales Orders** to bring up the sales order listing. Click on **Create** to create a new sales order:

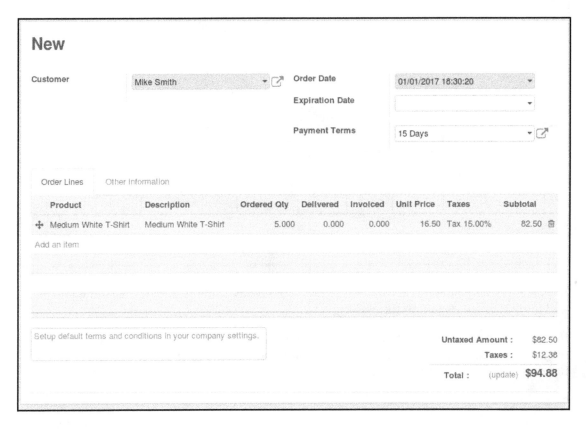

If you have followed along with our examples, then you will already have the customer and product entered to create the samples sales order. Otherwise, you will need to add a customer and a product if you wish to follow along on your computer. In this example, we have created a sales order for five `Medium White T-Shirts`. Make sure you click on **Confirm Sale** to create the sales order.

> Odoo will automatically number sales orders and other documents. In the preceding example, there have already been two sales order numbers used by the Odoo system. Therefore, depending on what you have already done with your current system you may not have the same sales order number for your sample.

At this point, if you were to go and look at the journal entry listing, you will not see any additional journal entries. *Why is this?* The way Odoo is currently configured, we must manually create an invoice. As long as you are in the **To Invoice** state you will not see any transactions in accounting.

Only when we click on the **Create Invoices** button at the top of the screen it will actually create accounting transactions.

Click on **Create Invoices** to generate a draft invoice for this sales order:

Odoo will present you with a wizard that allows you to determine how you wish to invoice. Please take note that the primary difference is in how down payments are handled. As we have no down payments, we are fine to take the default option **Invoiceable lines** (deduct down payments). If we did have a down payment, then it would be deducted automatically from the invoice total.

Click on **Create and View Invoices**:

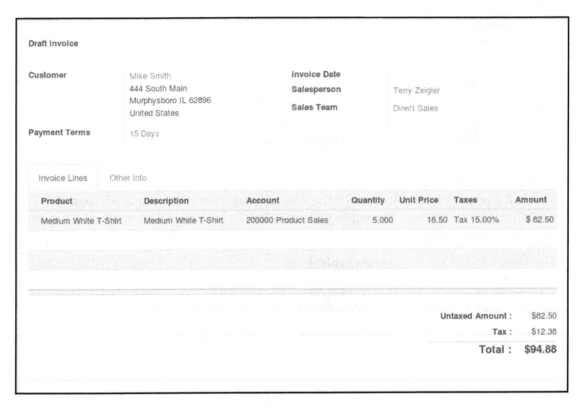

Because this is just a **Draft Invoice**, if you look at the journal entries, you will see no changes. However, if you look at the **Draft Invoice**, you can see exactly the transactions that will be created once you validate the invoice.

In the line item of the invoice, you will see the **200000 Product Sales** account. This will be the account that will be credited for the sale of the medium white t-shirts the customer has purchased.

Choose the **Other Info page** on the **Invoice** form. Notice under **Account** it reads `101200 Account Receivable`; this account will be debited to journal the amount the customer owes to the company once the invoice is generated.

You can also see this invoice will post $12.38 to the **111200 Tax Received** account:

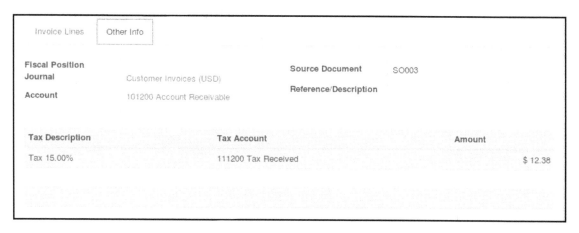

Click on **Validate** to post the invoice and create the transactions.

Viewing the transactions created by validating the invoice

Now that we have validated our invoice, Odoo has automatically created the accounting transactions to increase our **Accounts Receivable** assets and the accounting transaction to record the sale. We can now open back up the journal entries and see the newly posted transaction:

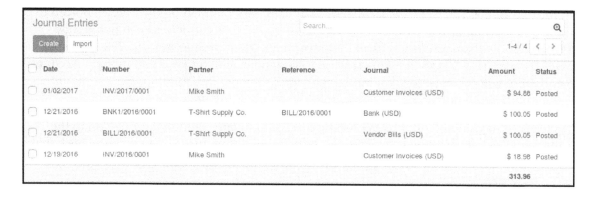

The number assigned to this specific invoice is **INV/2017/0001** and the amount is **$94.88**.

Under the Reference column, Odoo typically would include the sales order #. As you can see in the preceding screenshot, the reference is blank for our invoice. It's possible this is a bug and will be fixed in future builds of Odoo 10.

We can now click on this journal entry to see the details of the transaction:

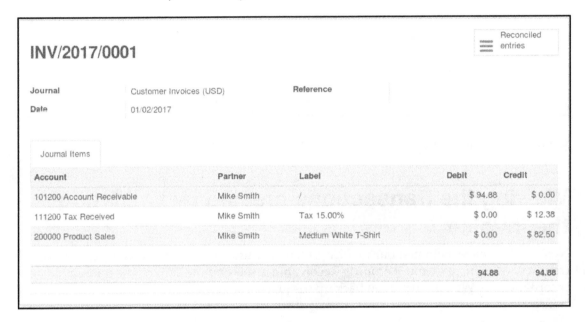

In **Journal Items**, you can now see the same figures we examined on the invoice posted to the correct accounts. The `101200 Account Receivable` account has been debited by **$94.88** to show the new current asset that represents this customer invoice. The customer owes the company **$94.88**. As you create invoices and customers owe you money, **Accounts Receivable** will continue to grow.

Next, you will see that the tax for the invoice is a credit to the **111200 Tax Received** account. Typically, you will then use this tax received account to later send that money on to the appropriate government agency. This, by the way, would require you to write a check that would credit your bank account (reducing its value) while posting a debit to the tax received account.

Finally, notice the **200000 Product Sales** account has been credited with **$82.50**. This account will continue to be credited for products you sell.

> For our example, we are using only one sales account to keep things simple. In most companies, you will have far more sales accounts to organize the various types of products sold.

Now let us see what happens to these accounts when a customer pays their invoice.

Go to **Accounting** and choose **Customer Invoices**, then click on the invoice to bring up the form. Click on **Register Payment** to bring up the **Register Payment** form:

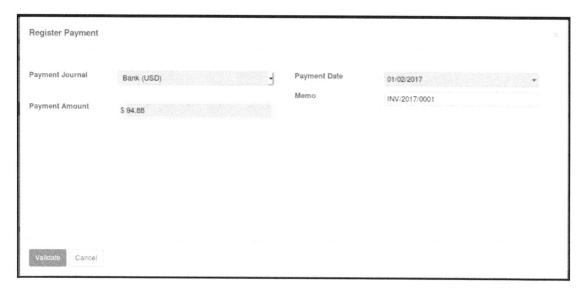

For our example, we have chosen the **Bank (USD)** payment method. You have the option to provide a memo to document that invoice payment. By default this will include the sales order number, but many businesses may wish to include a check number as well.

Click the **Validate** button to pay the invoice and create the appropriate accounting transactions.

The invoice is now paid and the journal entries have been automatically created, and we can now see the payment listed as a new journal entry.

As you did previously, use the **Accounting** menu and choose **Journal Entries** to bring up the list of journal entries:

Notice that we now have an entry number **BNK1/2017/0001** that is also for **$94.88**, the same amount as the invoice. The **Journal** allows you to more easily organize transactions and identify exactly which accounts will be affected.

Let's examine the details of the payment that has been posted by clicking on the journal entry:

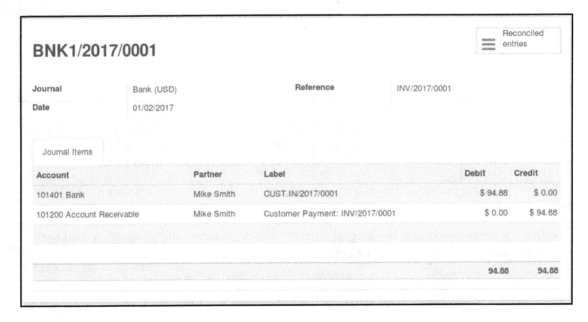

In this cash receipt, you will notice that we can see the details on exactly which accounts will be affected when we post the entry:

- `101401 Bank` is debited with **$94.88**. This will increase this asset account.
- `101200 Account Receivable` is credited with **$94.88**. This will decrease this asset account.

Essentially, this journal entry transfers the potential asset the customer owes the company from account receivable into the bank account. The customer's account balance is reduced to reflect their payment.

Practice posting transactions and tracking the results

Remember that people spend many years and even get full university degrees in financial accounting. It is important that you take time learning how each process you implement affects the accounts in Odoo. When implementing an ERP system for your company, take the time to get this right. It will save you a lot of pain in the long run.

Setting up your own accounts

For default English installations, Odoo installs the standard United States Chart of Accounts template. Most companies, however, will need to modify this chart of accounts or even set up an entirely different **Chart of Accounts** to match the needs of their business. As an example, we are going to add an additional sales account specifically for t-shirts so that we can better organize our sales into types of products.

To set up a new account, go to the accounting menu and then down to the **Adviser** section and choose **Chart of Accounts**. Odoo will present you with a listing of all your current accounts in Odoo. Click on **Create** to add a new account:

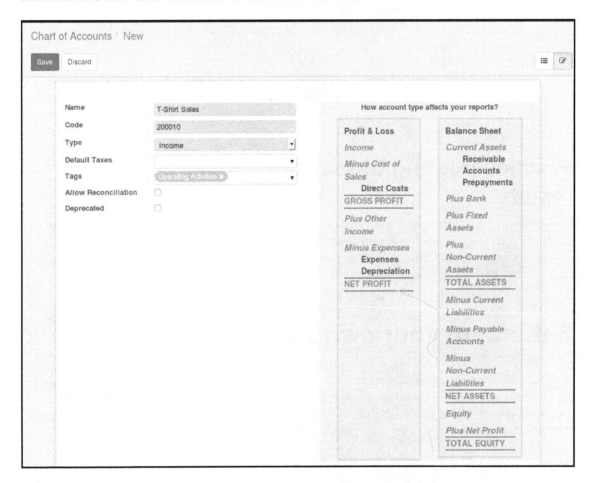

Notice in our screen that we have specified the account code as 200010. *Why did we choose this as the account code?* Odoo had already provided 200000 for the general **Product Sales** account. Therefore, 200010 was an appropriate account code to choose for our t-shirt sales. For the name of the account, we named it simply T-Shirt Sales.

The other important setting is the **Account Type**. Odoo needs to know the type of account you are setting up. So, for example, if you were setting up an account that was to track the costs of products you must purchase to produce your products, you would specify an expense account type.

> Take time planning your **Chart of Accounts** in Odoo. Even if your company has already been using an existing **Chart of Accounts**, it is always a good idea to evaluate the current **Chart of Accounts** and make any improvements given the current state of the business.

Specifying a new account for your product category

With Odoo, you can manage accounts at the product category level. Therefore, all products in a given category can utilize the same account settings. Let's create a new product category, T-shirts, for our Medium White T-Shirt, and assign that category to the 200010 T-Shirt Sales account we created. Later, we can add all t-shirt products to this category.

Go to the **Inventory** menu, and in the configuration section, choose **Product Categories** from the **Products** sub-menu. This lists the current product categories:

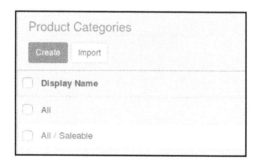

At this point, you will see we only have two categories. Click **Create** to create a new category for our t-shirt products:

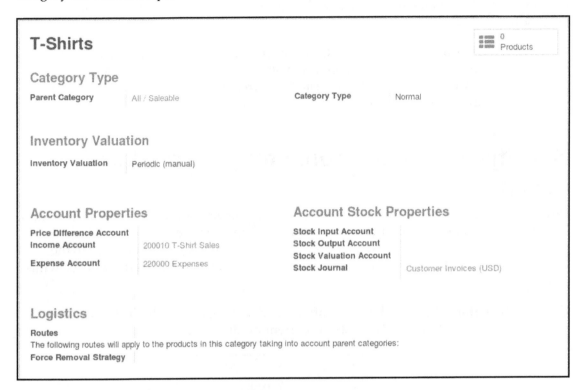

We have named our new category T-shirts. All t-shirt products can now be grouped under this category. Also notice that we have set a parent category of **All/Saleable**. This allows you to view the t-shirt products along with all the other products when you choose the parent category.

Most important from the accounting standpoint is we have assigned the **Income Account** 200010 T-shirt Sales that we have set up in the Chart of Accounts. When an invoice is posted that has a line item attributed to this product category, the amount for that line item will be posted to 200010 T-Shirt Sales. For the **Expense Account**, we have specified the built-in **220000 Expenses**. This will post our expenses related to products in this category to that account.

Exercise: Now try going into the product record for the Medium White T-Shirt and set the product category to T-shirts. Create a sales order, turn it into an invoice, and validate it. View the journal entries and you will see the income for your t-shirt in the specified income account.

Remember that it is important to practice using Odoo until you are comfortable setting up accounts and understand clearly where the transactions are posted. A little bit of time and effort put in during the configuration will save you a lot of time later.

Examining the available legal reports in Odoo

Like nearly all accounting and finance systems, Odoo provides the standard reports you would expect, including the following:

- General Ledger
- Trial Balance
- Balance Sheet
- Profit and Loss
- Financial Report

These reports are a bit buried near the middle of the **Accounting** menu in the **Reporting** section and then **Accounting Reports | Legal Reports**:

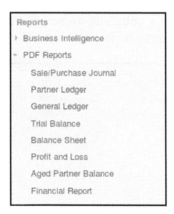

Each report you select will bring up an appropriate wizard to specify the criteria for a given report. After you have made your selections and generated the report you will be prompted to download the PDF file that contains the results. While going through each of these reports with all the screenshots is beyond the scope of this book, you are encouraged to spend some time examining each report and make sure you understand how it fits within the reporting requirements for your business.

As you add more and more data to your system, some of the accounting reports will take additional time to process. As part of the testing before you go in to production, you should take the time to make sure all your accounting reports run at acceptable levels of performance using data that will simulate real-world conditions.

Creating journal entries

While Odoo will create many journal entries automatically when you perform various operations in the system, it is inevitable at some point you (or your accountant) will wish to create a manual journal entry. A manual journal entry allows you to adjust account balances in a way that can easily be tracked and audited.

For our example, we are going to create a journal entry that will account for a small investment by one of the company owners. When someone puts money as an investment into a company, they are not buying anything and they are not selling anything. While there are other potential methods, a simple journal entry is a straightforward way to accurately record the transaction.

To enter a journal entry, go to the **Accounting** menu, select **Journal Entries** in the **Journal Entries** section and click the **Create** button:

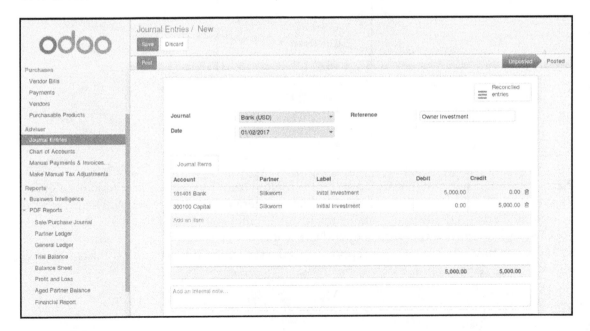

When you first create a new journal entry, you will need to pick which journal to post to. For this situation, we used an example of how we can post to the **Bank** journal to represent the owner's investment into the company.

We are considering the $5000 investment as a cash investment by the owner, so we have posted this into the **Bank** journal.

Whenever you create a journal entry, you will add at least two line items. Furthermore, the line items must balance out. In our example, we are putting $5,000 in funds from the owner into the company bank account.

Typically, any investment the owner puts into the company must also be recognized as a liability for the company. *Why?* The money really does not belong to the company. Instead, the $5,000 in this case is considered the owner's equity. The owner is entitled to get that money back, and therefore it is booked as a liability. You can verify this by opening up the chart of accounts and looking at the list of main accounts. **Liabilities and Equity** are grouped together, then are divided out as you drill down into the account hierarchy.

Odoo sets up a **Capital** account that allows us to post the $5,000 we have put into the bank as capital stock for the owner. Once you save your journal entry, it is in a draft form. To post the journal entry and have it appear in your reports, you must click the **Post** button.

Summary

In this chapter, we examined how Odoo generates transactions and how you can use the Chart of Accounts to look at how those transactions originated. We examined both the **Accounts Payable** and **Accounts Receivable** accounts and how an invoice is posted. There are certainly more advanced Odoo topics, such as bank reconciliation and recurring entries, that are beyond the scope of this book. Please refer to the Appendix to locate additional resources on more advanced Odoo subjects.

In the next chapter, we will look at the **Human Resources** (**HR**) application. HR allows us to keep track of employees, the hours they work, and the services they provide. Staff can be assigned to user-defined departments and designated as managers of other employees. And since your employees will often also be users of the Odoo system, the HR module is tied tightly to the user administration system, which manages access rights and messaging.

7
Administering an Odoo Installation

One of the greatest advantages of Odoo is that it is easy to get up and running with very little setup. Within just a few minutes you can have several applications installed and begin working with the system right away. In the previous chapters, we covered a great deal of functionality without having to spend a lot of time with configuration, access rules, languages, or other administrative topics.

Now we will take a closer look at important topics to consider when administering an Odoo installation. Topics we will cover in this chapter include the following:

- Basic administration of an Odoo installation
- Backing up and restoring Odoo databases
- Creating users and assigning access rights
- Internationalization, including currencies and language translation
- How to manage document sequences
- Multi-company configurations

Basic considerations for an Odoo administration

Like most IT installations, successful Odoo installations require proper planning and maintenance. Care must be taken in documenting important configuration details, and you must always have a business continuity plan in place that focuses on getting your Odoo installation back up and running within an acceptable period of time.

Have an implementation strategy

While you are learning Odoo and prototyping how you may use Odoo for your business, you may not care much about a clear implementation strategy; however, once you have made the decision to use Odoo for your business, it is important to plan your implementation strategy. While you may not have time to write out a 150-page detailed strategy, it is important to take the time to document your overall strategy and have a minimal plan in place before you begin setting up servers and installing Odoo.

While the total breadth of project management and administration that goes into an ERP system is beyond the scope of this book, there are several basic implementation considerations you will always want to consider.

Development, staging, and production servers

One of the first considerations you will need to make when contemplating an Odoo installation is how you will configure servers for various Odoo instances that may be required during planning, deployment, and final production operations. For example, you don't want to be making modifications to Odoo's functionality in your live production system. Instead, you should always make changes and modifications in a development instance of Odoo where you can test your changes outside of the live database.

In addition to a development server and production server, it is often desirable to have an Odoo installation that users (and in some cases, business partners) can use to train and learn the operations of the system. Sometimes, this installation is known as the staging server. This server will typically have all the tested changes and functionality of the live system but will be loaded with test data and configurations that are useful for training.

Each installation will have its own requirements and constraints. What is important is that you make these decisions early on in your Odoo configurations so that you can properly administer the installations all the way from development into production.

Clear documentation of all Odoo configurations

Once you have decided what Odoo servers you require and how those installations should be configured, it is important that you create a clearly defined method for documenting all the details that go along with the setup. This can be as simple as a text or Microsoft Word document that is in a known place and kept up-to-date. It can be as complex as using a full-blown project manager. Using cloud organization tools such as Dropbox, Evernote, and Google Documents provide you with a lot of options of how you can document your Odoo installations.

It will be up to your own business policies to determine exactly where you store this information and how much detail you keep. One bit of advice is that it is almost always better to err on the side of having too much detail rather than too little. You will naturally need to be aware of how you secure usernames and passwords and have a clear policy on how that information is securely stored.

Focusing on business continuity

Any business information system is only as good as its ability to recover from something going wrong. Despite having more reliable hardware and software, data can still get corrupted. Even the most dedicated employee can accidentally post bad data. The best security can be defeated. While everyone is making their best efforts, there are certainly still bugs lurking in Odoo's applications as you are reading this. No amount of planning can prevent a problem from occurring. This is why one of the most important tasks in administering an Odoo installation is making sure that you always have a clear recovery strategy.

Here are a few important considerations:

- Regularly test your backups for recoverability. Just because you are backing up your data, it does not mean that it is quickly recoverable. All too often, businesses may go months or even years without testing if the data they are backing up is recoverable.
- Have a strong archive of backups. Perform daily backups along with weekly and monthly snapshots as well. Often, data can be bad, deleted, or corrupted long before anyone knows anything has gone wrong. Someone might accidentally delete a set of old entries, and it may not be until a few months later a manager doing a report finds critical holes in the data.
- Have contingency system options. Even if you plan on hosting locally, consider having a cloud server configured where can run your Odoo installation in a pinch. Too often, you can have the backups ready to go but if you are waiting on hardware to be fixed or a part to be delivered, you are going to extend your downtime. If you plan to use your development server as a backup production system, make sure you have the proper procedures in place and tested. Don't make blindly optimistic assumptions about your system contingencies. Test them at least once or twice a year.
- Make sure you know how long it takes to fully recover your Odoo installation and what data would need to be re-entered into the system. If you back up nightly, and it takes you four hours to get your installation back up and running, make sure your internal business processes are clear on exactly what steps are required.

- Know exactly how much downtime costs your business, and plan accordingly. Companies such as eBay and Amazon are in crisis if they are down for even a few minutes. More than an hour of downtime for them would make international news. While you may not have their uptime requirements, it is important that you understand exactly what risk your business does face if your Odoo installation goes down for two minutes, two hours, or even two days.

Backing up your Odoo database

It is critical in a production environment that at the minimum you back up both your working Odoo application directories and the associated Postgres databases. Ideally, you will have server snapshots and a clear business continuity plan in place and tested. Still, it is valuable to know that Odoo provides a built-in database backup tool. I use it frequently in a variety of Odoo installations.

Before going ahead, it should be noted that this function will not be applicable to all Odoo installations. If you are running in a hosted Odoo environment where you have been provided a login and password to your database, then you will be provided a specific backup procedure. Make sure you fully understand how it works and have a way to test and make sure that it functions as expected.

The easiest way to get to the backup database function is to navigate directly to the database manager. By adding /web/database/manager to the end of your Odoo URL, you will be taken directly to the Odoo database manager:

Here you will see all the databases in your Odoo installation with the option to **Backup**, **Duplicate**, or **Delete** each of the databases.

 Sometimes, if you are having trouble with an Odoo installation, such as getting Internal Server errors and other system-related issues, you can navigate directly to the database manager to back up your database and perform operations that may help you recover from the problem.

Clicking the **Backup** button will bring up a simple wizard that will allow you to backup the database in ZIP format that will contain all the filestores associated with that database, or as a pg_dump file. A filestore could contain such things as document attachments or pictures associated with your products. The pg_dump format is a standard Postgres database operation that will make a backup of the database only without the associated filestore:

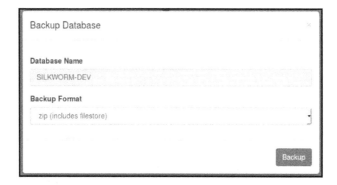

Click the **Backup** button to begin backing up the database. The database will then download through your browser just like any other file you may download off the Internet. (If your database is extremely large, there is a chance that the file may not be easily downloaded.)

Restoring an Odoo database

The ability to back up a database does little good unless you have the ability to restore the database to get up and running again. You can click the **Restore Database** button to bring up the **Restore Database** form:

Here, you specify the **Master Password** and choose the file you wish to restore. Once you have the file selected, you will need to specify a new database name to restore the database into it.

You also get the option to choose either **Backup Restore** or **Copy of an existing database** as the **Mode** for the restoration. As the instructions explain, Odoo will handle the restore slightly differently if you are restoring a database that has been moved rather than copied. Use the appropriate mode for your situation.

Administering users in Odoo

In any ERP system, it is important that you completely understand how users and user access rights are managed. When Odoo is first installed, an admin account is created automatically. This is a superuser account, and it is the only one like it. In some systems, any account can be specified to have full administration privileges. Odoo, however, gives permissions to the administration account that no other user in the system has.

Specifically, all access rights are bypassed when using the administrator account. Much like the root account in Linux or Ubuntu, you always need to protect your administration account by using a strong password and keeping it secret.

Selecting a user to administer

Let's begin looking at a user in Odoo and how they are tied to partner records within the rest of the Odoo applications.

To access the list of users, click **Settings** in the main menu and then choose **Users** from the **Users** section in the left-hand menu:

We can now click on **Terry Ziegler** to bring up the user so we can look at the additional options that are available:

When you pull up a user in your own Odoo installation, it is unlikely this screen will look exactly like yours. Depending on the exact applications that are installed, the available application and technical settings will change. Also, it is common to see modifications to this screen depending on the Odoo build you are running.

Managing user preferences

Now click on the **Preferences** tab so you can look at the available options:

In this section, we have the ability to specify important localization options that can dramatically change the user experience. We can specify one of the more than a dozen languages that Odoo supports, as well as the timezone and default sales team of the user.

Additionally, the preferences section lets you manage your **Messaging and Social** options for the user.

Currently, there are only two options for receiving inbox notifications by e-mail. Either he never receives notifications or the user receives all the notifications.

The **Alias** option will allow administrators to configure an e-mail alias for the user. By creating an alias the user can receive incoming messages from an e-mail that is different than the one assigned to the account.

Finally, you can use the **Signature** rich text area at the bottom to specify a signature footer for the e-mails sent by this user. If desired, the user can change their own signature at any time by choosing **Preferences** from the menu in the upper right-hand corner of the screen:

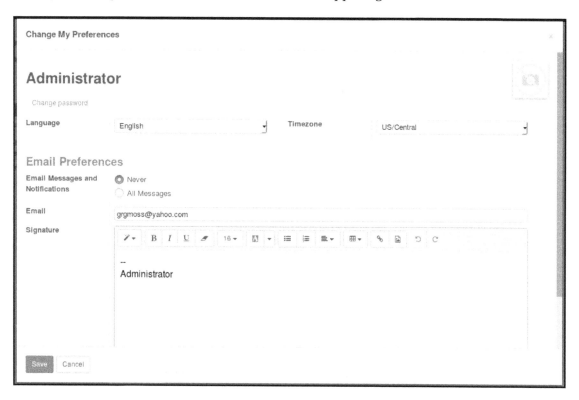

Remember that, if you are an administrator making these changes for another user, changing these settings will require that user to log out of the system so their session is updated with the changes.

> If you are setting up a lot of users, don't forget that you can use the **Duplicate** option under the **More** menu at the top of the form to make a copy of a user. This can be handy if a worker has left and has been replaced with another worker. You can deactivate the old employee and duplicate their profile for the new employee.

Understanding groups in Odoo

In Odoo, you give users permissions by assigning the users to groups. Once a user is assigned to a group then the user has all the permissions and options that are associated with that group. Users can belong, and often do belong, to more than one group. To see the list of groups that are currently available in your Odoo installation we will need to turn on the developer settings. To do this, go to the **Settings** menu at the top and then choose **Dashboard:**

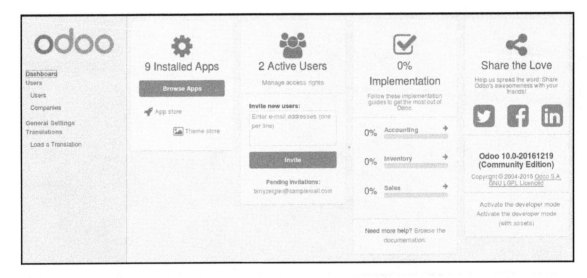

At the bottom right you will find a hyper-link to **Activate the developer more**. Clicking the link will then refresh the **Settings** menu providing you many more options for administering your Odoo installation.

Once you have successfully entered developer mode you can manage the user groups in Odoo by clicking the **Groups** link under the **Settings** menu:

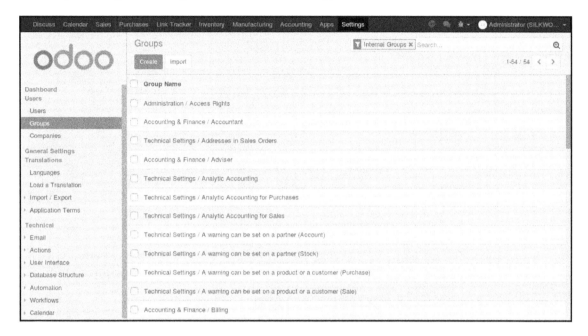

As you can see, Odoo has a lot of groups. Fortunately, once you understand how groups work, you will easily be able to determine exactly what options are available to a user when you put them in a specific group.

For our example, let's examine the **Sales / Manager** group. You can find this group by scrolling down the list of groups a little or using the search to narrow the list until you can find the group you are looking for.

Like other lists, clicking the **Sales / Manager** group brings up the form:

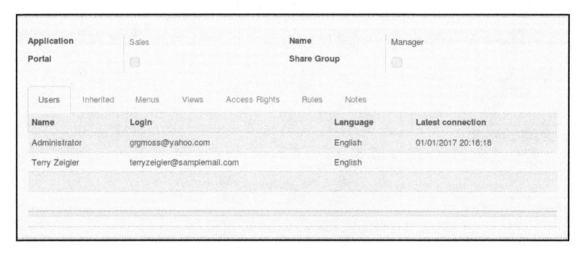

At the very top of the form on the left, you can see that a group is always associated with a given application. In this case, the group is associated with the **Sales** application. On the right is the name, **Manager**. Odoo automatically adds the slash (/) in between the application and the name when displaying the full name in the list.

As you can see, the first page lists the users that are assigned to the group. Naturally, you can add and remove users from this group as required. You will also notice there are seven pages on this form that you will be using to configure exactly what permissions this group will offer to users that are members.

Understanding group inheritance in Odoo

Managing access permissions in any ERP system is always a challenge. Odoo makes managing user permissions a little easier by allowing you to inherit permissions from multiple groups and then define a new group that automatically includes all the permissions from those groups. With proper planning, this allows you to create groups that provide your users with the permissions they require.

Let's take a look at the groups **Inherited** by the **Sales / Manager** group:

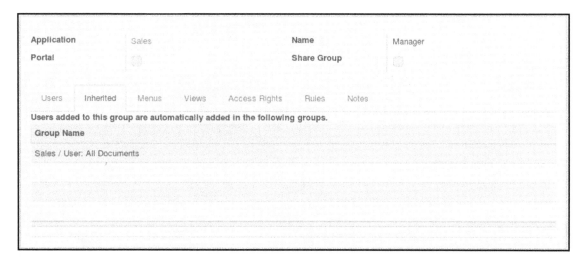

The **Sales / Manager** group has **Sales / User: All Documents** included in the inherited list. Just like the instructions say, users added to the **Sales / Manager** group will automatically be added to the **Sales / User: All Documents** group.

With this in mind, manager groups such as this will most often include all the other groups that have more restrictions in the system. In this case, looking at the **Sales / User: All Documents** group will let you see the most restrictive group permissions for the sales group.

Defining menus for your group

Groups provide a direct way to determine what menus users in that group should have access to. In the case of the **Sales / Manager** group, we have additional menu options listed. Members of the **Sales / User: All Documents** group would not see these menus unless they are also members of **Sales / Manager**: or they are added specifically to the **Sales / User: All Documents** group:

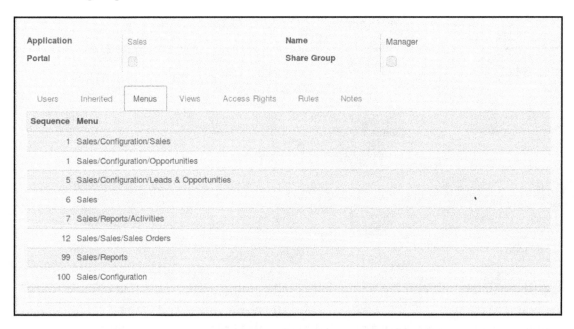

If, for example, you wanted to allow users in the group **Sales / User: All Documents** group to view the **Activites** report, you could remove the menu from the list in this manager group and add the menu to the **Sales / User: All Documents** group. Because the manager inherits from the **Sales / User: All Documents** group, they will still be able to see the menu in addition to users that are only in the **Sales / User: All Documents** group.

Understanding Access Rights in Odoo

So far we have seen how groups can inherit from other groups and how menus can be assigned to a specific group. Now we will look at the access rights that determine exactly which models the group has access to and what permissions they are assigned.

Below is the **Access Rights** page for the **Sales / Manager** group:

| Application | Sales | | | Name | Manager |

| Portal | | | | Share Group | |

| Users | Inherited | Menus | Views | **Access Rights** | Rules | Notes |

Object	Read Access	Write Access	Create Access	Delete Access	Name
Sales Team	✓	✓	✓	✓	crm.team.manager
Invoice	✓	✓	✓	✓	account_invoice manager
Sales Order	✓	✓	✓	✓	sale.order.manager
Sales Orders Statistics	✓	✓	✓	✓	sale.report
Partner	✓	✓	✓		res.partner.sale.manager
ir.attachment	✓	✓	✓	✓	ir.attachment.manager
Product UoM Categories	✓	✓	✓	✓	product.uom.categ salemanager
Product Unit of Measure	✓	✓	✓	✓	product.uom salemanager
Product Category	✓	✓	✓	✓	product.category salemanager
Information about a product vendor	✓	✓	✓	✓	product.supplierinfo salemanager
Pricelist	✓	✓	✓	✓	product.pricelist salemanager
Partner	✓	✓	✓		res_partner group_sale_manager
sale.layout_category	✓	✓	✓	✓	report_layout_category_1
Pricelist item	✓	✓	✓	✓	product.pricelist.item salemanager
product.price.history	✓	✓	✓	✓	prices.history sale manager

Access Rights is where you define exactly what models the group has access to. In Odoo, the term **Model** represents a business entity object and its related operations. You can determine for each object if the group should have any combination of **Read Access**, **Write Access**, **Create Access**, or **Delete access**. For example, in the preceding listing if you scroll down you will find the **Sales / Manager** group has the ability to read, write, and create meeting types, but they cannot delete meeting types.

Now let's take a quick look at the access rights of the **Sales / User: Own Documents Only** group:

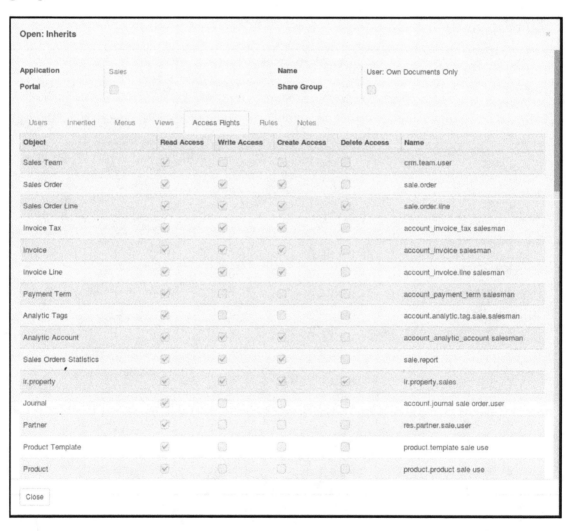

Object	Read Access	Write Access	Create Access	Delete Access	Name
Sales Team	✓				crm.team.user
Sales Order	✓	✓	✓		sale.order
Sales Order Line	✓	✓	✓	✓	sale.order.line
Invoice Tax	✓	✓	✓		account_invoice_tax salesman
Invoice	✓	✓	✓		account_invoice salesman
Invoice Line	✓	✓	✓		account_invoice.line salesman
Payment Term	✓				account_payment_term salesman
Analytic Tags	✓				account.analytic.tag.sale.salesman
Analytic Account	✓	✓	✓		account_analytic_account salesman
Sales Orders Statistics	✓	✓	✓		sale.report
ir.property	✓	✓	✓	✓	ir.property.sales
Journal	✓				account.journal sale order.user
Partner	✓				res.partner.sale.user
Product Template	✓				product.template sale use
Product	✓				product.product sale use

The manager group we looked at previously had a lot of permissions to create and write records, but the **Sales / User: Own Documents Only** group only has read access for many objects such as **Sales Team**, **Journal**, **Partner**, **Product Template**, and so on. This group can see the information, and it can be selected on forms and reports, but they do not have permission to modify records in those objects.

Understanding group rules in Odoo

Sometimes in a system you want users to have access to a particular model, but not to all records in that model. For example, you may want users to have access to phone calls within the system. But for some groups, you only want the user to have access to the records of their own phone calls, not the phone calls of everyone in the system. When you need to control user access based on the contents of records within a model, you can define **Rules**.

For this example, we are looking at the rules for the **Sales / User: Own Documents Only** group. Because this is a very restricted group, there are many rules that limit users in this group to only see the records that are associated with them personally:

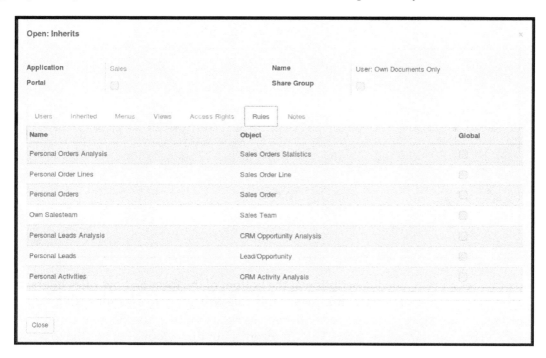

Typically, manager groups will have little or no rules because they do not have restrictions on what records they can access. Groups such as **Own Documents Only** have quite a few rules so that the users can't see records that do not belong to them. Let's take a quick look at the **Personal Orders** rule so we can see how we can construct a rule that limits what records a user can access:

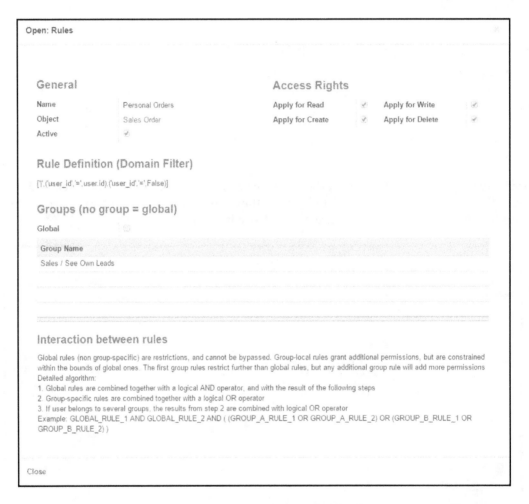

Odoo provides a pretty good description at the bottom of the form on how rules interact. If no groups are specified in the list, this means this rule will apply to everyone–all groups. As you can see on the right, you can specify the access rights for this rule. So, you could have a rule in which a user can access (read) certain records, but they would not be able to create, write, or delete records.

The most important part of the rule is the **Rule Definition** or **Domain Filter**. This is the filter that is applied to each record to determine if that record should be available. While the syntax may look a bit cryptic, you can see that the system is checking that **user_id** is equal to the current **user_id**. Specifically, this filter will be true if you are looking at your own records or records that have not been assigned to any specific user.

> When making your own rules, copy and paste rules from a similar rule to make it easier to get the syntax right. Also, be careful about changing rules in a live system. It is possible that an error in your syntax could make it impossible to access certain parts of the system.

Internationalization in Odoo

Even with a conventional English installation of Odoo it is possible to configure Odoo to work with a variety of languages, time zones, and currencies without downloading any additional add-ons. Odoo has very robust features for configuring a global ERP system that can meet the demands of today's multi-cultural business environment.

As with most Odoo features, you only need to configure the international features you require for your business. For example, you may do business entirely in US dollars but would like to offer Odoo in Spanish for some of your workstations, users, or portal customers. On the other hand, if you are purchasing from a supplier in an alternative currency, you may choose to create a special price list that allows you to do business in that currency.

Configuring language translation

Like many of the other options in Odoo we have discussed, business requirements should drive how you configure your system. For our real-world example, it has been increasingly desirable to offer a native Spanish Odoo interface for some employees. Let's see how we can configure Odoo to provide other language alternatives.

Fortunately, Odoo makes this very easy. Simply go to the **Settings** menu and choose **Load a Translation** in the **Translations** section on the left:

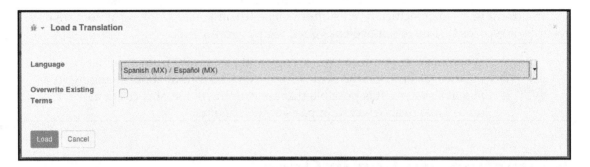

You will find quite a few languages to choose from in the list. At the time of writing, there are more than 80 languages to choose from.

 Many of these languages are community supported, and translation will certainly vary. Furthermore, ERP systems can often be confusing, even for users that speak the language fluently. Take the time to train users so they understand all their processes well.

You would use **Overwrite Existing Terms** if you have made custom modifications to a language translation and now wish to overwrite them.

After the language is loaded, you will get a confirmation message and instructions on the next step you need to take to begin using the installed language:

Now that we have installed the new language, we can assign that language to our users and even our customers and suppliers. In the following screenshot, we can see that we have set `Mike Zeigler`'s language choice to Spanish. Odoo also allows you to specify timezone by either the GMT offset or by common regions. In this case, we have chosen Cancun as the **Timezone**:

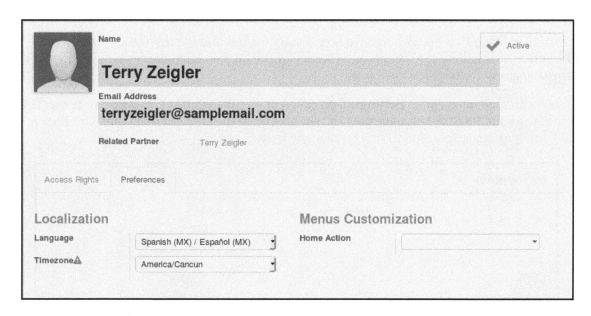

After the changes are saved and the user has logged back in, we will see their interface has changed over to Spanish:

Using translation features to customize Odoo for your business

Even if you do not plan to use Odoo's translation features for alternative languages, the translation features can be great for changing forms to better fit a given business requirement.

Starting in Odoo 10 the base language is no longer loaded into the translation framework. Therefore, you will need to synchronize terms for the English language if you wish to make any changes to the translations it uses.

To synchronize terms, go to **Settings**; then down under **Translations**, choose **Languages**. In the row for the **English** language you will see an icon at the far right that when you click it will bring up a confirmation to synchronize the terms:

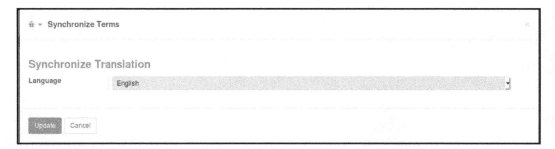

Once we load the translation for English we can examine the terms.

To see the translated terms for a given language, go to **Settings**; then down under **Translations**, choose **Application Terms / Translated Terms**:

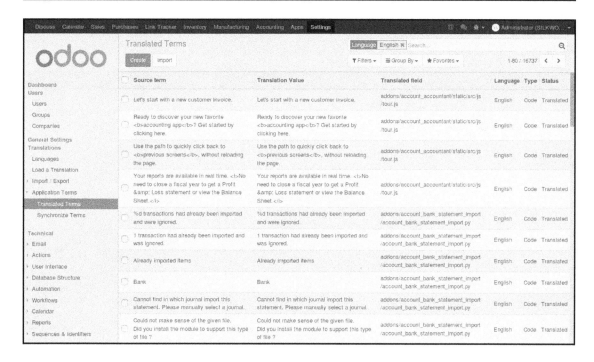

Notice that in the second to the last column we can see that the first page has all English translations and the record count is **16,737**. Nearly every message, menu, and label in Odoo is driven off the translations in this table. That is how Odoo can easily adapt and support dozens of languages, but we can also use these translations to change terms to make them more business-friendly for our requirements. For instance, you could change **Fiscal Position** in **Sales to Tax Status**, or change **Meetings** in the **Calendar** module to **Activites**. Neither will affect how the system works and are just labels.

International currencies

As you saw, it was quite easy and straightforward to configure Odoo for multiple languages. Currencies, however, are going to require more planning and more testing during your system configuration. Unlike languages, multiple currencies have the ability to directly modify the amount of money you are receiving or paying out. If the system has misconfigured currency settings, you are almost guaranteed to have inaccurate transactions within your system at some point. Make sure you thoroughly test all scenarios when working with multiple currencies in Odoo or any other ERP system.

To set up multi-currency in Odoo, go to the **Accounting** menu and select **Settings** in the **Configuration** section:

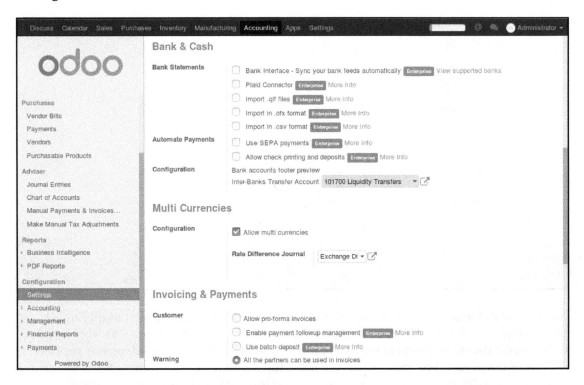

Under **Multi Currencies**, you will find **Allow multi currencies**. Check this, and you will get the option to select the accounts to which the differences between exchange rates will be posted. When setting up a full production system, you will want to assign appropriate accounts as discussed in Chapter 6, *Configuring Accounting Finance*. However, we can post to the default account **Exchange Difference** as an appropriate typed income and expense account for demonstration purposes.

Once you click **Apply**, Odoo will work for a few seconds and then return you to the same screen. Odoo has now added an additional menu option to the accounting configuration menu for currencies.

Clicking this option will bring up all the currencies that are available in your Odoo installation:

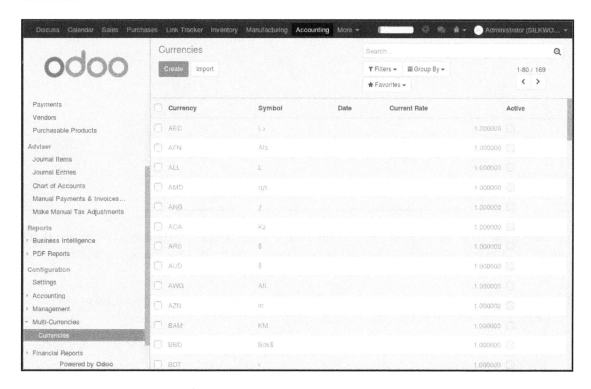

When you turn on multi-currency Odoo specifies both the USD and EUR currencies as active. You can activate any other currency by editing the appropriate record and checking the active option.

Let's go ahead and activate the currency for the Mexican Peso by finding the **MXN** currency record and setting it to active:

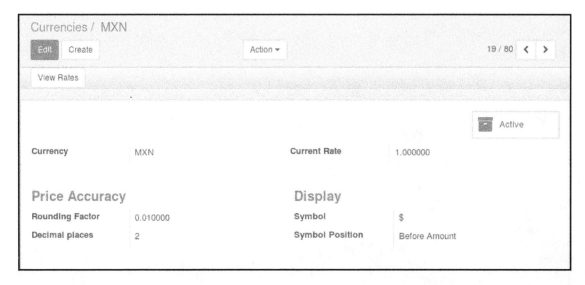

You will notice that this screen also contains the options to specify the rounding factor that will be used in converting from the **MXN** currency to the base Odoo currency. In this installation that is the US currency.

You will not notice the changes from multi-currency until we look at how some of our documents now appear in Odoo.

As when configuring other Odoo options, it is a good idea to *Shift–Refresh* your browser to force Odoo to display any new menus or settings resulting from your changes.

Purchasing in a different currency

Create a new purchase order and observe the new currency selection available at the top of the form:

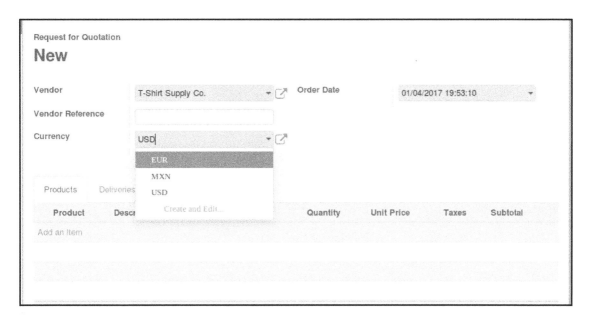

Once you choose a currency, you will see the symbol change at the bottom of the purchase order to show that you are now purchasing in the new currency.

If you continue, however, and try to add a product to your purchase order, you will quickly find out that unit cost does not auto-populate from the cost we have specified in the product file. As we are now using multiple currencies, we either need to provide more detailed pricing information, or we must enter the amount on each purchase order we create.

Managing supplier price lists

Now that we know we are going to have suppliers from whom we need to purchase in a different currency, let's see how we can set up a price list for this alternative currency so that when we order products we do not have to re-enter our costs.

We must first turn on multiple vendor price lists. Click on the **Purchases** menu and then click **Settings** within the **Configuration** section. There you can check the **Allow using and importing vendor pricelists** option under the **Vendor Price** section and click **Apply**:

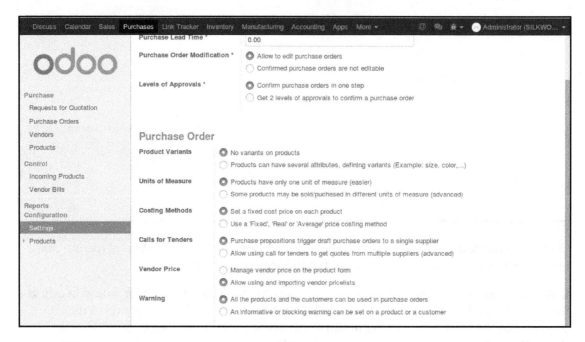

After we have turned on the option to manage pricelists per supplier, we can go to the vendor and set the currency for the vendor under the **Sales & Purchases** tab:

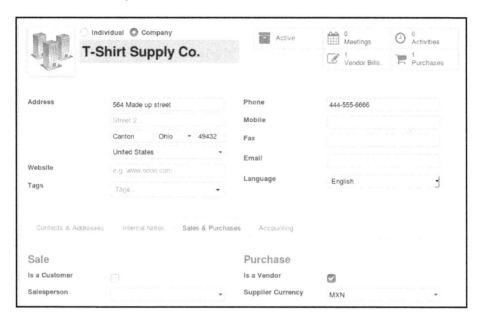

Once you save the vendor record and go back and create a new purchase order, the currency will automatically default to the new supplier currency we specified.

Let's see what happens when we add the line item for the Medium White T-Shirt:

If you look carefully you will notice that the **Unit Price** for our `Medium White T-Shirt` is set to **7.25**. This is the same price as the US currency. So what happened? While we have configured the vendor to use the **MXN** currency we have only specified a cost for US currency. Let's see how we can fix that.

Under the **Purchases** menu select the **Vendor Pricelists** option:

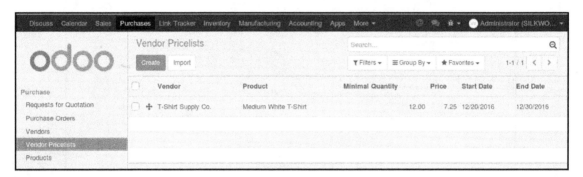

If you have worked with previous versions of Odoo, the pricelists in Odoo 10 have been greatly simplified. Rather than master price lists, you now just simply create a record for each product and vendor combination you require.

Let's make it so that this shirt is now priced by the Peso (**MXN**):

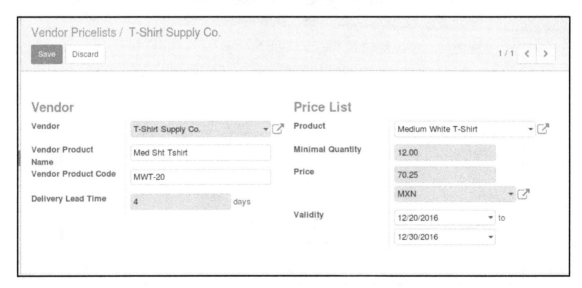

Once you **Save** and create a new purchase order the product will then be picked up and priced correctly in Pesos.

As you can see pricelists are flexible but you must be very careful to properly configure and test your configuration. It's very easy to end up pulling the wrong currency into a document.

Managing sequences in Odoo

When you are setting up a system for your business, there is a very good chance that the default naming of documents and the number sequences that Odoo defines may not be ideal. A simple example is that you most likely do not want your invoices starting at number 00001 when you may already have produced thousands of invoices. You would want the numbers to start where the old system left off

Additionally, sequences in Odoo don't just manage the numbering of your documents. They also manage how the document name looks inside of Odoo. To see the current sequences defined by Odoo, go to the **Settings** menu and choose **Sequences** under **Sequences & Identifiers**:

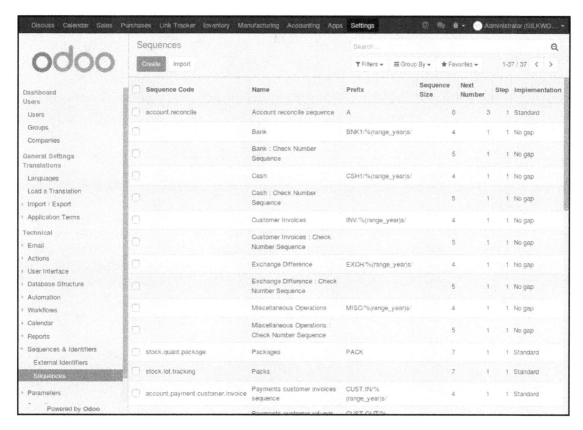

Here, we have scrolled down so you can see the **Sales Order** sequence. Click on the **Sales Order** sequence to bring up the details:

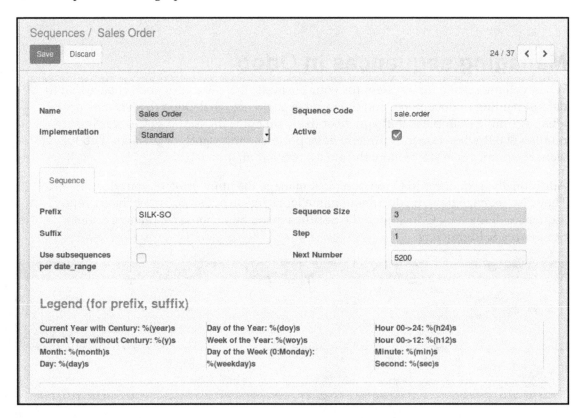

Using simply **SO** is very generic and could potentially match a document identifier from another company.

For this example, we have changed the **Prefix** of the **Sales Order** in our Odoo installation so that they will being with SILK-SO. It is common in a business situation that you may wish to prefix your documents with a notation that identifies that document specifically to your company. Also notice that we have bumped up the **Next Number** to 5200.

After you save the changes to the sequence, any new documents will now use the new sequence definition:

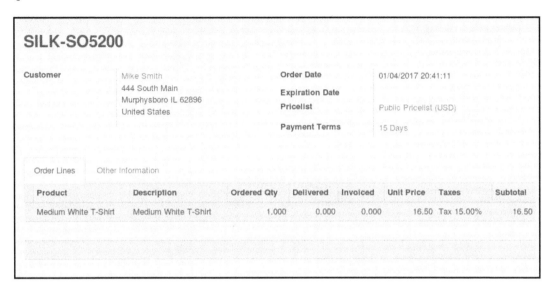

Multiple companies in Odoo

Odoo has the ability to manage multiple companies within the same database. This feature allows you to consolidate some of your system administration and manage more complex operations. As a general rule, multiple-company configuration is an advanced topic. You should be very comfortable with working with single-company configurations before you begin looking into multiple-company configurations. Also, Odoo's warehouse management and analytic accounting abilities can often be a preferable way to manage operations than by configuring multiple companies.

A good general rule is that if they are not separate legal entities, then most likely they should not be set up as multiple companies in Odoo. However, every business requirement is different, and the ability to use multiple companies in Odoo may allow you to easily implement a solution that otherwise may have been rather difficult with just a single company.

To set up Odoo to begin using multiple companies, go to the **Settings** menu then choose **General Settings**:

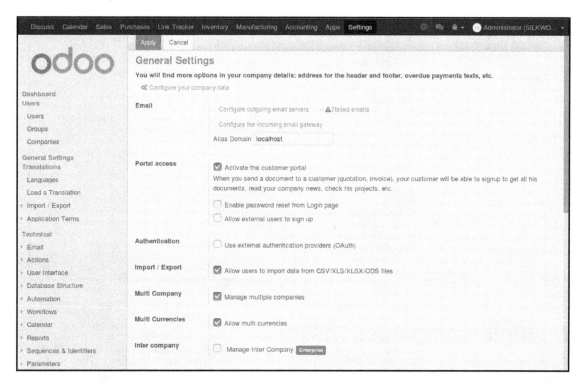

After you have checked **Manage multiple companies** and clicked **Apply**, Odoo will work for a few seconds to configure the installation for multiple companies. Please note that this operation can take more than a few seconds on some systems.

First off, by default Odoo does not turn on multi-company operations for a user even though we have configured multi-company operations through general settings. Even for the administrator user, you must go in and set multi-companies to on:

Setting up a second company in Odoo

Now we can create a second company. With Odoo, you can have multiple companies that are all independent of each other, or you can have child companies in which you can link a chart of accounts and other operations to roll up into the parent company. For example, we have created a new company named `Euro Shirts` and have set `Silkworm Inc.` as the parent company.

For our example, we are choosing France and using the Euro as the default currency:

Now that we have defined a second company, we need to go into our **Accounting** settings and see how we can define our **Chart of Accounts**:

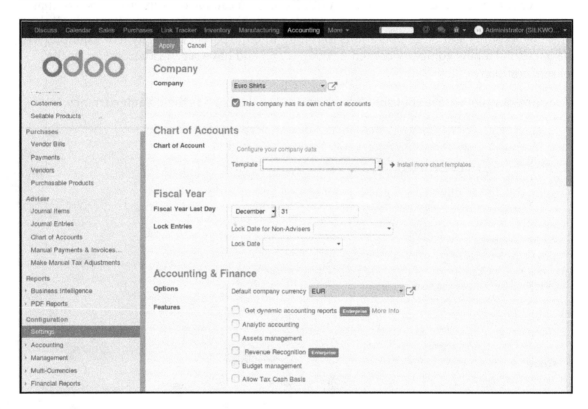

Notice that we now have an opportunity to set up a chart of accounts specifically for our new company along with its fiscal years. Also note that at the very top of the form we have specified that **This company has its own chart of accounts**.

Implementing a multi-company solution

As was previously stated, setting up a multi-company system is complex. While the system will work much the same as it did previously, it is important that you understand how a multi-company system impacts every operation within the system. Customers, users, suppliers, and the chart of accounts all tie into multiple company operations. This chapter has provided the very basics to get started configuring a multi-company setup, but final configurations will take a great deal of planning and fine-tuning to have a truly successful installation.

Summary

In this chapter, we examined some of the things you should consider when administering an Odoo installation, such as planning your server configuration and establishing good practices for ensuring business continuity in the case of failure. We discovered how to back up and restore databases as well as manage user access and group permissions.

Later in the chapter, we took a look at internationalization and configured Odoo to handle multiple languages and international currencies. We learned how to change Odoo sequences so your documents can have the formats and numbering that work for your business requirements. Finally, we took a brief look at setting up a multi-company configuration in Odoo.

In the next chapter, we will take a look at Human Resource applications and how you can configure Odoo to make it easier to recruit, interview, hire, and manage employees.

8
Implementing the Human Resources Application

Over the past few decades, companies have had increasing demands placed upon them to keep track of employee-related information. Odoo has a variety of modules that can help your company organize information involving your employees. Some of these applications, such as timesheets and attendance, can become critical processes that help a company contain costs. In this chapter, we will look at how you can integrate **Human Resource (HR)** applications.

We will cover the following topics in this chapter:

- Modular approach to Human Resources
- Installing the Employee Directory
- Creating new employee
- Timesheet and Leave Management
- Recruitment process

Modular approach to Human Resources

Like the rest of Odoo, the HR application allows you to implement the functionality you need today, and then later add additional modules. This approach makes it much easier to start using Odoo right away to solve specific company needs. The best way to be successful with implementing a system is to plan ahead and implement in stages. Once you are successful at putting one application in place, then you can move on to putting additional applications in place.

Installing the Employee Directory

When you install the base Odoo applications, you get the ability to manage system users, but you will notice that there are no menu options for entering and managing employees. To begin working with HR application, you will need to install the base **Employee Directory** application.

Go to the **Settings** menu and install the **Employee Directory** application using the same process as the previous Odoo applications:

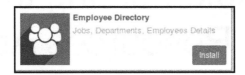

After you have installed the **Employee Directory** application, you will see a new menu at the top called **Employees**. Clicking on the **Menu** will take you to a dashboard that displays the **Employees** in a Kanban view:

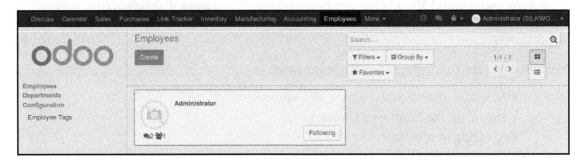

What you may notice first is that for better or for worse, Odoo does not consider users as employees. The only employee that is in the current Odoo installation is the Administrator. On top of that there is no built-in mechanism to automatically turn your users into employees.

Creating a new employee

Let's go ahead first and see how we can add a new employee to our system.

Click the **Create** button to bring up the form for you to begin entering a new employee into Odoo:

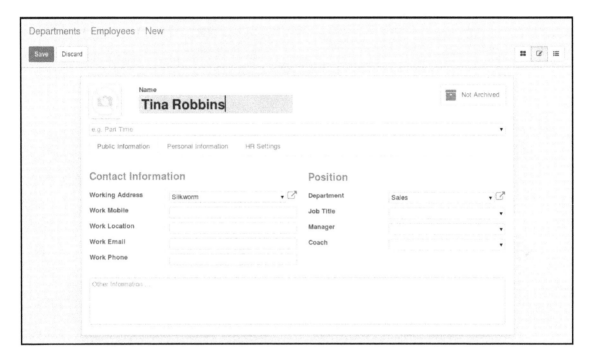

The only required field in the employee form is the name. All the other fields are optional. Odoo will default the working address to the company address. While most fields are self-explanatory, we will go over several of the more important fields to take into consideration.

Department

The employee department is a common way for a company to organize employees. While we currently have `Tina` assigned to the sales department, we can move her to another department. In our example, we are going to create a production department and assign `Tina` to that department:

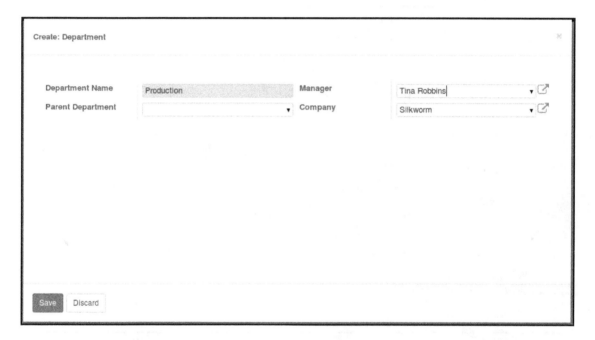

In this screen, we have set the **Department Name** to `Production` and set the **Manager** of this department to `Tina Robbins`. Please be aware that you must save the record first before you can assign Tina as the manager.

Also, you will notice the **Parent Department** field. This field allows you to create a hierarchical structure of departments for your company. Typically, you will wish to look at the organization chart of a company and take some time preparing the company department structure.

Job Title

The **Job Title** field allows you to manage job titles for employees inside of Odoo:

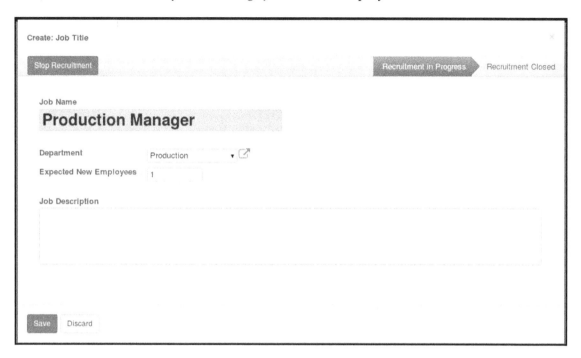

In this screenshot, we have created for Tina Robbins a job title of Production Manager. As you can see from this form, job titles are tied to departments. This means that to properly configure Odoo, you would need to create job titles across departments. Therefore, you do not necessarily want to name a job simply Manager. That would make it difficult, when looking at the list of job titles, to know with which department that manager may be associated.

You will notice that there is a place to enter the new employees that are to be expected and the default value is set to 1. You can also see that the status of this job title shows **Recruitment in Progress** as well as a **Stop Recruitment** button, which we will cover later in the chapter.

 If you try to save the record you may get an error **'Error! You cannot create recursive hierarchy of employee(s)**. It appears because Odoo knows Tina is in the Production department that the manager of that department should be Tina and fills in the **Manager** field. Clear the **Manager** field to proceed.

Manager and Coach

The **Manager** and **Coach** fields in the employee screen can be used to specify any other employees that are already in Odoo. The manager is often called the supervisor in some companies and may be involved in approving the employee's timesheets, leave requests, performance appraisals, and so on. The coach is just an optional field that you could use to specify another relationship the employee has that is valuable to the position.

Employee personal information

The **Personal Information** tab on the employee screen contains the individual's private details pertinent to the HR department, such as home address, date of birth, and citizenship status:

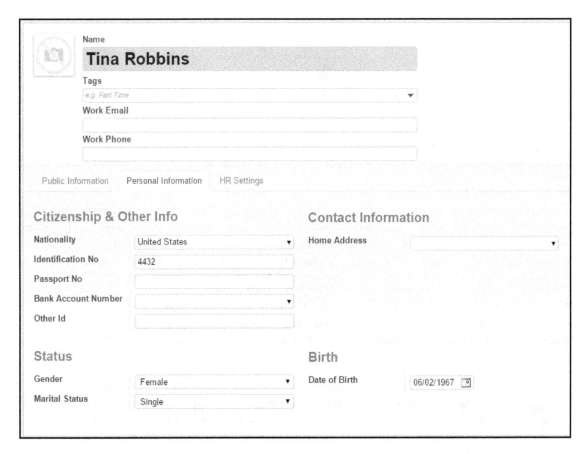

The nationality field allows you to select from the entire country listing that comes preloaded in Odoo. Typically, the **Identification No** field would be used for an employee badge. Odoo includes a **Passport No** on the form which may be required in some cases where a company is required to report citizenship information to the government.

If you do decide to enter a home address for the employee, you will be taken to another screen. Near the bottom of the form, you have the ability to specify **Gender, Marital Status,** and **Date of Birth for the employee.**

HR Settings

On the HR settings page, the **Related User** field will allow you to associate the employee with an existing user account in Odoo. Simply select the user from the pop-up list and choose which user you want associated with the employee. It is also possible to add user's on-the-fly by choosing **Create** from the **Related User** popup:

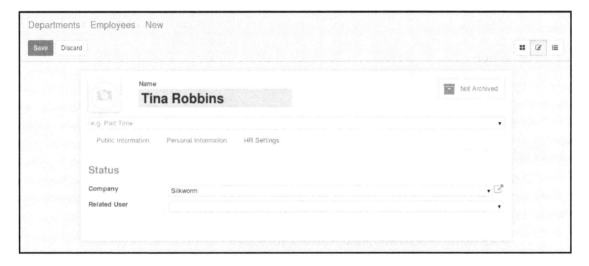

If the employee is not a user in the system, you can simply leave this field blank as we have in the preceding screenshot.

Managing departments

Earlier we saw how we can add a department on the fly as we are entering an employee. Odoo also provides a dedicated **Department** dashboard that lets you see and add departments to the system.

Click on the **Departments** link to bring up the form:

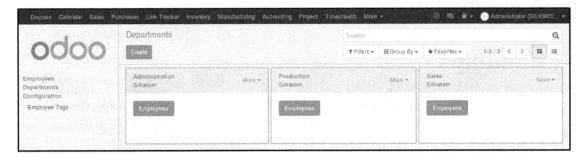

The default installation of the **Employee Directory** application comes with two departments, **Administration** and **Sales**. We have added the Production department in the previous section when we added Tina Robbins as an employee. Clicking the **Employees** button on either department will take you to the appropriate list of employees for that department.

Timesheets

Odoo allows you to install a HR module that will allow you to track employee time and attendance. **Timesheets** are most useful when you have jobs that require you to account for employees' work hours and assign those hours to projects or customers.

To utilize this feature, install the **Timesheets** application:

Once you have installed the **Timesheets** application, the menu bar will be expanded to include two new main menus, called **Timesheets** and **Attendances**. Currently, after installing the **Timesheets** application, Odoo just takes you to the standard **Discuss** menu just as if you have logged in.

Click the **Timesheets** menu to pull up the application.

The default installation of the **Timesheets** application is far more simpler than the **Timesheets** application in Odoo 9 with only two menu options. There are no weekly timesheet entry capabilities, no direct tie-in with analytical accounts, and no timesheet approvals. You essentially put in the activities through the **Detailed Activities** option and then use the **Activity Analysis** to report that data.

To begin recording employee activities, click on **Detailed Activities** then click the **Create** button:

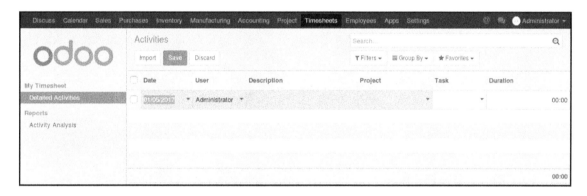

As you can see we get presented with a form that allows you to enter the activities line-by-line. Each line has four required fields. The **Date** is filled in with the current date by default, and the **User** defaults to the current user in the system. You must then enter a **Description** and provide a **Project** to attach the activity to.

A Project is how Odoo ties the duration of the activity to the appropriate accounting entries. We will learn more about projects in the next chapter on **Project Management**. For now, we will simply create a project to attach the activity to:

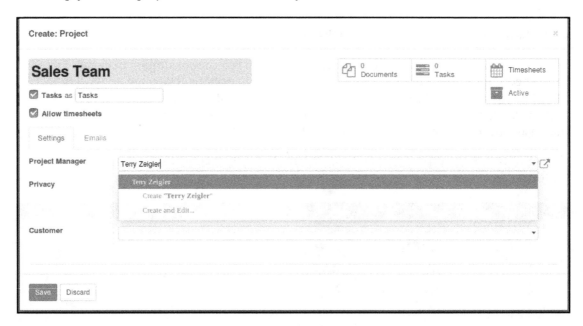

One thing you will notice is that you can assign a customer to the project as well. This can then allow you to more directly invoice customers based on a given project or activity. We are going to leave this blank for now and consider this an internal project that we need to track the time for.

Let's look at what the form looks like after has been filled in with a few activities:

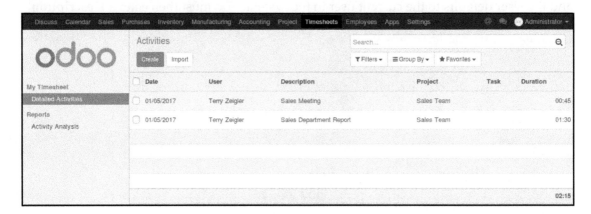

Leave Management

In addition to managing and approving daily timesheets, it is also possible to install an Odoo HR application that will manage holidays, leave, and other information related to employee time off. We install **Leave Management** the same way as the other Odoo applications:

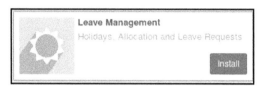

After you have installed the **Leave Management** application you will have yet another new menu, the **Leaves** menu. One departure from early additions of Odoo is now Odoo installs many of the HR applications as separate menus. This does lead to having more and more main menus within the Odoo application. Fortunately, the menu automatically collapses down into a drop-down list when there is not enough room to display the menu horizontally across the screen:

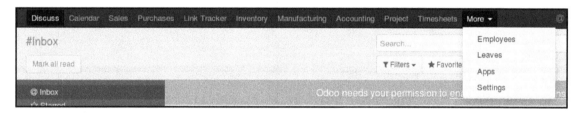

The primary purpose of this **Leave Management** application is to provide an easy mechanism for employees to request leave and for their managers to approve or deny the request.

Creating a leave request

When you click on the **Leaves** menu option, you are taken to a monthly calendar that will show you your current leave requests. Naturally, if there were no prior leave requests made, or there are none for the current month, then the calendar is empty.

Click on a day in the calendar to tell Odoo to schedule a leave request beginning on that day:

In this example, we have requested a **Sick Day**. It's possible to configure leave types to only allow a specific number of days or time. The personal days leave type, for example, is configured this way by default in Odoo.

Leave Type

For our example, we have chosen the **Sick Day** leave type. This implies that the employee is taking this leave with pay. Alternative leave types can be managed for reporting purposes.

Duration

When you change the **Duration** using the date range fields, Odoo will automatically recalculate the **Days** field.

Mode

The **Mode** field deserves special explanation and dramatically changes the way in which this leave request is submitted. For our example, we are submitting the leave request for a single employee. By using the **By Employee Tag** mode, you can submit leave requests that match all employees that share that same employee tag. This can be useful if you need to schedule leave for entire sets of employees.

Employee

This field lets you set the employee for whom leave is requested.

Department

This field lets you set the department for which leave is requested.

Submitting for approval

When requesting leave, clicking the **Save** button is all that is required to save the information and send it on to the assigned manager for the employee for approval.

Once you have saved the leave request the form will close and you will see the updated calendar:

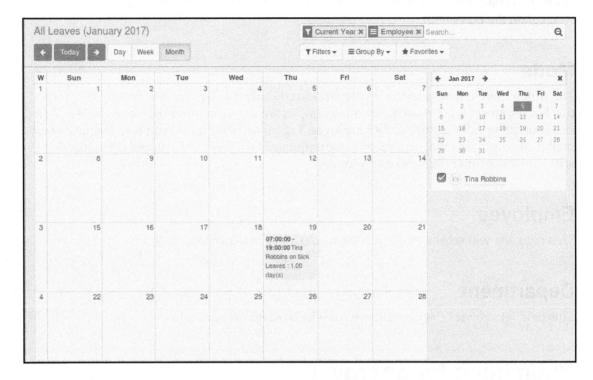

As you can see our leave request is presented on the calendar with the appropriate information.

Approving leave requests

Clicking on the **Leaves** option in the **Leaves to Approve** section of the HR menu pulls up the list of leave requests to approve. You may have to clear the **My Department Leaves** filter if the leave is not showing in the list. In our example, we see the leave request we have submitted for Tina Robbins:

To approve a leave simply click on a request and then choose **Approve** to approve the request or **Refuse** to deny the request.

Recruitment Process

Many HR departments can spend a great deal of time managing the recruitment process. Odoo provides an application that can help organize the information and make it easier to keep track of the communication required when hiring new employees.

Install the **Recruitment Process** application as you have the other Odoo applications:

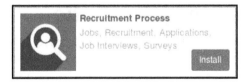

After the **Recruitment Process** application has been installed, you can access the application by selecting the newly added **Recruiting** menu.

You are then presented with the Job Positions form:

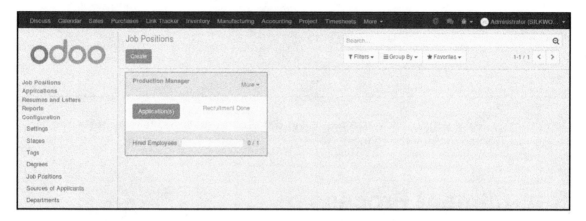

You will then see the **Production Manager** job position we added early in the chapter. Like the other Kanban setups in Odoo, each position provides various options to color the panel, and perform other common operations.

Recruiting for a new job position

Tina Robbins has been very busy in her position of Production Manager. It has been decided that there is a need to hire a Production Assistant to assist her in her duties. With the new recruitment application installed, we can now create a new job position and start the recruiting process.

Click on **Job Positions** under the **Recruitment** menu and click the **Create** button:

Here, we have filled in the details for our **Production Assistant** assigned the position to the **Production department**.

When we go back and look at the **Job Positions** in Odoo, we will find that the Kanban view now displays details about the job position we created:

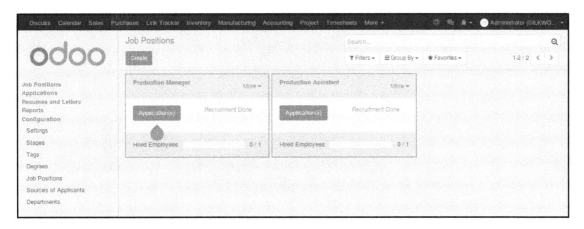

Creating an employment application

When a potential employee sends in an application, resume, or another trigger that will allow you to document their interest in working for your company, you create a recruitment application.

Click the **Application(s)** button for the **Production Assistant** to bring up the application list for the job position:

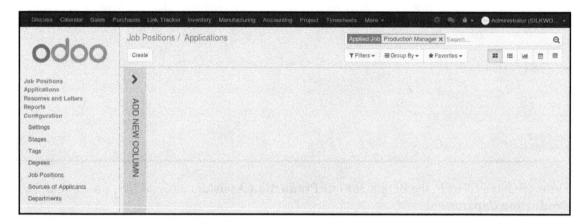

Because there are no applications, naturally this list will start out empty. Also, notice that there is a filter applied that is restricting the applications to only those that are associated with the `Production Assistant` position.

Click **Create** to add a new application:

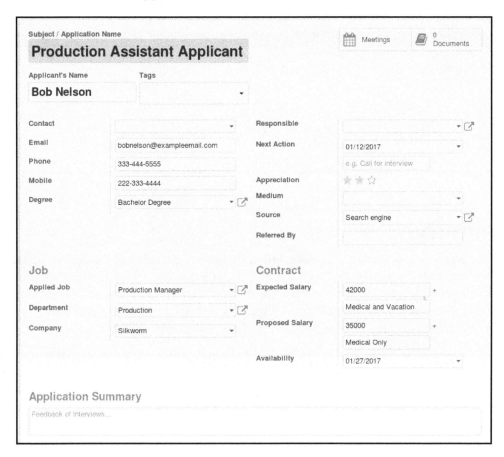

This form has a lot of fields to be potentially filled out. By default, the only required field for the application is the subject. The rest of the information can be collected throughout the recruiting and interviewing processes.

Hiring employees

Let's go ahead and hire this Bob Nelson guy. Thankfully, Odoo's recruitment module will create the employee for us by simply clicking the **Create Employee** button near the top of the form.

Looking at the **Employees** list, we can now see that `Bob Nelson` is an employee in the **Production** department with the title of **Production Assistant**:

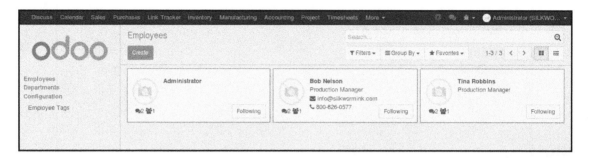

Summary

In this chapter, we examined the various HR applications available in Odoo. We installed the base **Employee Directory** followed by applications that managed time and attendance, as well as leave requests. Finally, we installed an application that allowed us to manage the recruiting processes of new employees. We walked through completing an employment application and finally turning the potential applicant into an employee.

In the next chapter, we will look at the **Project Management** application in Odoo and how it can be used to improve service quality for customers. **Project Management** allows you to organize the simplest projects to complex projects involving multiple tasks. Furthermore, you can even track time related to projects and display project information in a variety of graphical formats to make it easier to track your deadlines.

9
Understanding Project Management

In this chapter, we will explore a very flexible application that allows you to manage projects and tie them into other applications in Odoo. The **Project Management** application allows your company to manage project stages, assign teams, and even track time and job costs related to projects. Analytical accounting features give you even greater control over how project costs can be tied to your company's general ledger.

This chapter covers the following topics:

- Discovering the various uses for Project Management
- Linking projects with customer accounts
- Assigning teams to projects
- Creating custom project stages
- Adding, assigning, and organizing tasks
- Tying into analytical accounting and employee timesheets

Basics of Project Management

Depending on your industry and the types of projects you may encounter, the **Project Management** application can be set up to manage independent projects, or instead, it can be configured to manage projects related to customers or sales orders. With additional modules, it is possible to tie the **Project Management** application into virtually any aspect of Odoo.

For example, you could simply use the **Project Management** application to track the various stages and tasks involved with a company event. Who is going to be responsible for finding the location? When will you need to order the invitations? Who is going to set the agenda? When is an employee going to go and pick up the sound system? In this instance, the **Project Management** application is simply being used to track a single project that is not associated with the customer.

In other instances, you may wish to utilize the **Project Management** application to track projects that are organized around your customer records. A common example would be a construction firm. After assigning the project to a customer, you can track various stages of the project life cycle. Employees can be assigned tasks and using the Odoo messaging system, you can share project details with your customers. It is in this configuration that the Odoo **Project Management** application can add real value to an Odoo installation and provide better integration with your accounting system with less effort than a standalone project management tool.

Installing the Project Management application

To access the project managing features, if you have not followed along in Chapter 8, *Implementing the Human Resources Application,* you will need to install the **Project Management** application. In Odoo 10, Project Management is automatically installed when you install the **Timesheet** application.

If Project Management is not installed, go to the **Settings** menu and install the **Project Management** application using the same process as the previous Odoo applications:

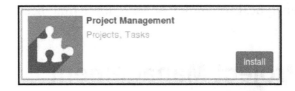

Understanding the Project dashboard

After installing the **Project Management** application, the screen will be refreshed and you will see the Project dashboard. The dashboard provides an overview of the active projects and comes with the project we added in the previous chapter; **Sales Team**:

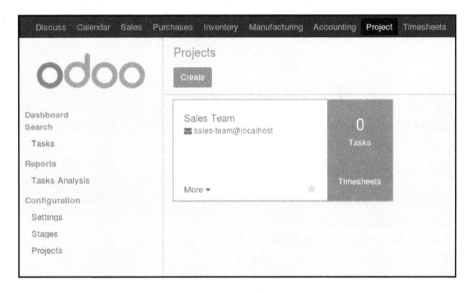

We can see in the summary that the project we created in the previous chapter has **0 Tasks** as we never added any tasks to the project when we were using it enter timesheets. If you do click on **Timesheets** you will get taken to the two activities we created.

While this project was useful for an internal example of using a project to time for various employee activities, let's see how can use the project management application to manage various tasks for a customer.

Real-world project example for a customer

As in other chapters, we will use a real-world example to demonstrate the functionality of Odoo's **Project Management** application. In the silkscreen industry, it can be common to have extremely large projects that span across many types of apparel and print designs. For this example, we are going to create a project to manage creating an entire line of sports jerseys for an organization called `Sunny Hill Lil League`.

In defining our project, it is important to look at the scope of our project and why it will be valuable to use the project manager to organize the various tasks involved. With our `Sunny Hill Lil League` organization, we have multiple teams that can vary in logo design for the team, the number of players, the sizes of the apparel required, and the printing of different players' numbers and even players' names. There are often multiple deadlines to manage and a number of people that may need to approve various phases of the project as they are completed. Using the **Project Management** application, we can better track this information and tie it into sales orders and other Odoo functions.

Creating our first project

After the **Project Management** application has been successfully installed, we can go to the **Project** application and create a new project.

The basic steps we will follow are:

1. Create a new project record.
2. Give a name to the project.
3. Assign the project to a specific customer.
4. Assign team members to the project.

To begin, under the **Project** application, select **Projects** in the menu on the left, and then click the **Create** button:

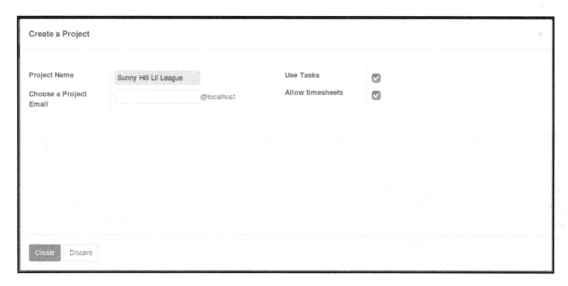

In previous versions of Odoo, you were taken to the Project editor after clicking Create. Like many processes in Odoo 10, it is now greatly simplified and you are presented with a very simple wizard that prompts for a **Project Name** as well as a **Project Email**. For our example, we will use `Sunny Hill Lil League` as the name for our project.

The **Project Email** is useful when you want a specific e-mail assigned to the project. If you leave the **Project Email** field blank, Odoo will automatically create an e-mail based on the project name. Leave the **Project Email** field `blank` so that Odoo will create our e-mail address for us automatically. As this e-mail is only used for potential incoming e-mails, there would be no harm in this as long as the e-mail does not conflict with another you may be using for a different purpose.

Typically, tasks are used to break down a project into several steps. If you choose not to check the **Tasks** checkbox you still get to manage the main settings of the project but there will be no tasks associated with it.

For our example, we will leave the **Tasks** checkbox checked. A little later we will go through how to define the various stages for our project.

As you may expect, checking the **Timesheets** checkbox will allow you to associate timesheets with the project as we did in the previous chapter. We will go ahead and leave this checked so that our project can manage the labor that is spent on the project and then bill it to the customer when required.

Once you create the project, the dashboard will refresh revealing the project you just created:

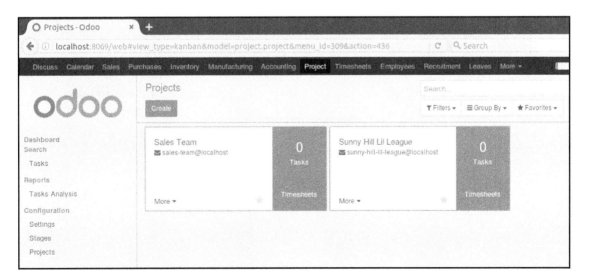

Understanding project stages

Project stages allow you to track a given task through different phases of its completion. These stages often will vary from project to project depending on the types of tasks involved. For example, a project involving software development would likely have different task stages than one that involves planning a real-estate development seminar.

In Odoo 10, a new project does not provide default stages for your project. Fortunately, it is very easy to create new stages. Let's go ahead and create some stages for our new project.

Click the **Tasks** button at the top of the new project you have created to bring up the tasks:

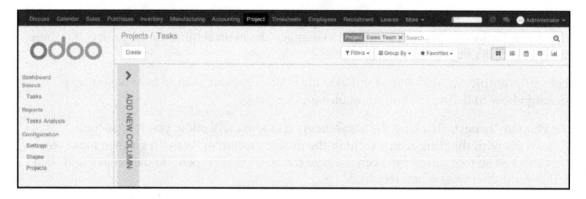

Naturally, we have not added any tasks to the project yet. We can, however, begin defining stages for the project by clicking the **ADD NEW COLUMN** button. A small panel will come up for you to enter the description for the stage.

For our example, we are going to create stages for Specifications, Art Design, Approval, and finally Production.

Simply type in the stage, in this case Specifications, and then click the **Add** button:

The screen will refresh to show the new column added. Use the same process to add the additional stages to the project:

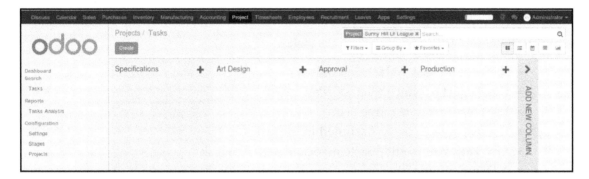

When you are finished adding, your project stages should look similar to the preceding screenshot. Now we are ready to begin adding tasks to our project.

Defining project tasks

The main unit for tracking the various activities involved with a project is a project task. Odoo provides a quick way to add a task to the project by clicking the large plus button under the appropriate project stage.

Click the plus button inside the **Specifications** stage and create a task for Determine Team Names:

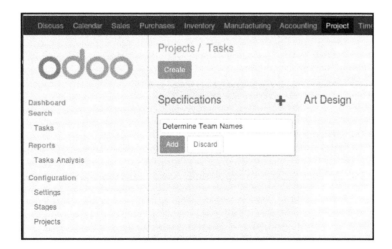

Similar to adding a stage, you simply enter the title of the task and then hit the **Add** button. The screen will then refresh and you will automatically be prompted to add the next task. Once you have created the task, you can use the menu on the task to pull the task up to edit it and provide additional details.

Here, we'll define additional aspects of the task:

- Name of the task (which is required)
- The **Project** to which the task is assigned
- The **Deadline** date of the task
- The responsible party **Assigned to** the task
- Any **Tags** you would like to associate with this task
- A **Description** of the task

For our example, we have filled out the task as shown in the following screenshot:

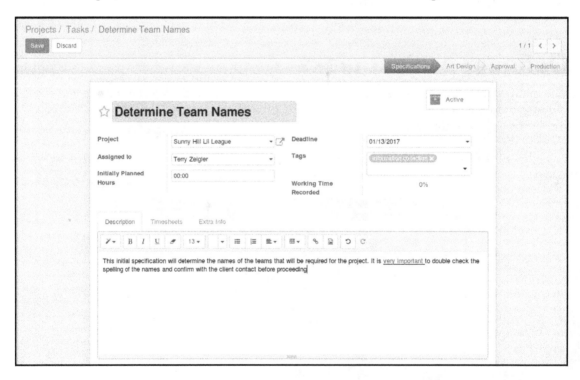

At the top of the form, you will see all of the project stages with the current stage highlighted in blue. In this example, **Specifications** is the currently selected stage. When in edit mode, you can click on these stages to directly assign the task to a given stage. This can be changed as the project progresses so you are not locked into keeping a task assigned to the same stage throughout the project.

One of the important aspects of good project management is assigning responsible parties for each task. The **Assigned to** field allows you to specify who is ultimately responsible for the completion of the task.

The **Tags** field can be valuable for better tracking and organizing tasks. In our example, we have defined an **information collection** tag. This tag can then be assigned to any task that is related to collecting data regarding the project.

Creating additional tasks

For our real-world example, we are going to define several tasks at various stages. These tasks include:

- Identifying suppliers
- Designing the logos for each team
- Approval of team logos
- Final inspection
- Packaging and shipment

Now that we have created generic tasks for the entire project, let's go ahead and assume we have received a draft list of team names. This will allow us to track the progress of each team as it goes through the various stages in the project. For our example, we will use the following team names and leave them in the **Specifications** stage to start:

- Bulldogs
- Falcons
- Wolf Pack

After entering our tasks and assigning them to the various stages, it should look something like this:

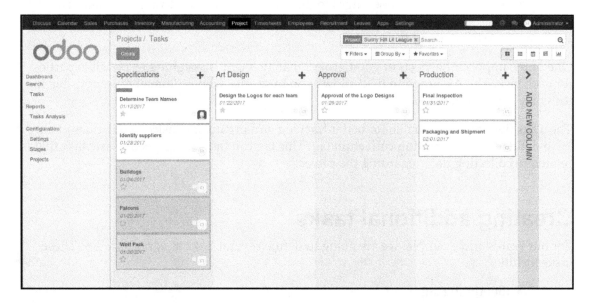

The **Kanban** interface allows you to pick up a task and move it to another stage or reorder it within a current stage by just clicking and dragging. You can reorder the stages by clicking on the title of the stage and dragging it to the position you like.

Also, notice that we have added in deadline dates to the tasks. We can then view the tasks in the calendar view for the project.

Click on the **Calendar** icon on the right of the form to bring up the calendar view.

Completing project tasks

As you complete project tasks, you can bring them up and mouse over the **Active** button. It will then change to **Archive** as you hover over it. When you click the button, the task will be archived. This method will remove the task from the project entirely and hide it from view.

 If you ever need to see tasks that have been archived, you can use the advanced filter skills you will learn about in Chapter 10, *Creating Advanced Searches and Dashboards*, to set a filter that displays records in which active records are false.

Previously in Odoo, there was a done status that was provided by default. If you need to keep track of completed tasks and not have them fall off the project, you will need to set up a **Done** or **Completed** stage for your project.

Calculating project costs and time

To assist the process of calculating project time and costs, you can install the human resources application, **Timesheets**. This application lets you create timesheets for your employees that let you specify hours worked by day. If you have been following along, this application should have already been installed in Chapter 8, *Implementing the Human Resources Application*.

If you click the **Timesheets** page on a given task, you will get a list view in which you can create new timesheet entries. In this example, we have attributed one hour to **Determine Player Names** to the Bulldogs task:

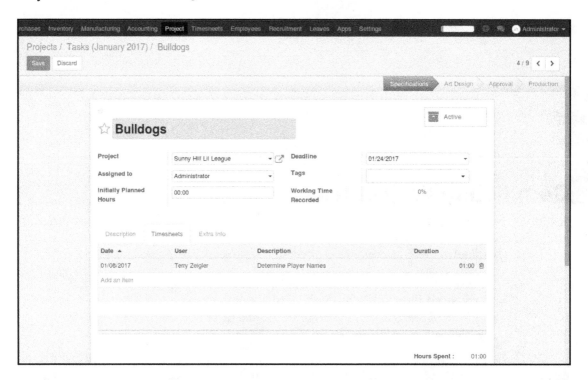

You can learn more about using timesheets and analytical accounting in Chapter 8, *Implementing the Human Resources Application*.

Summary

In this chapter, we examined the **Project Management** application by taking a look at the project dashboard. We then created an example of a real-world project involving our Lil League organization. After setting up our project and assigning team members, we defined the various stages that would be involved in completing the project. With the stages defined, we were able to go through and assign various tasks to the stages along with their dates of completion. Finally, we looked at the various ways you can view the tasks and how you can complete them.

In the next chapter, we will explore how you can create advanced searches and custom dashboards in Odoo. As a company uses its system from day to day, the amount of collected data can grow quite rapidly. Being able to locate pertinent records in a speedy fashion is vital for optimum business operation. We'll discover how to utilize all of the handy searching, filtering, and dashboard presentation tools that are at our disposal within Odoo.

10
Creating Advanced Searches and Dashboards

In this chapter, we will cover advanced searching, custom filters, and dashboards. We begin by looking at how Odoo searches the various data sets within the system. Next, we explore more advanced searching options and discuss how you can save these filters so they can be easily accessed when you need them. Finally, we discuss the Odoo dashboard capabilities and how we can improve usability for users.

The topics covered in this chapter include the following:

- Identifying users' search requirements
- Understanding default filters versus custom filters
- Grouping items in a list
- Setting and saving advanced search conditions
- Creating dashboard content and layouts

Determining the search requirements for your business

One of the tasks that can often be frustrating and time-consuming for users is trying to find the information they need. When data sets are small and simple there is not much of an issue. As the number of records in the system grows, it can become increasingly hard to find information.

When implementing an ERP system, you will want to take the time to work with users and get familiar with the data they use each day. If you are working with a purchasing system that only produces an average of ten purchase orders a day, you will have far less concern over advanced searching in that application. However, if you have 20 purchasing agents cutting 450 purchase orders a day, it will be critical that the users have a firm grasp on the search functionality of the system. Trying to locate a specific order can be like trying to find a needle in a haystack.

Take the time to sit with users and watch them use the system. Often, users will need to look up the same types of data repeatedly in their daily interaction with the system. These are the activities that you will want to set up custom filters for and perhaps even include on the user's dashboard.

Fortunately, Odoo offers a robust searching mechanism as well as the ability to create dashboards for displaying information that the user may need to look at frequently.

For the purposes of this chapter, we will create a new database with the demonstration data so you can better see the searches in action.

Creating a database with demonstration data

Often, it can be valuable to test certain features in Odoo without having to enter a lot of data. Odoo offers an option to populate a database with demonstration data when you create it. Since this chapter is focused specifically on searching and displaying data, we will load up a database with the sample data provided by Odoo.

Accessing the database manager

While it is possible to access the database manager by clicking on links in the login screen, there are times when that link is not available. One reason could be because the website application has been installed, and the manage databases link is hidden from the home page.

Sometimes, if your Odoo server is throwing internal server errors or you are having other problems with your database, you can resolve the issue and at least make backups of your data by going directly to the database manager.

To access the database manager directly in the default installation of Odoo, you use:

```
http://localhost:8069/web/database/manager
```

You will then get presented with the database manager screen:

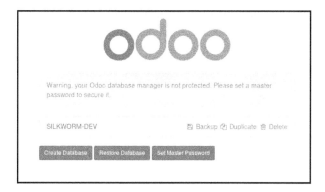

Naturally, you will need to change the server address and port to match your Odoo installation by following these steps:

1. Click the **Create Database** button to create a new database.
2. When creating our database, we check **Load demonstration data** so that our database is pre-populated, making it easier to present example search techniques:

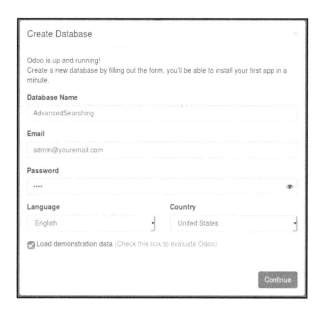

3. After you click **Continue**, Odoo will set up the new database. So we have an application to work with, we will install the **Sales** application:

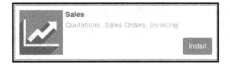

Searching in Odoo

Odoo provides a standardized search box in the upper-right corner for all of the list and Kanban views. Depending on the menu item, some forms come with predefined filters already set for the list.

If you navigate to **Sales** and select **Customer**, you can see the search box in the upper-right corner with the **Customers** filter preassigned:

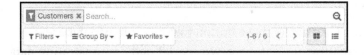

Some lists open with a predefined filter that will limit the primary data set. In the prior screenshot, you can see that the list view, **Customers**, has a customer filter applied by default when you open the form. Odoo stores customers, vendors, and employees in the same central database table. The customer filter prevents those other types of data, such as vendors or employees, from displaying in the list:

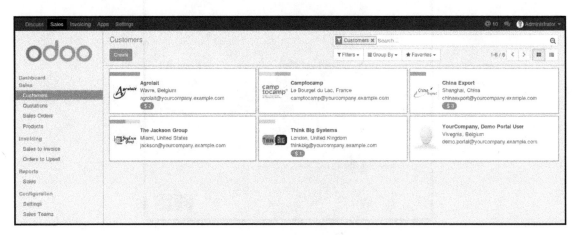

In this instance, if you clear the **Customers** filter by clicking on the small close box in the tag, you will have a list with not only customers, but partners, users, suppliers, and contacts as well. The **Customers** filter is applied by default in this view.

> Sometimes, users can get confused if they accidently remove the filter. If you are not getting the results you expect, always double-check the filter in the upper-right and if necessary navigate away from the view and back again to refresh the default filter.

Basic searches are handled easily in Odoo. Just go into the search box, begin typing, and press the *Enter* key. Odoo will then look at the primary search fields for the type of data you are searching and show you the results in the list or Kanban view.

In the following screenshot, you can see a simple search:

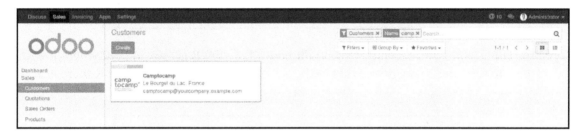

In this example, Odoo has returned all the customers that have **camp** in their name.

Now we can see that there are two filters applied. The default filter, **Customers**, that was there when we opened the customer list and the **Name** filter that will limit those customers to just the names that include **camp**.

> The small space between the two filter tags means that both conditions are required for a record to be included in the results list (A and B). When two filter tags are butted up against one another without a space between them, it denotes records may meet either condition (A or B).

Odoo will remember your search criteria as you move between list, Kanban, and form views. Once you go to another menu item, the search criteria will reset to the default search when you return.

As you type in the search box, before hitting the *Enter* key, Odoo will display the available filters in a small drop-down list directly under the search box:

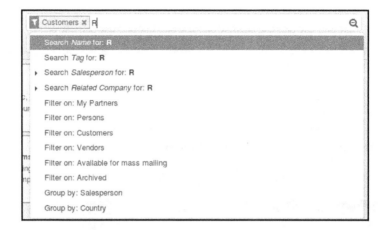

Type the letter R into the search box. You will notice how the **R** is now in bold where it will be applied to the filter. Also, notice that to the left of **Search Salesperson for: R** there is a small triangle. Clicking on this triangle will expand the results in the list:

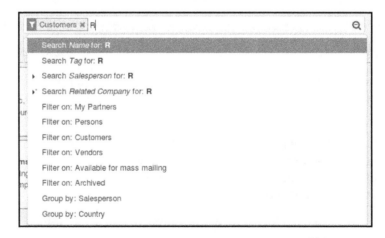

Using filters in list views

Odoo provides default filters for all of the list views. Applying a filter will limit the records that Odoo displays. You can apply one or more filters depending on your needs. The available filters, and by what fields you can group, will vary depending on the data you are viewing.

For example, the **Products** view will have a completely different set of filters and group options than the **Customers** view:

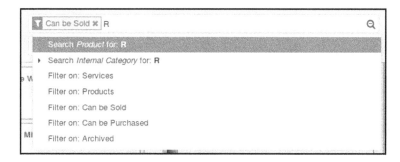

While each search box will have different default filters and **Group By** options, the functionality is the same. In Odoo 10, you access all the search features by clicking the small magnifying glass symbol in the search box:

When you click this, Odoo will expand the search area to show all the search features. Let's return to the customer list and click the small triangle to bring up the advanced search options:

In Odoo 10, the advanced search tools have been consolidated into **Filters**, **Group By**, and **Favorites**. Let's first explore using **Filters** to limit the records that are displayed:

In the example drop-down in the preceding screenshot, you can see a check mark next to the filter that has been applied, **Can be Sold**. The tag for the currently selected filter is also displayed inside the search box. Clicking on a filter applies the filter immediately and refreshes the result list.

Naturally, the list of available filters will change depending on which set of records you are viewing. Clicking on a filter that is already highlighted will remove that filter from the search.

Grouping information

In addition to filtering your results, you can also group data in most Kanban and list views using the **Group By** option. When you group data in a Kanban view, you will get a column for each category. You can then use the horizontal scrollbar at the bottom of your window to look through the items. This will be ineffective for items with a very large number of groups:

The preceding screenshot shows **Customers** in a Kanban view, demonstrating how a user will need to scroll, not only up and down, but also left and right to get a view of all the items.

You need to be somewhat careful when grouping in a Kanban view. If you group on a field that has many results, you will have a long way to scroll to the right to even turn off the filter. In this case, it is usually faster just to click over to another menu and come back to restore the default search settings.

Grouped data is often more easily represented in a list view.

When you group data in a list, a little triangle appears to the left of each group header. Clicking on this triangle will display the rows grouped under that header:

As shown in the previous screenshot, we have filtered by customers that are companies by selecting the **Companies** option in the **Filters** section; we also grouped our data by category by selecting **Country** in the **Group By** section. Next, we expanded the **France** country section by clicking on the small triangle to the left. You can then see the list of companies that are in France. As with filters, clicking on **Companies** again will remove the grouping. You can also nest groups inside other groups simply by selecting additional items under **Group By**.

Grouping can be a great way to look at data. Unfortunately, with extremely large data sets, grouping lists can be very slow because far more records must be processed if you are filtering and browsing data.

Performing a custom search

While the default filters may help us find most of the data records we seek, it is inevitable that there will come a time when we will need a more customized search. To create a custom search, open up the filter pop-down menu and then click on **Add Custom Filter** to expand the available options. Here, we will get a drop-down list of fields that can be used to set our search criteria:

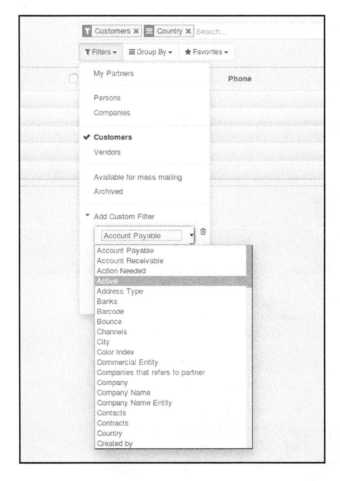

Choosing a field from the list will allow you to select from the available search operators as well as specify the data for which you wish to search. Click on **Add a condition** to enter further criteria. Clicking on the small **x** to the right of a search condition will delete that condition from your custom filter.

In Odoo, you will often find it best practice to make records inactive when they are no longer required. For example, if you discontinue a product, you will often find yourself unable to delete that product because there are transactions tied to it. Therefore, you will wish to deactivate that product record. By default, Odoo will hide inactive records. If you need to retrieve inactive records, use a custom filter to create a condition where the **Active** field is false and then apply to this filter.

You can continue to add additional criteria to your custom filter. When you have specified all the criteria you wish to use in your search, click on the **Apply** button to apply the custom filter:

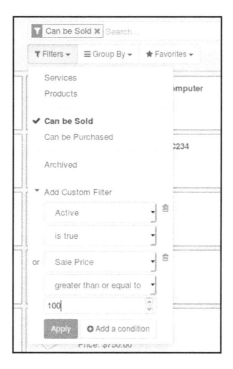

In the custom filter option we have specified two conditions: **Active** must be **is true** or the **Sale Price** for the customer is **greater than or equal to** a value of **100**. Many users can get confused and believe that this filter would imply both **Active** and **Sale Price** must meet our criteria, but it is not so. Notice the **or** to the left of the second condition.

Specifying multiple advanced searches

As you can see in our previous example, Odoo will always use an **or** operation between each of the conditions you add to the search. But what if we wanted to have a search where the record is active and the sale price is greater than **100**? To accomplish this, you must first apply the custom filter with only the active condition defined. That will limit the results to only active products. Then you can go back and add a second custom filter that only contains the **Sale Price** greater than **100** condition.

Just remember that if you want both conditions to be true, then they must be applied separately. If you want either of the conditions to be true, then add them together in one search:

In the previous screenshot, we created a search that will return **Products** that can be sold and are active or have a sale price greater than or equal to $100, and the cost of the product must be less than $50.

Saving your favorite filters

While advanced searches are quite powerful, they can often take a bit of time to configure and to get the results just like you want them. Fortunately, Odoo allows you to save your searches so that you will not have to build them from scratch each time. To save a custom search, click on the **Favorites** drop-down, which is the little triangle next to **Save current search**, provide a name for the search, and then click on **Save**:

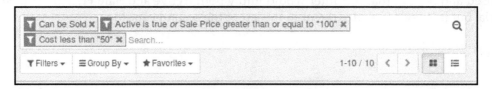

Once you click on **Save**, the filter is added to your list of **Favorites** and can be applied just like the default Odoo filters. In addition, you also have the option to save the custom filter for all users and even set a custom filter as the default filter to be applied when you bring up the list:

In the preceding screenshot, we applied the custom filter, **Special Products**, that we just saved. As you can see, the criteria at the top no longer shows all the detail in the advanced search and instead uses the name you provided when you saved the custom filter.

 There is no easy way for an end user to see what the criteria of their search is after they have named and saved their search for later use. Like in our example, credit customers is all we will see when returning to the search later. Until Odoo provides an easier method, users should be encouraged to document their searches.

The ability to save advanced searches into your own custom filters and make them available for other users allows you to better customize Odoo for your business requirements.

Creating custom dashboards in Odoo 10

Dashboards allow you to take information that you need to look at frequently and put it together in one place. In previous versions of Odoo, the installation came with dashboards even if you never used them. In Odoo 10, you can add custom dashboard support by installing the **Dashboards** module:

Odoo has a very flexible dashboard system. Each user has a personal dashboard named **My Dashboard** provided when you install the **Dashboards** module. Initially this dashboard will be empty except for some useful instructions on customizing your dashboard:

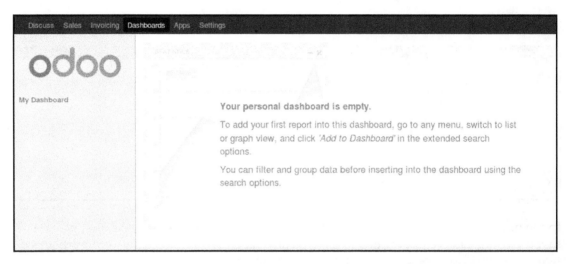

Let's see how we can add our custom filter from the previous section to our dashboard. Return to the products and choose the list view and apply the custom filter:

To add a new result set to your dashboard, open up the **Favorites** drop-down menu and simply click on the little triangle next to **Add to my Dashboard**. By default, Odoo will prompt you to add the search list to your own personal dashboard. However, if you wish, you can add the results to any dashboard by selecting the name of that dashboard in the list and clicking on the **Add** button:

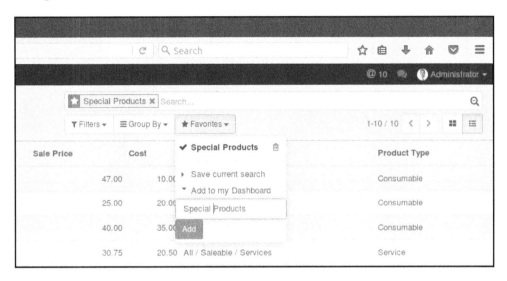

In this example, the current **Special Products** filter we created in the previous step will be added to **My Dashboard**, which can be found as the first option under the **Dashboards** menu.

The build of Odoo 10 that we are running requires you to *shift*-refresh your browser for any new additions to the dashboard to show up:

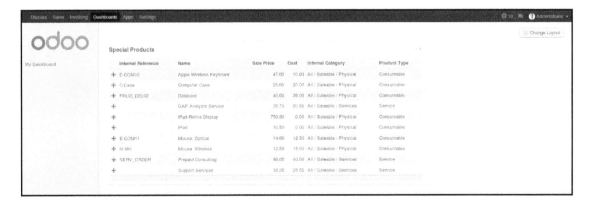

Odoo provides a variety of layouts so you can customize the appearance of the dashboard according to your preference. For example, you may wish to have two columns of lists summarizing your sales or, if there are view columns, you may choose to have a column of three lists.

Clicking on the **Change Layout** button will bring up a small pop-up window to allow you to select an alternate layout:

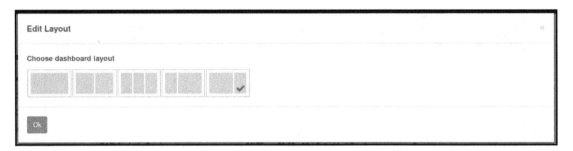

In the top-right corner of each item added to the dashboard, you can click on the little underscore icon to collapse the report area down to just its title. To arrange items on your dashboard, simply click and drag the item to drop it in the desired location. Finally, you can remove an item from the dashboard by clicking on the close box in the upper-right corner of the item:

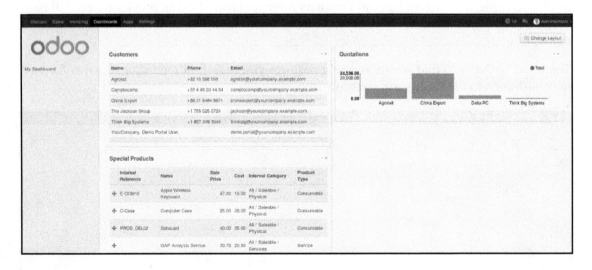

In this example, we have added a few more items to the dashboard and arranged them into two columns. Adding a graph is just as easy as adding a list view to the dashboard. In this example, we went under opportunities, changed the view to graph, and then added it to our dashboard.

Summary

In this chapter, we examined Odoo's advanced searches and dashboards. Advanced searching allows you to search on a variety of fields as well as save your searches so you can easily pull them up later. Using these features, you can more easily find the data you are looking for and place data that you need frequently into your own personal dashboard.

In the next chapter, we will look at Odooâ©©s integrated website builder that allows you to easily create great looking websites.

11

Building a Website with Odoo

In this chapter, we will look at perhaps the most important business applications that were added to Odoo in version 8, the Odoo **Website Builder** application.

Topics covered in this chapter include the following:

- A brief introduction to **content management systems** (**CMSs**) and how they make it possible to manage websites
- Modifying pages with Odoo's **Website Builder**
- Inserting and customizing blocks
- Important Odoo website blocks and how to use them
- Editing the menu of your website and organizing pages
- Selecting themes for your website
- Promoting your website

What is a CMS?

The **Website Builder** application available for Odoo 8 through Odoo 10 can be considered what is commonly known as a CMS. A CMS is a collection of tools that allows you to structure, organize, and manipulate your website without having to interact directly with the inner workings of your website. A key feature of a CMS is the ability for non-programmers and those with little technical expertise to create and edit content on the website once the initial structure of the site has been designed.

In many ways, Odoo is coming into a very crowded market that has a great variety of both open source and paid CMSs you can choose to build your website. Here are few of the more popular website CMSs, all of which at this point have considerably more configuration options and greater levels of adoption.

WordPress

WordPress is arguably the most popular CMS that companies may choose to deploy for their websites. More than a decade of maturity and a massive install base means there are plenty of themes, add-ons, and professionals that can support a WordPress website. In addition, WordPress is open source, based on PHP, and continues to be developed aggressively, and in more recent versions is targeting improved social networking features.

Joomla

Also enjoying great popularity in the crowded CMS market, written in PHP and open source as well, is Joomla. This CMS, while perhaps not as often deployed as WordPress, has thousands of available plugins and can be found under some very prominent sites on the Internet. A few of the more high-profile sites that use Joomla for their CMS include Harvard University and the Guggenheim Museum.

Drupal

No list of popular CMS solutions would be complete without including Drupal. Like the other two, this CMS is also PHP-based and open source. For the most part, Drupal has more advanced capabilities and would be considered for more complex sites than perhaps you would use to build in WordPress. While there are fewer available themes for Drupal than for Joomla or WordPress, that has not kept Drupal from being the CMS for very popular websites, including Popular Science and Sony Music.

Evoq or DotNetNuke

This CMS was previously known as **DotNetNuke** (**DNN**) has recently been through its own re-branding effort, much like the way OpenERP became Odoo. So, according to their own news release, DotNetNuke is no more and is now to be known as **Evoq**. While not nearly as popular as the other three listed, Evoq has the distinction of being a Windows Server-based solution that uses Microsoft's .NET platform. Some big names using Evoq for their CMS include Hilton and Samsung.

Why use Odoo Website Builder for your CMS?

With so many CMS solutions available that have far better support and mature features, a very valid question is why would I use Odoo **Website Builder** for my CMS? Not only is this a good question ask, it is vital when building a website for your company that you pick the tools that work best for your given situation and requirements. So let's quickly look at some of the pros and cons to get a quick look at the strengths and weaknesses of using Odoo as the CMS to build your website.

Potential advantages to using Odoo as a CMS

While Odoo is still new and does not offer the proven track records and successful websites as the CMSs that have been previously mentioned, there are still some very compelling reasons to consider Odoo as your CMS:

- One-click setup if you already have Odoo installed.
- Very easy-to-use features, such as fast page editing and simple controls.
- Great support for mobile devices.
- Powerful built-in language translation support.
- Integrates seamlessly with Odoo to leverage many of the applications already available for Odoo. This is especially true for the e-commerce application that will be covered in the next chapter.
- A growing number of professional themes will make the Odoo **Website Builder** an attractive option in the years to come for those who are already using Odoo.
- Good built-in promotional tools.

Current limitations of using Odoo as a CMS

Despite a growing list of positive reasons to consider Odoo as your CMS, there are also some reasons why it may not be the CMS for every solution:

- Very limited support among hosting companies, website designers, and consultants. If your Odoo website breaks, you are reliant on Odoo experts to fix your website.
- Limited CMS functionality for version control of your web pages.

- Complex and confusing security of web pages and assignment of access permissions to content.
- A very limited set of themes available that work directly with Odoo and the professional themes that are available are expensive.
- Immaturity of the CMS itself may cause volatility in the years ahead as new features are added, making it challenging to move your website between databases of various Odoo versions.
- There is no easy way to move websites or web pages between Odoo databases, which can add to integration, testing, and deployment challenges.

Deciding what is best for your company

Currently, Silkworm, the company we are using for our real business example, does not currently use Odoo for their CMS. That said, we expect that could change in the years ahead, and the previously mentioned positive benefits of using Odoo for your website may be enough to make it a good choice.

Backing up the website you make in your Odoo database

If you do use Odoo's **Website Builder** for your website, as has been stated in many of the other chapters, back up your database often. All of the web pages you create are stored inside your database, so you must back it up to make sure you have a copy of your website. Additionally, you want to make sure you keep your Odoo application backed up as well because static themes, images, and CSS files that are located there must be available to properly display your website.

Installing the Odoo Website Builder

One of the greatest reasons to give Odoo's **Website Builder** consideration is you can try it out in a matter of seconds. Just install the **Website Builder** application like you would any other Odoo application. Go to **Apps** and search for **Website Builder**:

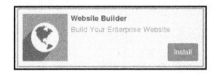

Once you click **Install**, Odoo will install the required modules and take you to a new screen that will allow you to choose the basic theme for your website:

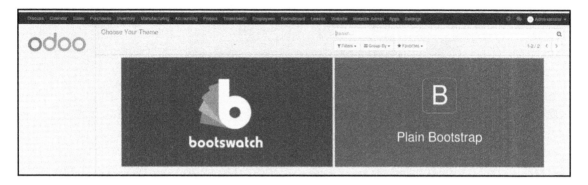

In this build of Odoo 9, you can choose between **bootswatch** themes or **Plain Bootstrap**. We have decided to use **bootswatch**, which will allow more flexible theme selection than **Plain Bootstrap**.

 The **Website Builder** installed for this chapter was Odoo 10 Community Edition. Depending on your specific Odoo build, you may have an alternate selection of themes, or may in fact get taken directly to the your Odoo homepage.

Hover your mouse over the **bootswatch**and click on the **Install** button that appears. This will automatically re-direct you to the home page of your new website. Also, you should be presented with a **Website Builder** tutorial that will walk you through some of the basics of building your website.

Here we can see initial web page presented by Odoo:

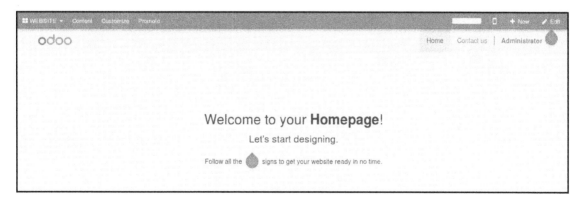

In the middle of the screen, you will see a **Welcome to your Homepage!** title along with an invitation to follow the signs for a simple walkthrough that will assist you in building your first website in Odoo. We will go ahead and use some of these tips to highlight the basic features of the Odoo **Website Builder** application:

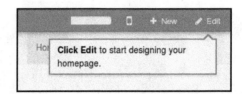

Clicking the in the top right directs your attention to the **Edit** page button at the top right corner of the screen as shown in the preceding screenshot. This button is available on every page while you are on your Odoo website as an administrator. Clicking this **Edit** button will toggle your page into edit mode so you can make changes to your website.

Click the **Edit** button to begin editing your home page.

After clicking the **Edit** button your page should refresh to display the tool bars and options available to edit your web page:

Here, we will see that the tutorial is prompting you to **Drag the Cover Block** and drop it into your page. This is the action you will take any time you want to add additional content to your web page. Also note that the tips that walk you through each step are just for the tutorial that is run the first time.

Click and hold your left mouse button over the cover block and drag it out onto your web page. The web page will immediately update to show you the banner, along with a snippet of text to the left:

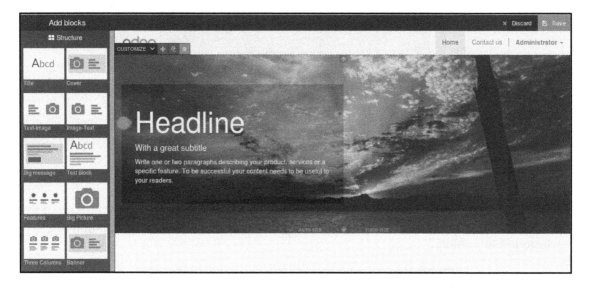

Odoo's simple tips still follows along, prompting you to now change the title of your text to whatever you choose. All of the editing is performed right in the page itself. Just use your mouse to select the text, like you would in any simple text editing program. Notice, too, at the top you have the ability to modify text to make bold, underlined, italic, or change other property such as color.

After a few changes, the Odoo **Website Builder** tutorial will come back once again, calling attention to the **CUSTOMIZE** tool bar menu at the top left of the block. This is a very important menu that allows you to edit properties of the container as well as select the parent container of any object you are editing:

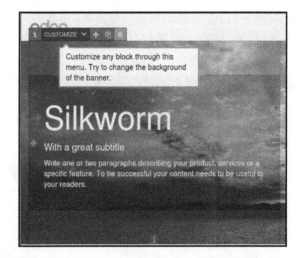

Following the tip, we can use the customization menu to now change the background of the cover block. There are several options including uploading a graphic or changing the background to a color:

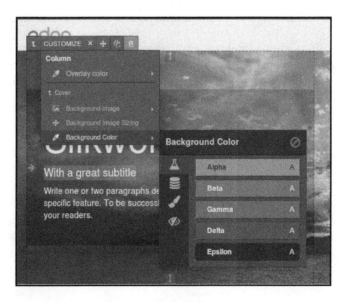

As you mouse over the colors you will see the background change to reflect your choice. Pick a background that you like and the Odoo tip will then prompt for you to drag an **Image-Text** block on the page:

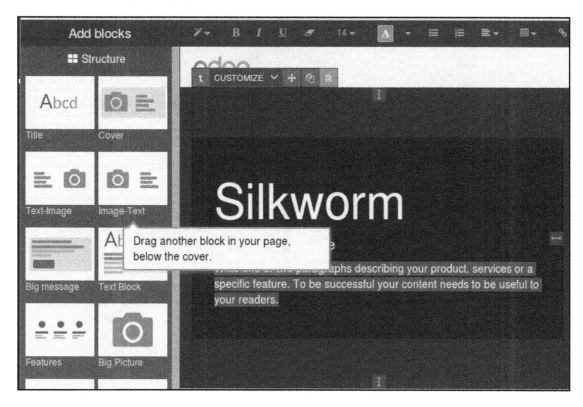

Follow the instructions and drag the block below the cover image in the previous step.

You can feel free to change the block as you wish and practice with the various options that are available:

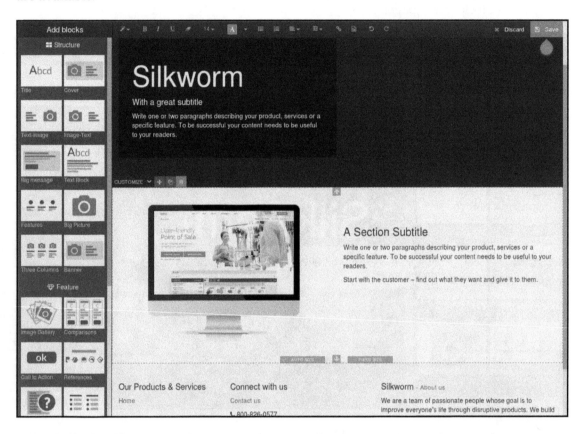

Saving your web page

Once you have had a chance to practice with editing your web page use the **Save** button on the very top right of your page to publish your changes:

After you click the **Save** button, the page will refresh, and we can see our web page as it will look to the visitors that come to our site:

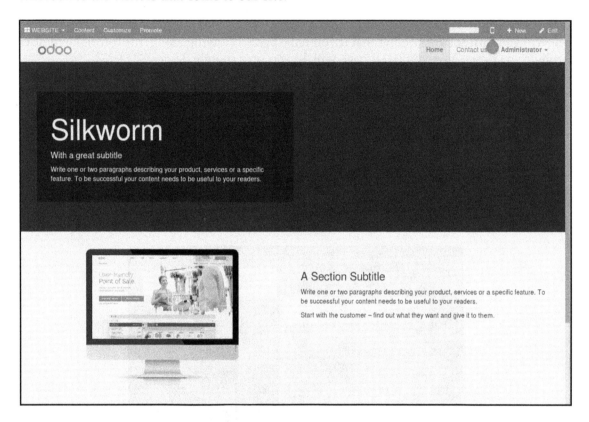

Odoo's tutorial will give you a little congratulations message for successfully saving your website and completing this part of the tutorial. We've now learned how to edit our web pages, add new content blocks to those pages, and save those changes back. As you can see, it is pretty easy to create web pages in Odoo using the **Website Builder**. Still, expect to spend a bit of time learning how the various objects can be combined and edited to get the results you desire.

Previewing our website on a mobile device

Certainly one of the compelling reasons to consider Odoo's **Website Builder** for your CMS is that it was built from the beginning to support mobile devices. This feature is so central to the **Website Builder** application that if you have been following along, the tutorial will now prompt you to see how your web page will appear on a mobile device:

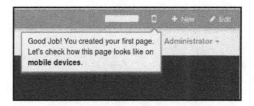

Click the mobile preview button to see how your web page will look on a typical mobile device:

While you should still double-check all of your web pages on real mobile devices before you deploy your website, this feature is very valuable because it allows you to get an idea of what your pages will look like on mobile devices.

Adding new pages and menus to your website

Next, it is time to take a look at how we add new pages and menus into our website. Typically, it is a good idea here to lay out your ideas ahead of time and decide what pages you need and how the menu structure for your website should look. I personally believe that it is better to start out simple and add additional complexity as you go. Still, there are some pages you may already know you must have on your website, so you may as well go ahead and add them.

Odoo's tip guide prompts you to use the **New** menu to add menus and pages or the edit pages to make changes to an existing page:

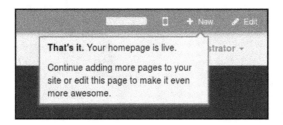

At this point, it is the end of the tutorial provided by Odoo. Still, this brings our attention to the **New** menu option, which we will use to add a new page to our website and continue exploring some more advanced aspects of Odoo's **Website Builder**.

Adding a new page

Clicking **New** brings up a large icon in the center of the page to confirm you wish to add a **New Page** to your website:

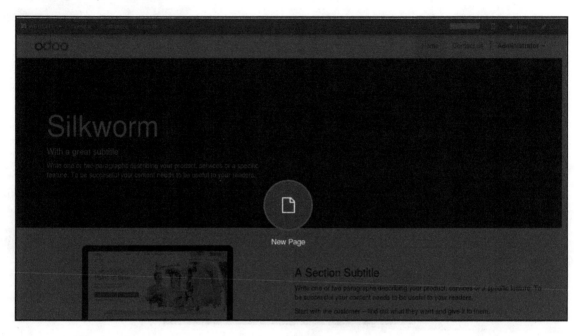

In this example, we will name our page Frequently Asked Questions, a page that is common on many websites. We will also leave the **Add page in menu** checkbox checked so that our page will be added to our menu automatically when the page is created:

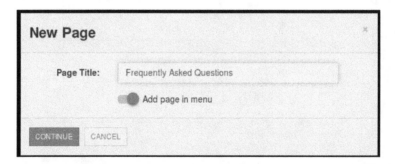

Simply click the **Continue** button and the web page is added and ready to be edited, just like we edited the previous web page.

Creating our frequently asked questions web page

In the following example, after creating the page, we inserted an **Accordion** block found under the **Feature** section in the blocks area. We then edited the block with some of Silkworm's frequently asked questions content:

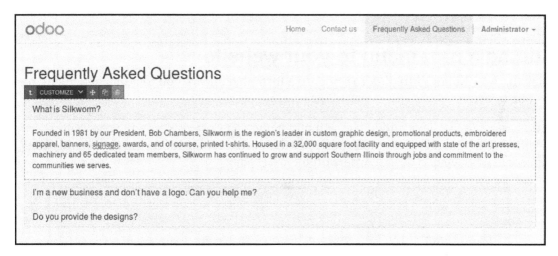

Once the page is the way you want it click the **Save** button to publish your changes.

Managing menus on your website

In the **Content** menu you can choose **Edit Menu** to organize the menu structure for your website:

Using this simple **Edit Menu** form you can re-organize your menus by using the sliders on the far left to click and drag them to the order you desire. Any menu you drag to the top will automatically become the home page of the website and get the little icon of the house on the far right to designate the page.

Dragging a menu to the right will nest menus within other menus. Using these basic methods, you can create a hierarchy of menus to contain your pages in any structure you choose.

Adding a new menu to your website

Click the **Add Menu Entry** link to bring up a form that allows you to add a new menu item to your website.

In this example, we have added a new menu named `Silkworm Design Tool` and specified an external link to connect directly the design tool that Silkworm currently uses for people who wish to design orders on their website:

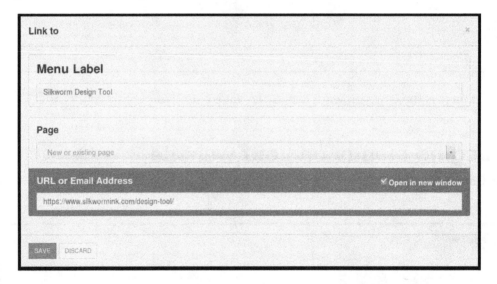

The form allows you flexibility in assigning a menu to an existing page, creating a new page, or specifying a **URL or Email Address** to link to the menu. You also have the option to specify that the menu should open the page in a new window.

Changing themes in Odoo

One of the attractive features of most CMS solutions is the ability to change the theme of your website without having to modify your content. Odoo's **Website Builder** provides the ability to modify your theme by selecting the **Customize Theme** option from the **Customize** menu:

With this build of Odoo 9, you have the option to select from a variety of free bootstrap themes using **Bootstrap 3 CSS**. Simply click **Apply**, and your website will then be updated with the new theme.

Here, we can see how our **Frequently Asked Questions** page looks after we have applied the **Cyborg** theme:

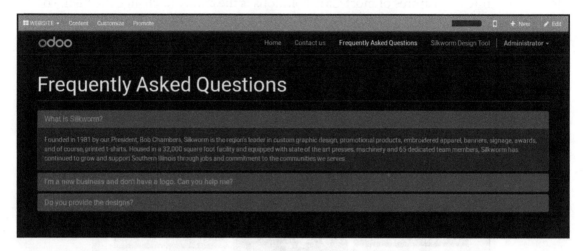

As you can see, simply by changing the theme of your website, you can create a dramatically different look.

Promoting your website

Some of the other nice features of Odoo's **Website Builder** are the built-in promotion tools for your website. Not only is it helpful to use the promotion option for each of your web pages, it is vital. If you don't go in and specify the title, keywords, and descriptions for your page, Odoo will provide default information to search engines such as Google. This is never a good idea. Make sure to take the time to at minimum provide a proper title and description for your web pages.

To promote your web page, go to the web page you wish to promote and click **Promote** in the **Website Builder** menu and choose **Optimize SEO**. Odoo will then bring up the promote form:

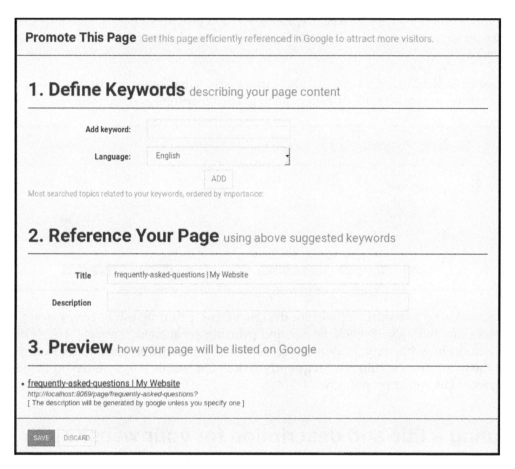

For this example, we have intentionally left the fields as they were when the form is brought up so you can see why it is so critical that you specify the title and description for each of your pages. Notice how Odoo has named our page and that the preview at the bottom is nothing like what we would want to have listed with search engines.

Specifying keywords for your website

Search engine optimization (**SEO**) is a huge topic that could fill an entire book all on its own. One of the major aspects, however, of good SEO is that it knows what keywords are most popular for the page you wish to promote. Odoo provides a handy little tool so that as you specify keywords, Odoo will let you know associated keywords that are also popular within Google.

Here, we enter the `t-shirt` keyword and can see associated keywords that may be good to include within the content of our web page to get better results in search engines:

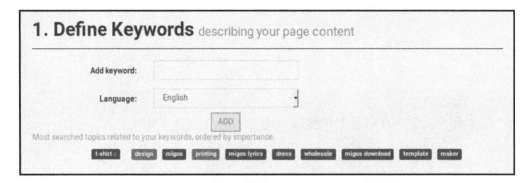

In the results, next to **t-shirt** you will see **design, migos, printing, migos lyrics, dress, wholesale**, and more. Notice how design and **printing** are shaded in purple. This is because Odoo is indicating that these keywords are located within our web page. If, for example, we added the word **dress** within our **Frequently Asked Questions** page, we would then see the keyword colored appropriately.

Creating a title and description for your website

Take time to make a description that includes good keywords and accurately describes the content of your web page. There are many good books available to help you better promote your website and provide advice on how you can get the best results in search engines.

In the example shown in following screenshot, I have added a few keywords to the title. The purpose is to try and have as many keywords as possible in your title and description so that you can get better results for your page. In this case, **design** and **printing** are important keywords that I have included in the title, based on the feedback from Odoo's keyword research:

Note that this is only an example, and it is far more important to have accurate descriptions than to simply make a title based on popular keywords.

Once you've edited your titles, descriptions and keywords for all of the pages of your website, you can visit a website like WooRank.com to check your site's SEO score and get suggestions on how to improve your ranking in search engines. Also if you have a **Google Adwords** account, you can use Google's **Keyword Planner** to find the best keywords to use within your website pages and within Google Ads to drive quality traffic to your website.

Summary

In this chapter, we took a look at Odoo's exciting new **Website Builder**. We discussed CMS a little bit, and some of the other more popular options. We then demonstrated how to install the Website Builder and followed along with Odoo's simple but effective interactive tutorial to learn the basics.

We then learned how we could add new pages to websites, configure and edit menus for the website, and how to add additional blocks and content to our pages. Finally, we finished up by learning how to change themes to give our website a new look and promote our web pages for good search results and a proper description within Google.

In the next chapter, we will look at how we can use our new website to host an e-commerce shopping cart that integrates directly with our products in Odoo.

Implementing E-Commerce with Odoo

12

In the previous chapter, we took a look at the new **Website Builder** application and saw how it can be used as to easily create a website. Now that we have the basics for getting the website up and running, this chapter will show you how you can extend a simple website to become a full e-commerce site that can take and manage orders. Even better, this functionality ties directly into sales management, which you learned about in `Chapter 3,` *Exploring Customer Relationship Management in Odoo 10*.

Topics covered in this chapter include the following:

- An overview of e-commerce and how it is implemented in Odoo
- How to install e-commerce and view the default web store
- Configuring and modifying your online store
- How to use product variants such as color and size to provide customized options for the products you sell
- Advanced product options such as alternative products, accessories, and categorizing your product
- How to set up a payment processor

E-commerce and Odoo

As I'm sure you are already well aware, e-commerce is a term that describes offering your products and services to customers electronically, typically on an internet website. Over the years, e-commerce has expanded to more and more markets. There are increasing ways to take payment on websites, and now many mobile applications include the ability to take micro-transactions. Now even applications and games include the ability to perform micro-transactions. E-commerce now covers a very wide field of options.

Popular e-commerce platforms

Like Odoo's late entry into the Website Builder/CMS market, Odoo is also introducing e-commerce functionality into a very mature market with several options. While there are hundreds, if not thousands, of viable e-commerce platforms out there, here are a few of the more popular ones.

Magento

A list of popular e-commerce applications would not be complete without Magento. Magento is open source, very popular, and is often the choice to integrate with Odoo. Even with Odoo's new e-commerce option, Magento will continue to be the selection for Odoo customers who need more advanced functionality than what Odoo can currently offer.

Volusion

Volusion is also a very popular e-commerce platform that takes an entirely different approach. Instead of an open source solution, Volusion is a hosted solution in which you configure your website and cart using their tools. They offer many different pricing models, as well as a free 14-day trial. While not for all companies, Volusion can be a fast solution for companies to get up and running without having to worry about installing software.

Shopify

While Shopify is very popular and is a hosting solution like Volusion, Shopify also directly markets Point of Sale solutions as well. This means it could be a good solution for companies that want to have an online presence but also have retail operations in which Shopify would be an appropriate Point of Sale solution. Also like Volusion, Shopify offers a variety of pricing options and a 14-day free trial.

Yahoo's Aabaco Small Business

Also a hosted solution, Yahoo's Aabaco Small Business offers a straightforward online shopping cart and what you would expect in a basic e-commerce solution. With Yahoo, you get some advantages from other services they offer, including easy advertising integration, local marketing options, and robust e-mail handling options.

Odoo as an e-commerce platform

In Odoo, e-commerce is implemented within the **Website Builder**. This means the **Website Builder** is a dependency to use Odoo e-commerce and Odoo will install the **Website Builder** if it is not already installed in the database. Also, in addition to adding a great deal of functionality to the **Website Builder**, e-commerce also adds a lot of additional options to products in Odoo so they can have variants, can appear in multiple categories, create associations with alternative products, and other options as well.

While other e-commerce platforms may have more features, there are some significant advantages to using Odoo e-commerce, especially if you are already using or are planning to use Odoo as your primary accounting/ERP system. Products you enter into Odoo automatically integrate with your e-commerce website. Orders you get automatically come into Odoo.

Best of all, Odoo e-commerce is extremely easy to set up.

Installing Odoo e-commerce

You install Odoo e-commerce like other Odoo applications:

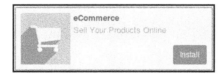

After clicking **Install**, Odoo will refresh the browser and you will be taken to the store page that Odoo has added to the website menu. Like before, Odoo has a tutorial that takes you through the basics of the Odoo website. Here, we can see the basic Odoo shop setup that has been displayed using data we've entered throughout the book so far:

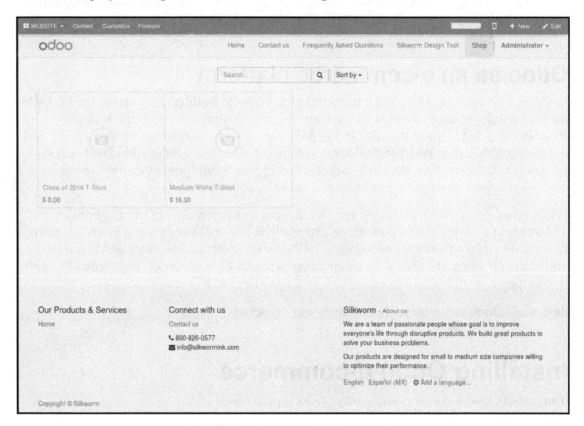

You will notice there is a placeholder to show you where the pictures for your product will display once you add a picture for the product. We will see how to do that a bit later in the chapter.

It certainly is an easy setup, and the fact that all your products come in and everything is tied into the base Odoo applications is much less complex than alternate solutions such as syncing Odoo to an external e-commerce system such as Magento.

Basics of Odoo e-commerce

You will notice a few things right away. There is a search box at the very top of the page that will allow you to search for products on the store. It is also worth mentioning that the footer is shared between all pages on the website.

Odoo has a handy feature that allows you to enter products directly from the website. In other words, you don't have to go into the **Sales** menu in Odoo and click products and add the product there. You can do it right from this shop page.

Click the **New** button at the top of the form and you are prompted to either add a **New Page** or a **New Product**:

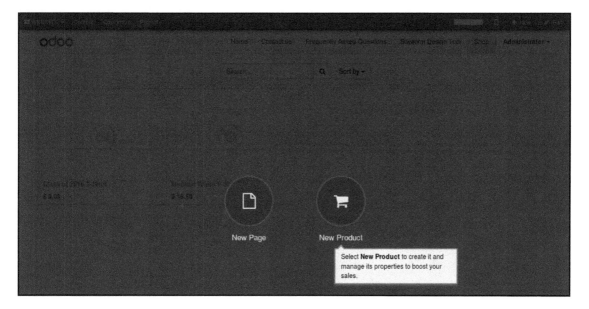

Let's go ahead and click the **New Product** button to bring up the form:

In this case, we have filled in the name of a new product we want to add to our store and we are now prompted to click the **Continue** button to add the product.

Odoo then refreshes the web browser to show the new product page your users will see when they navigate to the product. Here, you can edit and add content to the product page, just like in the previous chapter on the Odoo **Website Builder**:

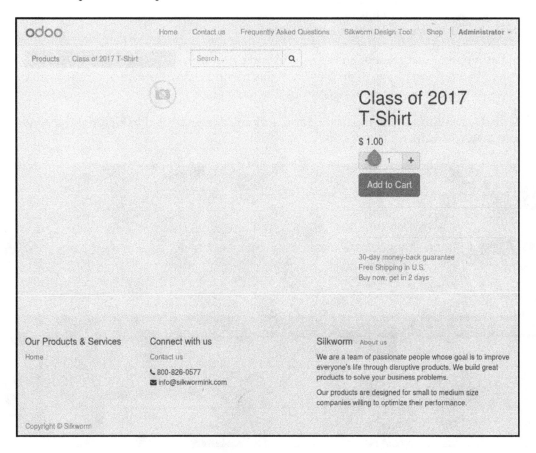

While the page is not much to look at yet, you can see the basics. The price is right under the name of the product, under that is a place to change your quantity, and then there's the button that will add that product to a shopping cart. Using what you have learned in the previous chapter, you can drag and drop blocks from the left to add content to the product page.

Setting the product price from the e-commerce page

Another nice feature of Odoo e-commerce is that you don't have to go all the way back to the product list back inside of the standard Odoo business applications. You can change the price right on the website:

While it may seem like a small thing, the ability to change the price right on the webpage can help with workflow and not having to switch back and forth between the two different views.

Adding a picture to your product

If you are going to have an e-commerce site, you are going to have to have a picture for your product. Following Odoo's tutorial, you are prompted now to add a picture for the product:

When you get presented with Odoo's picture selection wizard that allows you choose pictures for a gallery, your own computer, or even through a URL:

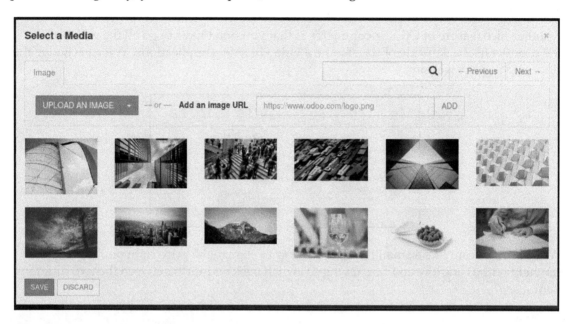

Notice, the **Upload an image** and **Add an image URL** near the top. These you will probably use more frequently than the built-in gallery pictures that Odoo provides.

We are going to use the **Upload an image** from your computer to select a simple blue t-shirt. We are using Firefox within Ubuntu Desktop to upload **Blue_Tshirt.jpg** that was obtained from the creative commons image library:

Once you click **Open** the page will refresh and you will see your product image has been successfully uploaded as shown:

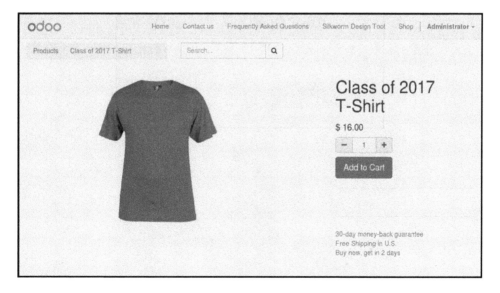

Describing the product

Following the tutorial, you could now **Add Blocks** and drag the **Text Block** onto the page. Take some time to learn what blocks are available and use them to make a product page that meets the needs of your customers. You can review `Chapter 11`, *Building a Website with Odoo*, to learn more about inserting blocks into web pages.

After you have finished inserting blocks and editing pages, click the **Save** button to commit your changes.

Publishing your product

By default, both new and existing products that were already in Odoo are not published to the website. You can see them when logged in as administrator or another user with appropriate permissions. But until you publish the product, they will not be seen by anonymous website users:

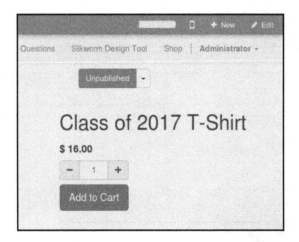

When you click the red **Unpublished** button, the button will change to green and will now display **Published**:

Your product is now published and visible to anyone who can access the website store. By clicking the button again, you can set the product back to the **Unpublished** state.

Additional configuration options for your Odoo shop

When you first install Odoo e-commerce, it provides you a default layout to get you started. However, there are several options available that you can use to alternate how your shop looks and the information it displays. Let's take a look at a few of those now.

You will want to choose **Shop** from the main menu so you can see your changes. Clicking the **Customize** menu on the right, you get a list of several options that you can check or uncheck to change appearance of your online store.

The **Customize** menu is available on every page, but the options that are available in the menu change depending on what page you are on.

Let's check the **Add to Cart** option to add a small image to each product that will allow visitors to click and easily add the product to the shopping cart:

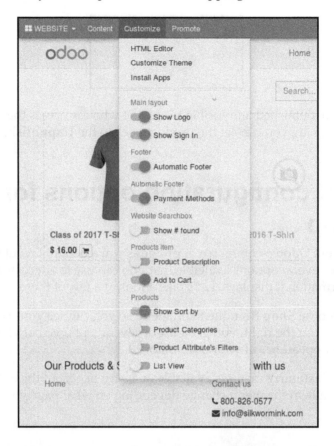

In the previous screenshot, you can see the available list of options and now can see that the little shopping cart icon is to the right of the price on each product. Experiment with the other options available inside the **Customize** windows to get the appearance you want.

Modifying the order of the products on the store

There are also other store options available to you if you edit the shop page. One of them is the ability to re-order the products. Click **Edit** at the top of the page and then hover over products to see the options menu show.

We will choose **Promote** and then **Push to top** to send the **Medium White T-Shirt** to the top of the page:

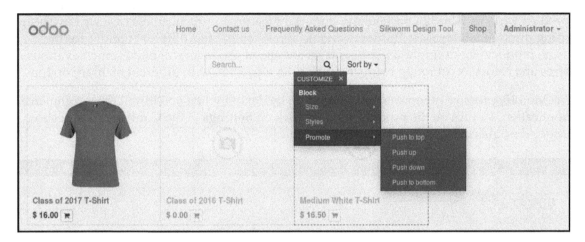

As you can see in the menu, it is possible to promote a product to the top quickly, but it could get time-consuming moving around a lot of products.

 In Odoo 8, inside the product page, you could quickly adjust the order of the products by setting sequence numbers directly. Unfortunately, this has been removed from Odoo 10. Using the skills you will learn in `Chapter 13`, *Customizing Odoo for Your Business*, you can add the sort order field to the product view.

Take a few minutes to explore the other options in the menu. The size options allow you to change the size that product shows up in the grid, giving you the opportunity to make more interesting shop layouts. The **Styles** options give you the option of adding a sale ribbon to the product, like we can see in the following screenshot:

Setting up product variants

Another nice feature that comes with the e-commerce application is the ability to create product variants. This is a particularly important feature for the business case we have been using throughout the book. Product variants allow you to offer different options for the same product. For example, a t-shirt and most apparel products will often come in various sizes and colors. A computer company may offer a product with different memory options.

In Odoo 10, product variants are not turned on by default when you install the e-commerce application. To turn on the product variants click on **Settings** in the **Configuration** section under the **Sales** menu:

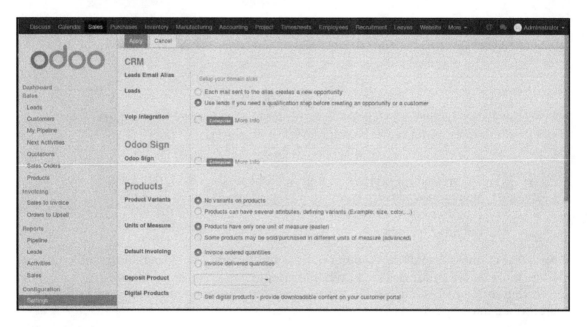

Under **Product Variants** change the selection to **Products can have several attributes defining variants (Example: size, color,....).** (If you turn this option off again after creating some product variants, those variants you've created will still display throughout the system. You will not be able to edit them, add or delete them.)

To create product variants for our t-shirt, we need to navigate to the product for which we wish to create the variants. Let's create variants for the `Class of 2017 T-Shirt`.

After you are out of edit mode in the **Website Builder**, choose **Sales** from the **Website** menu in the top left corner of your screen. Then choose products and bring up the `Class of 2017 T-Shirt`.

Choose the **Variants** page, and you will see the grid where we will be adding the variants:

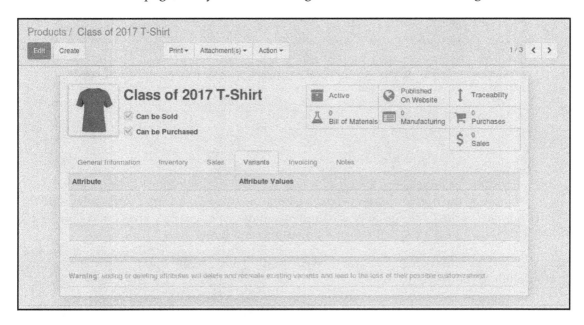

Now that we are where we need to be, click the **Edit** button at the top of your page and let's add some variants to our product.

To add variants, simply edit the product, choose the **Variants** tab, and click **Add an Item**. In the **Attribute** column, you provide the label you want to use for your attributes. We will create attributes for both **Color** and **Size**. In the product's **Attribute Values** column, you add each of the available values.

Here, we will list the available sizes and colors for our product:

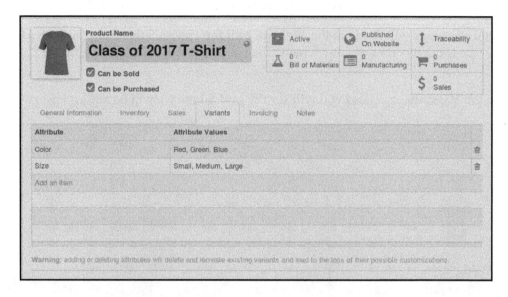

As you can see in the previous screenshot, we have created two attribute categories, one for **Color** and one for **Size**. For the color attribute, we have specified red, green, and blue. For the size attribute, we have specified small, medium, and large.

Save the product and then go back to the website shop and see the options now as they appear on the product page:

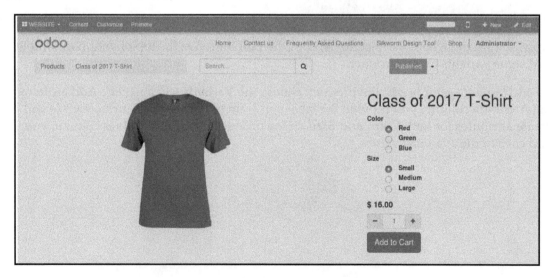

Advanced e-commerce product options

In addition to the basic options we have covered so far, Odoo also offers several advanced options on the product page that give you more control over how it appears on the store. These options include specifying multiple categories, alternative products, and accessories, as well as direct control over the position of the item on the store.

Once again you will need to go to the product page:

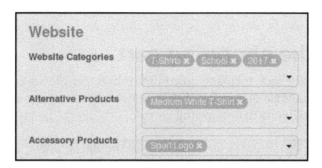

We can see in the preceding screenshot that we have specified quite a few advanced options. Instead of our product now just showing up inside of one category, it will show up in **T-Shirts**, **School**, or **2017** categories. This gives you more flexibility in designing your e-commerce store.

 To see your categories on your website you will need to go under customize while on the store page and check the product categories option.

Alternative products

Often, when customers purchase one product, it is likely there are alternative products that may also be appropriate. Maybe it is another brand of product or perhaps a deluxe version of the model they are currently viewing. For our example, we choose the medium t-shirt as a potential alternate.

Now when the user comes to the product page they will see the alternative product displayed at the bottom.

Accessory products

These are products that would probably accompany or compliment the purchase of the product on the page. For our business example, we have chosen a sports logo that would perhaps be a pin or an extra print location on the shirt. A more standard e-commerce example would be if you purchase a tablet computer that you would get prompted to purchase a case, a stylus, or perhaps a warranty.

The accessory products are presented when you add a product to the cart.

Looking at the shopping cart

While we have primarily been focusing on configuration, people are coming to your store to (hopefully) buy merchandise or services. Let's see how the shopping cart looks for them by adding the Class of 2017 shirt to a shopping cart:

You will notice that the sports logo has been added as a suggested product to our shopping cart along with a link to add it to the cart. Odoo's shopping cart works like most e-commerce shopping carts do. After you adjust your quantity here and are finished shopping, you can click **Process Checkout**, which will take you to the form that collects your shipping and billing information. A progress bar at the top right of the form keeps user informed of the steps in the process.

Seeing the draft sales order in Odoo

As soon as an item is added to the shopping cart, the order will appear as a draft within Odoo in real time. Just go into sales and look in the list of quotes and you will see your e-commerce order listed at the very top. Click on it to see the details of the order so far:

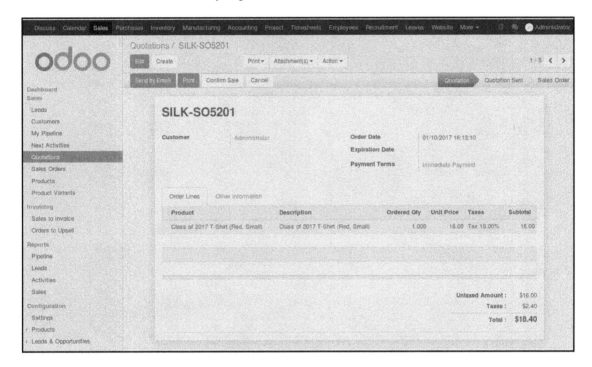

If the user abandons the order without checking out, it simply remains in draft mode and you can delete it later. This can actually be good to see how many of your users may have added something to a cart but didn't make it all the way to checkout.

Even if the user doesn't check out, this information can be valuable to see what customers are looking for.

Checking out

Like every other shopping cart application, after you have decided what you want you must provide your billing address and shipping address. Odoo by default assumes that the shipping address will be the same as the billing address:

In Odoo 10, all of the fields on this form are required except for zip code.

After clicking **Next** you are prompted to verify your address information:

You are presented with both the **Billing Address** and **Shipping Address** which will both be the same when you first coming to the screen. If you use the small icon in the upper right corner of the address box to make to edit the address, those edits will apply to both the Billing and Shipping Address. To add an alternate shipping address that is different than your billing address the customer will need to click **Add an address**.

As customers are using these forms they are for the most part easy to understand. It is important however for you get to get very familiar with the checkout process as it is ultimately up to your company to make sure it works just as you wish. Depending on your sales volume and the nature of your business, it may be necessary to customize the checkout process to maximize your sales.

When you click **Confirm** the status in the top right changes to **Payment** and we are taken to a page titled **Confirm Order**. By default, Odoo installs **Wire Transfer** as the one and only method of payment:

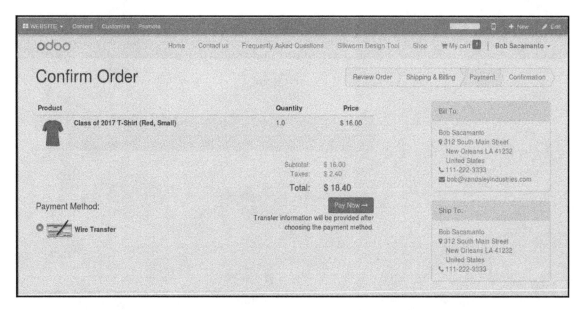

Now that we have reached this point, the remainder of the process is just like any other e-commerce system. You will notice, however, that the only payment method that is available is a **Wire Transfer**. Next, we will see how we can add PayPal as a payment processor.

Adding PayPal as a payment processor

While Odoo by default only includes **Wire Transfer**, the framework is modular and can be extended with additional payment methods.

One of the most popular e-commerce payment processors, PayPal can be quickly installed and integrated into your Odoo e-commerce system.

We install a PayPal payment processor a little differently because it is not a full application, but a module. You still go to setting and local apps, but you will want to uncheck the **Apps** filter from the search.

After clearing the **Apps** filter, simply type in `PayPal` and you will see the standard **Install** button:

Once you click **Install**, the screen will refresh and you will be left on the **Apps** screen with the apps filter back in place. We now need to go to the **Website Admin** menu and choose the **Payment Acquirers** option in the **eCommerce** section to bring up the list of payment acquirer. You will see the **PayPal** provider in that list.

 As you can see it is possible to install a Payment Acquirer though this list rather than having to go into the Apps form and install it there.

Click **PayPal** to open the form and see the available options:

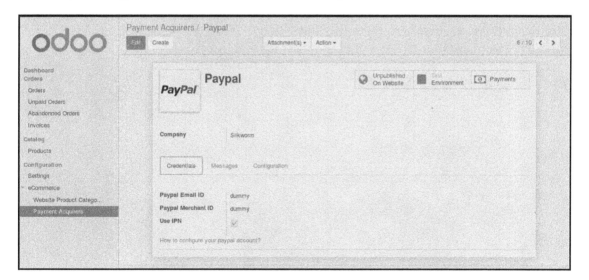

You will see under the **Environment** option that Odoo defaults to the **Test** environment which PayPal calls the sandbox. This allows you to configure your **Paypal Email ID** and **Paypal Merchant ID** at the bottom and begin testing your store. Once you have everything worked out, you can turn the environment from **Test** to **Production**.

Naturally, you will need to set up a PayPal account and use the credentials they give you to fill out the form.

Summary

In this chapter, we learned how Odoo e-commerce fits in with the **Website Builder**, how to get it installed, and the basic configuration options. Next, we looked at product variants and how they could be used to make it easier to present products that come in multiple styles.

We spent a little time learning about the advanced product options Odoo offers, such as alternative products, accessories, and defining multiple categories. After looking at the checkout process, we learned how to add an additional payment processor, PayPal, and where you need to go to set the options required to make it all work.

In the next chapter, we will look at one of the more exciting aspects of working with Odoo: how to use Odoo developer mode to add additional fields to your models and modify views to customize Odoo to fit the requirements for your business.

13
Customizing Odoo for Your Business

In this chapter, we will begin covering one of the greatest advantages of Odoo – the ability to customize the software to meet the unique needs of your business. Fortunately, Odoo provides a great deal of flexibility in which you can customize Odoo without writing any code or developing a module.

We've already discussed some of the ways to make Odoo display your company's data in a more useful manner. For example, in Chapter 10, *Creating Advanced Searches and Dashboards* we examined ways to configure Odoo to perform advanced searches, save them, and display them on dashboards designed for individual users. In Chapter 11, *Building a Website with Odoo* and Chapter 12, *Implementing E-commerce with Odoo* we created a website featuring our own products and added a shopping cart capable of accepting credit card payments. Now we will explore more advanced ways to customize Odoo to collect additional data for your business.

We will begin this chapter by learning how to activate Odoo developer mode and then back up our database. This is a very important practice when customizing Odoo. Next, we will learn how to add fields to our database and display them on forms and views. Note that customizing Odoo is a very broad topic that would take many chapters to describe. You might consider this an introduction to customization.

The following topics are covered in this chapter:

- Understanding the Odoo architecture
- Entering and exiting developer mode
- Backing up our database
- Restoring data from a backup
- Appending custom fields to models
- Displaying our newly added fields upon forms and list views

Understanding the Odoo architecture

Before you can begin understanding Odoo, it is important that you have a basic understanding of the underlying architecture that makes up Odoo applications. Fortunately, you don't have to be an expert developer to understand how the Odoo framework fits together. Each Odoo application has three primary components that make up the final Odoo application. These are **models**, **views**, and **actions**.

Models

In the Odoo framework, models are what hold and manage the data that make up your Odoo application. When you save a sales order in Odoo, the data for the sales order header is stored inside a model appropriately named **sale.order**. Individual data items such as order date and customer address are known as **fields**. In this chapter, we will be adding a few fields to the **sale.order** model inside Odoo.

Views

Models by themselves do not display any information to the end user. Models simply hold and manage the data for the application behind the scenes. Data that is stored from these models is displayed in your applications using views. This allows the **sale.order** model information to display in a variety of different ways. Want to make a very simple custom order screen that summarizes orders for the day? Create a custom view to show the model information however you wish.

Actions

The third and final component that pulls together the framework is actions. Actions are what trigger appropriate views to be displayed or for specific actions to take place on a model. For example, when you choose **Quotations** from the **Sale** menu, you are triggering an action that tells the Odoo framework to display the appropriate **sale.order** view. Without actions, the Odoo framework would not know which view to display. Another example of an action would be posting or confirming the sales order. When you click **Confirm**, the Odoo framework calls the appropriate function that will update the **sale.order** model.

Activating developer mode

To customize Odoo the first step is to activate developer mode. Once you enter this mode, Odoo will provide you with a lot more onscreen information as you navigate through the interface. This mode also allows you to make changes to the database and store that information in a file.

To activate developer mode, click on the **Settings** menu. On the far right you will see a panel that contains information about the Odoo installation. At the bottom of the panel you will see the link to **Activate the developer mode**:

Once you have entered this screen, you can click on **Activate the developer mode** to begin customizing Odoo.

Odoo recognizes that you are in developer mode by adding `?debug` to the URL in your web browser. Additionally, Odoo changes the information that is provided when your mouse cursor hovers over various fields in the interface. For example, when viewing a sales order record while in developer mode, you can move the cursor over the label for the **Order Date** field to reveal details about how that field is represented internally in Odoo:

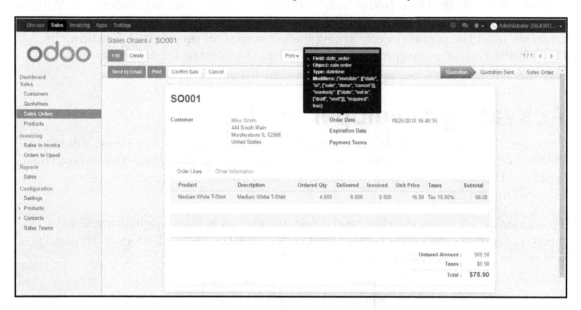

The preceding screenshot demonstrates how Odoo displays information while you are in developer mode. In this example, we can see that the **Order Date** field is named `date_order` and that the field belongs to the `sale.order` model object. Additionally, we can see the field type is date and there are modifiers assigned to the field. This type of information will be of great value as you continue to customize Odoo.

Getting out of developer mode

Now that you are in developer mode, there will come a time when you want to exit developer mode and work with Odoo as you normally would. To exit developer mode, simply go back to the **Settings** menu and choose the **Deactivate the developer mode** link.

Alternatively, you can simply remove `debug` from the URL string in your browser:

Make sure you leave all `?` and `&` symbols in place when you remove the debug tag from the URL. If you get any errors or other unusual behavior after removing `debug` from your URL, you can typically use your browser's back button.

If this also fails, you can always restart the browser and log back in to Odoo.

Backing up your database

When you make changes while in developer mode, those changes are written into the database associated with the company. One of the major advantages of this approach is that you do not have to write code in Python or create a custom module to implement simple customizations. One of the major disadvantages, however, is that there is the potential that you could make a change that is undesirable and perhaps difficult to reverse.

Therefore, it is very important and highly recommended that you make backups of your database both before and after you make any customizations through developer mode.

 Do not skip this step!. It is always a good idea to frequently back up your database. However, it is absolutely imperative that you back up your database before undertaking any customization.

To back up your database, you must first log out of Odoo. After you have successfully logged out, click on the **Manage Databases** link. (Don't see that link? If you have installed the **Website Builder** app, you may first need to click on the **Select** button that appears next to the name of your database on the login form before a **Manage databases** link appears.)

From this screen, you click on the **Backup** link which appears to the right of the name of your database:

To back up your database, select the database from the pop-up menu and enter the master password for the Odoo installation, if one is set. (By default, the master password in Odoo 10 will be empty; however, in prior versions it was admin.) You can also choose to save to a .zip file or a pg_dump file. ZIP files will be bigger because they include an encrypted copy of the filestore, while dump files only include the data stored in ProgreSQL. Next, click on the **Backup** button.

After you click on the **Backup** button, Odoo will save your database to your local drive. Depending on the browser you are using and the settings in your browser, the prompt you get to save your file will vary. The default filename will end with the .dump extension if you selected the pg_dump backup format and .zip extension if you selected the zip format.

After you save your file, Odoo will download it into the directory you have specified. If this is the first time you have backed up your database, you should also take the time to verify that you can successfully restore the database. While this may seem like an unnecessary exercise, it is important to remember that a backup is only as good as your ability to successfully restore it.

Restoring a database in Odoo

To restore a database in Odoo, click on the **Restore Database** button.

To restore your database, you need to provide three pieces of information: the backup file you wish to restore, the master password of Odoo, and a new database name. Clicking on the **Choose File** button in the file selection area will prompt you to select the .dump or .zip file created when you performed the backup.

After you have specified the file and the other required fields, click on **Continue** to begin restoring the database. A small progress bar may appear in the bottom left of the browser to update you on the progress of the restore. Once the database restoration is complete, log in to the database to make sure everything is working as expected.

Now with a successful backup and restoration, you are ready to begin customizing Odoo. If something goes wrong, you will have the ability to restore your backup. While customizing Odoo, remember to back up the database frequently and test the restore process often.

Adding a custom field to Odoo

One of the most common reasons for customizing Odoo is to collect additional information that is specific to your company. If you are running an insurance company, perhaps you want to specify the policy number on your sales order. If you are working in property management, perhaps you would like to store the date on which the lease agreement will expire.

For our working example, we will be adding fields that will help us better manage the data and processes for our silkscreen company. Specifically, we will be adding the following fields to the sales order header:

Field name	Label	Field type	Purpose
x_daterequired	**Date Required**	Date	In the screen printing industry, deadlines drive when production must begin and when the product should be delivered to the customer.
x_rush	**Rush Order**	Boolean	Related to **Date Required** is the necessity to flag some sales orders as rush orders. A **Rush Order** can then be prioritized and given expedited treatment.

Custom field names in Odoo should be preceded by x_. This is so that field names in future Odoo versions and standard updates will not accidentally conflict with the custom fields you have added.

Viewing the model in Odoo

Odoo allows you to add custom fields to the model if you are in developer mode. Click on **Settings** and then, in the **Database Structure** sub-menu, choose **Models**. You will get a list of all the models that make up your current Odoo installation:

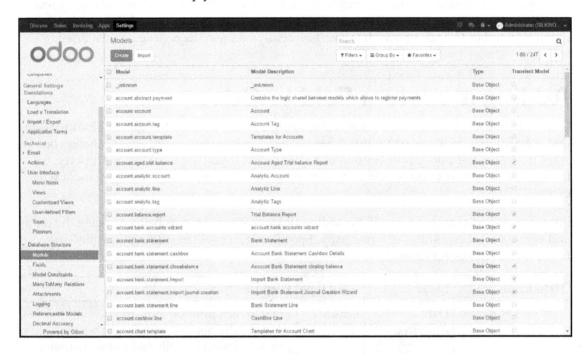

Using the standard search tools in Odoo that you have learned about so far, you can now limit the results to just show the **sale.order** model:

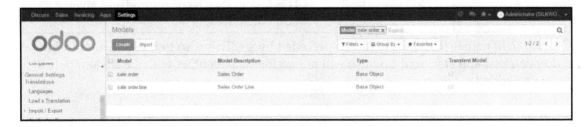

You can now click the **sale.order** model to open up the model and display all the fields that make up the **sale.order** model:

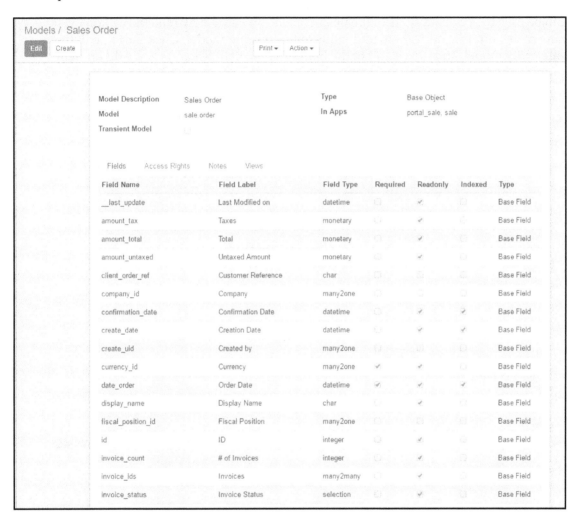

Model Description	Sales Order	Type	Base Object
Model	sale.order	In Apps	portal_sale, sale
Transient Model			

Fields   Access Rights   Notes   Views

Field Name	Field Label	Field Type	Required	Readonly	Indexed	Type
__last_update	Last Modified on	datetime		✓		Base Field
amount_tax	Taxes	monetary		✓		Base Field
amount_total	Total	monetary		✓		Base Field
amount_untaxed	Untaxed Amount	monetary		✓		Base Field
client_order_ref	Customer Reference	char				Base Field
company_id	Company	many2one				Base Field
confirmation_date	Confirmation Date	datetime		✓	✓	Base Field
create_date	Creation Date	datetime		✓	✓	Base Field
create_uid	Created by	many2one				Base Field
currency_id	Currency	many2one	✓	✓		Base Field
date_order	Order Date	datetime	✓	✓	✓	Base Field
display_name	Display Name	char		✓		Base Field
fiscal_position_id	Fiscal Position	many2one				Base Field
id	ID	integer		✓		Base Field
invoice_count	# of Invoices	integer		✓		Base Field
invoice_ids	Invoices	many2many		✓		Base Field
invoice_status	Invoice Status	selection		✓		Base Field

Here, you can examine the name of the field as well as the field type and whether the field is required or not. Some fields are also designated as **Read only** fields. These fields are often automatically generated or calculated by Odoo.

 Examining the models in Odoo is a great way to learn more about the structure of the data and how it is organized. This is particularly vital for anyone who wishes to customize Odoo.

Creating a new field in the sale order model

Let's go ahead and start adding our custom fields to the **sale.order** model. Please be aware it can be easy to accidentally click **Create** and create an entire new model. We don't want a new model but instead want to add fields to the existing model. Click **Edit** to edit the **sale.order** model, and then scroll to the bottom of the field list and click **Add an item**:

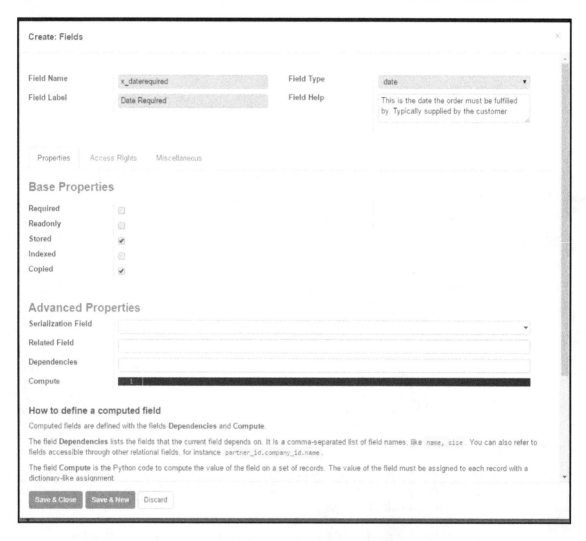

In the preceding example, we have specified our **Date Required** custom field.

The x_ prefix is already specified in the **Field Name** by default to encourage the use of good naming conventions. We have filled in the other data required for the field including setting the **Field Name** to x_daterequired, the **Field Label** to Date Required, and the **Field Type** to **date**.

Click on **Save & New** to finish adding our new field to the **sale.order** model and proceed to enter the remaining x_rush field:

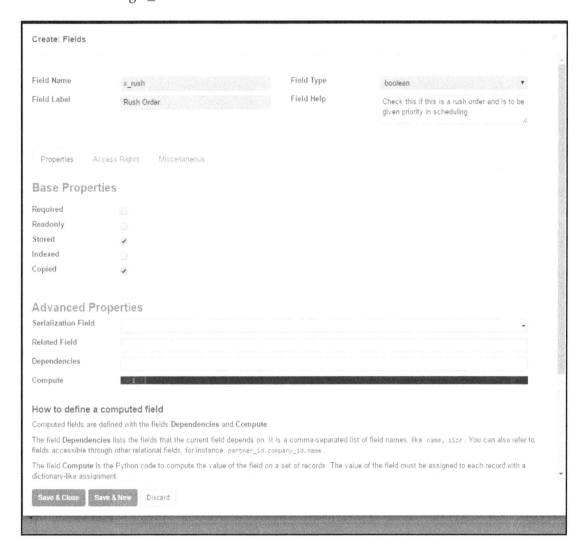

You will see this field is very similar to the **Date Required** field, except that we specified the field type as **boolean**. This will tell Odoo's framework to display the field as a checkbox. Click on **Save & Close** to finish adding our new **Rush Order** field. You must also click the **Save** button at the top of the screen to save both new fields into the **sale.order** model.

Editing the form view

Now that we have added our fields to the model, we want to display them on the form. Fortunately, Odoo provides an editor that makes it easy to add the fields to your view. It is helpful if you have a bit of experience using a text editor and have some familiarity with XML. If you don't, please see the Appendix, where you can find some basic information on editing XML.

The easiest way to edit a view–in this case the sale order form–is to go to the form you wish to edit. Simply pull up any sales order in Odoo, and from the debug menu choose **Edit FormView**:

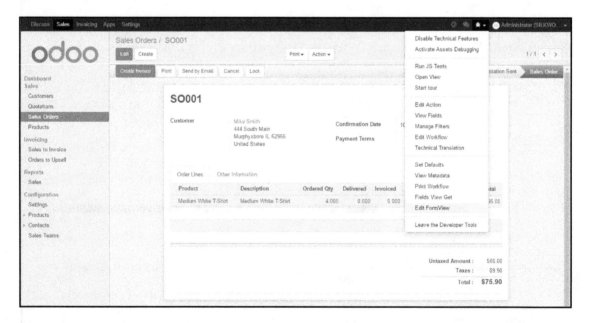

This will bring up the actual XML code that makes up the sale order view. It is going to look somewhat intimidating at first if you are new to XML, but the changes we are going to make are very easy. Even better, you can copy and paste an existing field so you don't have to type all the special characters and understand the syntax.

Now scroll down until you find the line that displays the payment terms on the sales order form. Note the line number (**40**) displayed on the left. We will add our two custom fields directly below that line:

To simplify, you can copy and paste the `payment_term_id` line and then edit it to include the custom field we wish to add. Here, we have added the field for **Date Required** to our view:

```
32          <field name="partner_shipping_id" groups="sale.group_delivery_invoice_address" context="{'default_type':
33        </group>
34        <group>
35            <field name="date_order" attrs="{'invisible': [('state', 'in', ['sale', 'done', 'cancel'])]}"/>
36            <field name="validity_date" attrs="{'invisible': [('state', 'in', ['sale', 'done'])]}"/>
37            <field name="confirmation_date" attrs="{'invisible': [('state', 'in', ['draft', 'sent', 'cancel'])]}"/>
38            <field name="pricelist_id" groups="product.group_sale_pricelist"/>
39            <field name="currency_id" invisible="1"/>
40            <field name="payment_term_id" options="{'no_create': True}"/>
41            <field name="x_daterequired"/>
42        </group>
43      </group>
44      <notebook>
45        <page string="Order Lines">
46            <field name="order_line" mode="tree,kanban" attrs="{'readonly': [('state', 'in', ('done','cancel'))]}">
47                <form string="Sales Order Lines">
```

Notice that we have removed the options tag for the purpose of this example. Now you can save your changes, close the editor, and refresh the form.

Please be aware, that you may have to hold down the *Shift* key when you refresh your browser to see the change. Notice how the form now appears in edit mode:

As you can see, it is pretty easy to create new fields and then add those fields to views and forms.

Customizing search operations in Odoo

In addition to having the ability to modify the forms and list views in Odoo, you can also customize searching in Odoo to better fit the needs of your organization. For example, when customers place orders, it is common in a business-to-business scenario that you will be provided a purchase order or another source document that the customer references internally.

By default, Odoo does not include the source document field in your search. You must use the advanced search function each and every time in order to look up a customer's order by the source document that they have provided to you. As in much of this book, this example comes from a real-world scenario. When customers call, often they may not have an invoice number or sales order number from your company; instead, they may only have their internal source document number. Let's see how we can customize Odoo to more easily search on the **Source Document** field in the sales order.

Specifying additional fields you want Odoo to use in the search

One of the greatest features of Odoo's developer tools is that you can move your mouse over any field in a form and see important information about that field. For our example, we are going to hover over the **Source Document** field to learn how this field is represented within Odoo's database:

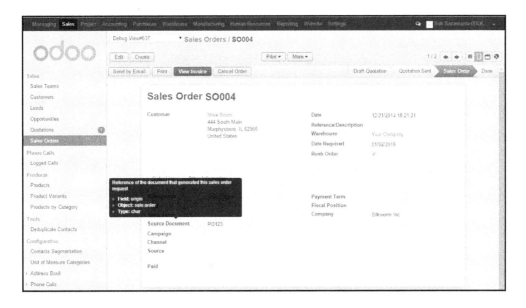

As you can see, the **Field** name for the **Source Document** in the sales order is **origin**. We can also verify that this field belongs to the **sale.order** object, and it is of type **char**.

We will use this information to modify the search view so we can add the ability to search for the source document in our list view without using the advanced search.

Editing the search view

You edit the search view by navigating to the list for the search you wish to modify. In this case, we will simply click on **Sales Orders** under the main **Sales** menu. Then under the **Debug View** menu, choose **Edit SearchView**. Find the **Inherited View** field and click on the "open" icon next to it.

The XML for the search view will now appear for you to edit:

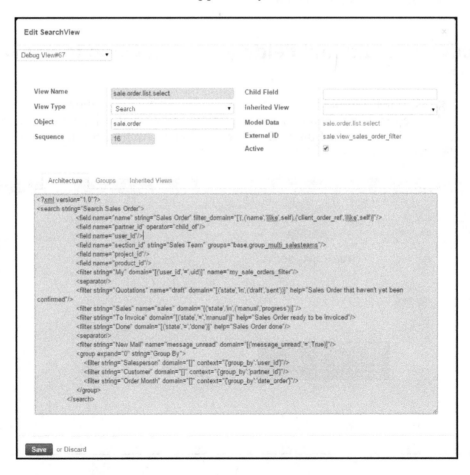

Take a little time to look at the structure of this form. You will see that many tags start with `<Field name="`. Each of these fields define what search fields are available to you in the list's search box.

To search on **Source Document**, we only need to add a field tag for **origin** to the list. Here, you can see we have added it directly under the `project_id` field and above the `product_id` field:

```xml
<?xml version="1.0"?>
<search string="Search Sales Order">
    <field name="name" string="Sales Order" filter_domain="['|',('name','ilike',self),('client_order_ref','ilike',self)]"/>
    <field name="partner_id" operator="child_of"/>
    <field name="user_id"/>
    <field name="section_id" string="Sales Team" groups="base.group_multi_salesteams"/>
    <field name="project_id"/>
    <field name="origin"/>
    <field name="product_id"/>
    <filter string="My" domain="[('user_id','=',uid)]" name="my_sale_orders_filter"/>
    <separator/>
    <filter string="Quotations" name="draft" domain="[('state','in',('draft','sent'))]" help="Sales Order that haven't yet been confirmed"/>
    <filter string="Sales" name="sales" domain="[('state','in',('manual','progress'))]"/>
    <filter string="To Invoice" domain="[('state','=','manual')]" help="Sales Order ready to be invoiced"/>
    <filter string="Done" domain="[('state','=','done')]" help="Sales Order done"/>
    <separator/>
```

After you save the form and close the editor, *shift+refresh* the page. If you begin typing in the search box, you will now see **Source Document** available in the search list:

When making changes here in these forms, all of the previous warnings apply. Make sure you do not make changes in live systems, and make sure you have good backups.

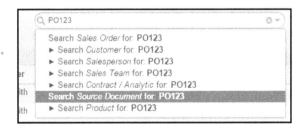

As you can see, the **Source Document** is added to the search under **Analytic Account**, which is the description associated with the `project_id` field in Odoo.

Understanding actions

We've seen already how we can modify views and how to create custom search criteria. From here, you're well on your way to making customizations that are quite useful. At some point, however, when you wish to create a new view or a specific type of filter, you are going to need to understand actions so you can change the way an Odoo application behaves.

As we learned earlier, we can use actions to trigger views. Let's begin by getting a look at the list of actions that are already in your Odoo installation. While in developer mode, under the **Settings** menu under **Technical | Actions**, choose **Window Actions**. You will be presented with a list:

In the preceding screenshot, we have filtered the list of actions to only those named **Sales Orders**. (Be sure to type the plural: `sales`!) Let's now create our own custom rush order action that will allow us to create a menu to easily pull up only the sales orders that are rush orders. This is a perfect example of simple customization that can save a lot of keystrokes and improve usability depending on the operation.

One nice thing about customizing in Odoo is you can often use an existing record as a template to copy/paste and then simply make the custom changes you require. This dramatically reduces the risk of making a typing error.

It is recommended when you are first starting out that you consider making only one change at a time and testing it thoroughly before making additional customizations. This practice helps you narrow down the cause of the error.

Let's duplicate the top sales orders action in the list that has the domain value
`[('state','not in',('draft','sent','cancel'))].`

Click on the **Edit** menu and choose **Duplicate** from the **Action** drop-down menu:

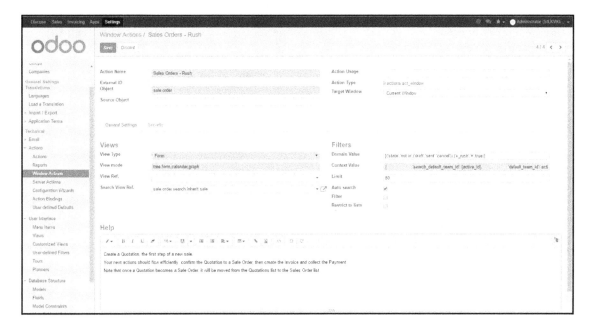

Notice that after we duplicated the action, we changed the action name to **Sales Orders – Rush,** so it is easy for us to recognize that this action will only show orders that are designated as rush orders.

To actually filter the **sale.order** model by orders that have been marked as rush orders we need to change the domain value of our new action. Notice how the domain value already has a limit that says this cannot be a draft order. We will leave that filter in place and add the additional condition that the order must also in fact be a rush order.

In a large operation, a simple modification like this could reduce a screen that has thousands or even hundreds of thousands of records and limit it to a manageable size for that process.

Make sure you save the change to your new action. Now we can add our new menu.

Create a new menu

When customizing Odoo it is inevitable at some point that you are going to have to create a new menu to pull a new view you have created or perhaps an alternative action that will filter or limit a view in a different way. The ability to create new menus and tie them to your own custom actions can create a better user experience that is more customized to your specific business requirements.

While in developer mode, go the **Settings** menu and choose **Menu Items** under **User Interface**:

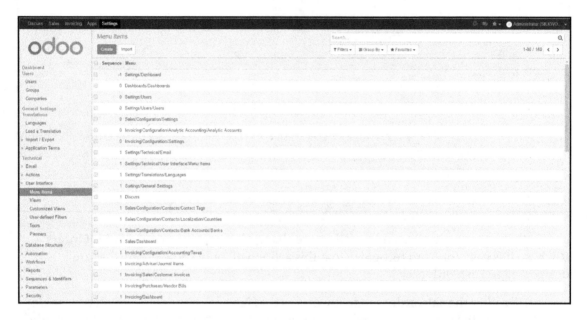

Like before, you can use the search feature to limit the menu to the sales orders menu item. Just like we duplicated the sales orders action to make it easier to create our custom sales order action, duplicate the sales order menu item as a starting point for our new Rush Sales order menu:

Notice how we have changed the name that will appear in the menu and have assigned the **Sales Orders – Rush** action to this menu. Odoo now knows that when you select the **Sales Orders – Rush** menu item, the **Sales Orders – Rush** action will be triggered. Because we modified the domain value of the action to only include rush orders, we only see the records that match that criteria.

Summary

In this chapter, we started by learning how to activate Odoo's developer mode. Next, we walked through how to make a backup of the Odoo database and how to restore that database using the manage database tools in Odoo. It was emphasized how important it is to back up databases prior to performing any customization in Odoo. Next, we went through step-by-step how to customize Odoo by adding fields to the database and ultimately to your forms and views. This is by no means a comprehensive guide to Odoo customization; it is merely an introduction to common ways to easily customize forms, lists, and searches.

In the next chapter, we will explore how we can use the Odoo report designer to customize reports and export data from Odoo. We begin by looking at how to customize our company headers and footers that will appear on our standard documents. With Odoo, we can use dynamic fields to automatically put values from our database into our reports. Using the new **QWeb** template language we will get a great deal of power and flexibility in building reports that integrate well with Odoo.

14
Modifying Documents and Reports

Regardless of how great the built-in reports are in any ERP system, it is inevitable that most companies will need to do some custom modifications to the standard documents and reports. Of course Odoo is no exception. The goal of this chapter is to provide the reader a solid introduction to the Odoo reporting framework.

In this chapter, we will cover:

- How to make simple changes to headers and footers of your reports
- The basic framework of how Odoo organizes reports and forms
- How to modify and make changes to reports using the Odoo reporting framework and the **QWeb** template language

Within Odoo, it is possible to make some changes without modifying the documents themselves. For example, you can change the headers and footers that appear on all your reports throughout the company.

A powerful template language called QWeb allows you to integrate data from Odoo into your report. This chapter walks through these steps and shows you how to modify exisiting Odoo reports.

 Like in other areas of Odoo development, make frequent backups of your databases. In some of the examples we will change the database in ways that can make it difficult to recover if something goes wrong.

Getting the skills required to modify reports

In my experience, many end users believe that with perhaps an hour or two of training, they will be able to create their own reports. This is not just an Odoo issue; it is a common perception that many end users have when working with an ERP system. Unfortunately, creating or modifying reports is often not easy and should be considered more of a developer task than an end user task. Be prepared to spend considerable time to acquire the skills required to make significant changes to the documents and reports in Odoo.

Furthermore, reporting has changed dramatically in the past several years. Previously, many companies were dependent on paper reports and Excel sheets to properly communicate information through the company. Very often in Odoo, what was previously a physical report can better be managed through filtering and grouping views properly, or using the business intelligence features built into Odoo. Be sure to carefully consider your report options from many different angles.

 Scope creep, refers to projects that continue to grow in complexity beyond the original design. Pay special attention to report requests, as it can be an area in which you can end up with many additional requirements you did not anticipate.

What is the QWeb template framework?

The QWeb template framework is actually far more useful than just for basic reports. The QWeb template is also the main way that all of the website builder's and new CMS generate the HTML to create the page. In reports, QWeb works exactly the same way as HTML gets generated, but instead directs the output into a PDF file.

The great part about this is once you learn how to modify reports in QWeb, that same skill will allow you to create dynamic web pages that can tie directly into Odoo.

Company report configuration

When Odoo is first installed, you are presented with a default template that will appear on many of the standard reports. Even if you don't plan to make a lot of major changes to the standard reports in Odoo, it is very likely that you will wish to modify the headers and footers and other parts of your report template to be more specific to your company.

To begin editing Odoo headers and footers, login as an Odoo administrator. Navigate to the **Settings** menu and click **General Settings**. Scroll to the bottom and you will find the **Report Configuration** area:

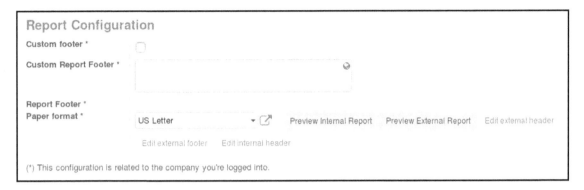

Before we make any changes at all to our reports, let's go ahead and get a look at one of the default reports by clicking **Preview Internal Report.**

Odoo will then process the report into a PDF and allow you to download it in your browser.

Problems with Wktohtmlpdf installation

While a majority of Odoo installations go smooth for the primary operations, it is quite common for installations to have problems with a library called **Wktohtmlpdf**. If you have this problem with your own installation you will see a message like the following:

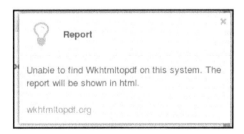

Follow the link to `http://www.wkhtmltopdf.org` and the resources in the *Appendix* to learn more about how to install this package so Odoo can properly display the PDF file.

After the PDF is downloaded, you can view it to see the default internal report:

As you can see, the default internal report is extremely basic with only a simple header and no footer. This report is used as the name suggests; for internal reports that will be shared with other employees of the company or perhaps with close contacts to the company such as sub-contractors.

Now let's take a look at the default external report by clicking **Preview External Report:**

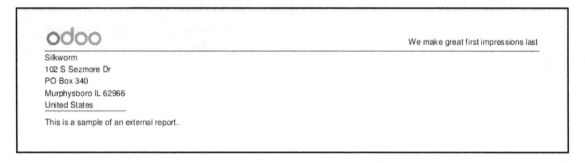

Here we see the header of the external report has quite a bit more information than the internal report. This makes sense, as reports we would distribute to vendors or customers need to have information necessary to know what company the information belongs to. In addition to the report header, external reports also provide a footer as shown in following screenshot:

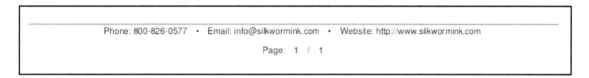

By default, the footer provides additional contact information as well as the page count. The first two options in the **Report Configuration** settings allow us to change the footer on the external report:

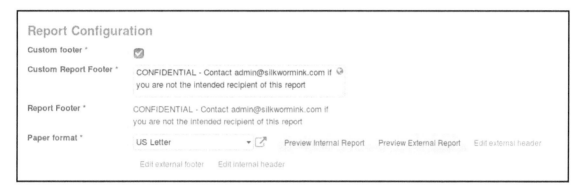

In this example, we have modified the report footer to display a message that asks anyone who has received the report in error to contact the company through an email address. You can then click the **Preview External Report** to see how the message will appear on your report.

Even if you specify a custom footer it will not appear on the internal report. Using what you learn in this chapter you can change that if you wish.

Specifying the paper format for your reports

Depending on your specific business requirements, it is possible that you will need to have custom paper formats. Fortunately Odoo allows you to specify a default paper format as well as indicate which reports should use a given paper format. While you may not need to use this feature, to configure a paper format simply click the standard edit icon to the right of the **Paper format*** dropdown list, and you will see the available options:

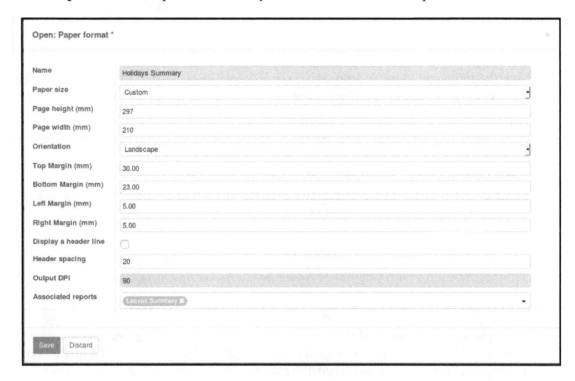

In the above example we can see the custom paper configuration for the `Holidays Summary`. Most importantly notice how the associated reports includes the `Leaves Summary`. This is how Odoo can associate a given report with a specific paper size.

Troubleshooting printers and paper sizes can be tricky. Even if you have your settings correct here in this Odoo configuration, you will need to consider the settings in the application you use, to print the report, as well as the settings on the printer itself.

Modifying the internal report header using QWeb

From the options we have seen so far, it is clear that while we can create a custom footer, that we must do something else in order to change the header for our reports. To make this change we must edit the actual QWeb source that makes up the header of the report.

Let's look at the QWeb for the company header by clicking the link **edit internal header**. The following is a screenshot of the QWeb used for the internal report header:

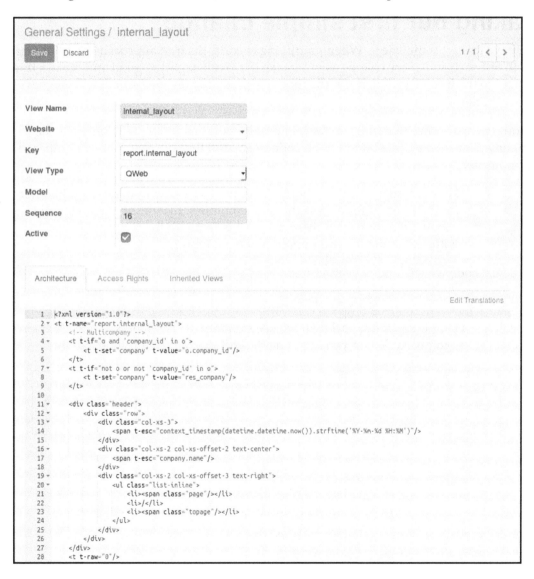

Here we can see the actual QWeb code that displays the report header in HTML which is then converted into a PDF report. As was mentioned earlier in the chapter, modifying reports is not something that should typically be attempted by end users. This example is to demonstrate how you can make a small change to a report. By analyzing other reports in Odoo it is possible to make your own custom reports. Just be prepared for a considerable learning curve if you are new to XML and template languages.

Making our first simple change

You have to start somewhere. When modifying reports, the best approach is to start simple and to test each and every change as you make it. Do not expect to go in and make a dozen changes to the header and then run the report without any testing — not until you have a lot of experience.

For our change, notice that in the default internal report header in Odoo only has the company name. Let's add a bit of QWeb code to append the company phone number to the report header.

 Here we can use a little shortcut, because we know that the default footer for the external report has the phone number. By editing the footer and copying the code from there, we can paste it into the internal header without having to worry about making a typo.

The actual code we will add is very simple:

```
: <span t-field="company.phone"/>
```

The colon is a simple separator and then we use standard QWeb syntax to specify the phone number for the company. When you are done the edited code should look like this:

```
13    <div class="col-xs-3">
14        <span t-esc="context_timestamp(datetime.datetime.now()).strftime('%Y-%m-%d %H:%M')"/>
15    </div>
16    <div class="col-xs-2 col-xs-offset-2 text-center">
17        <span t-esc="company.name"/> : <span t-field="company.phone"/>
18    </div>
```

Now you can preview the internal report to see the change:

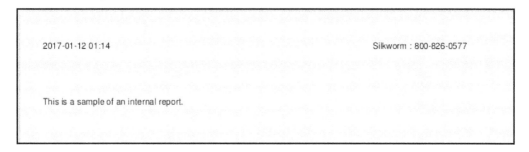

As you can see, the report now includes the colon separator as well as the phone number for the company. Remember to start with simple changes and examine other reports to learn how to make more complex changes.

Learning how Odoo organizes reports

Unfortunately, the ability to edit the header and footer of the company information does not get you very far. If you spend time with Odoo, it is inevitable the time will come when you need to make changes to specific Odoo documents. For example, a company may need to customize their quotation or sales order to make it more visually attractive to their customers. Perhaps a company would like to change the appearance of their invoice, or the picking ticket they use to pull products from inventory.

However, before you can begin going in and start modifying reports or adding new reports, it is important that you have an overall understanding of how reports are organized within Odoo. First make sure you have activated developer mode, as you have learned how to do in the previous chapter.

With developer mode active, you can get access to the reports within Odoo by going to the **Settings** menu, then in the **Technical** section further down in the menu you will find the **Reports** option. Clicking it will list the **Reports** in Odoo, as shown in the following screenshot:

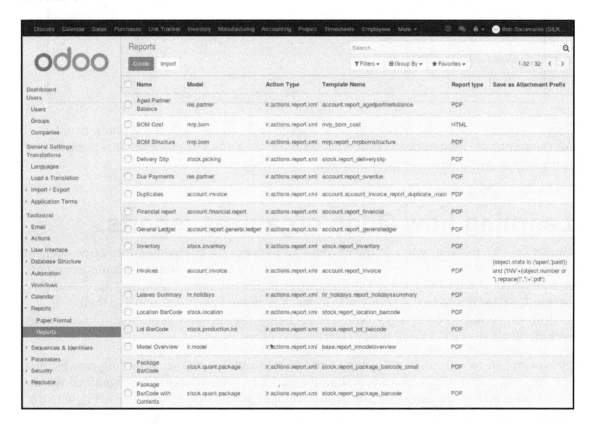

Here you can see the list of reports in the view with critical information that tells you which model the report is associated with, the type of action used to trigger that report, the template for the report, and the report type.

The **Save As Attachment** prefix can be used to append a prefix to the beginning of the report name when it is saved.

Understanding the report types

Each of the past few major upgrades to Odoo has brought with it upgrades and new improvements to the reporting engine. Odoo 10 is no different and many of the old reports are gone. However, Odoo still provides support for those older types of reports. In the previous screenshot, when you see a report type of RML or PDF (depreciated), that is a report that is still using the old reporting mechanism. You can still open up those older reports and make changes to them. However, most of the reports now use Odoo's new Odoo report framework, QWeb templates.

Looking at the definition for the Sales Order form

As with other examples in this book, we are going to choose a very common business requirement for this example. Most companies are not going to want to use the default sales order. In fact, after involvement in hundreds of accounting and ERP systems, I cannot recall any system implementation that involves sales orders that did not customize the sales order at some point.

Using what you have learned in previous chapters, you may wish to bring up a quotation or a sales order and have it ready to print so you can see your changes as they happen. Any changes you make will modify both the quotation and the sales order as they share the same QWeb template.

 Odoo is quite friendly at allowing you to use more than one tab in your browser for most operations. I often keep one tab open with the document I want to print and then keep another tab open with the report I am editing.

When you are ready to edit the sales order, scroll down the report list and find the **Quotation / Order** and click on it. It is also the only report in the default list of Odoo reports that is built on the **sale.order** model:

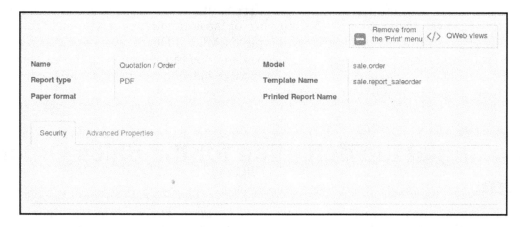

You will notice there is some basic information at the top of the page and then a **Security** tab at the bottom of the report that is empty. You can use this tab to put additional restrictions on the report beyond what has already been specified in the **sale.order** model.

The previous screen is primarily the configuration of the report. The views that make up the actual report itself can be found by clicking **QWeb views**:

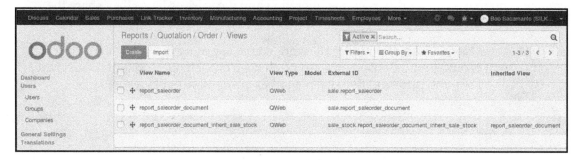

This brings up all the **QWeb views** associated with the report. While there are three views listed, the one we are interested in is **report_saleorder_document**. The **report_saleorder** view is basically a container that holds the content of the document view and you would rarely need to modify that unless you were an experienced Odoo developer.

Click on the **report_saleorder_document** view to open the view:

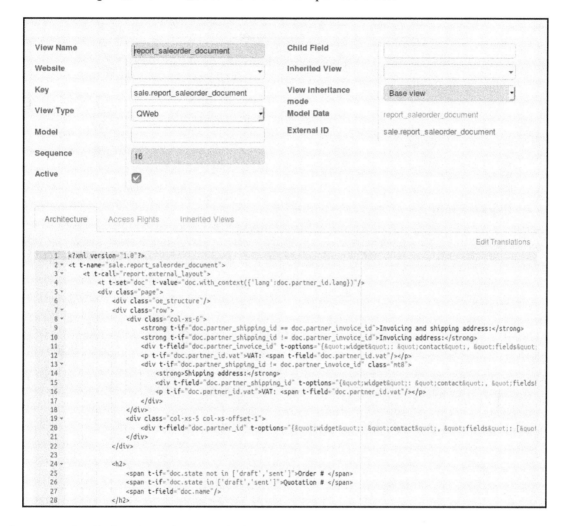

So we are finally here! You have to drill down a little bit to get to them, but after you have done it a few times it really is pretty easy. Now we are looking at the actual QWeb report template. Odoo calls these templates views, when they are associated with Odoo reports.

If you look through the architecture you should quickly find elements within it that compare directly to the standard quotation or sales order report.

Here is a sample quotation that was produced using the default QWeb template we are viewing:

So like we should always do, let's make a small change and see the result. I cannot emphasize enough how important it is to back up frequently and make small changes when you are first getting started.

So let's assume for this change we want to have **Quote #:** instead of **Quotation N°** on our report.

This is relatively simple. Click **Edit** as you would on any Odoo form to edit the template. Then scroll down into the template until you find `Quotation N°`:

```
<h2>
    <span t-if="doc.state not in ['draft','sent']">Order # </span>
    <span t-if="doc.state in ['draft','sent']">Quotation # </span>
    <span t-field="doc.name"/>
</h2>
```

Replace the selected text you see in the preceding screenshot, `Quotation N°` with `Quote #:`, and then save the document. Be very careful of the changes you make until you understand XML. A less common but worst-case possibility is that a mistake you make will still allow the document to save, but it will break the application.

> The XML is represented with ordinary text, a little trick you can use is to copy and paste the XML into a text editor to have a quick backup in case you make a mistake or do not get the results you expected.

After you have saved, you should be able to print the document and see your change when you print the quotation again:

		We Make Great First Impressions Last
Silkworm, Inc.		
102 South Sezmore Drive		
Murphysboro, IL 62966		
United States		

Invoice and shipping address:
Mike Smith
444 South Main
Murphysboro, IL 62966
United States

Mike Smith
444 South Main
Murphysboro, IL 62966
United States

Quote #: SO015

Quotation Date: **Salesperson:**
04/23/2015 04:09:41   Administrator

Description	Taxes	Quantity	Unit Price	Price
Medium White T-Shirt		21.000	7.00	$ 147.00

Total Without Taxes	$ 147.00
Taxes	$ 0.00
Total	$ 147.00

We have successfully changed it. This change is small, but even just knowing how to do this will allow you to often add many things you need to a report.

Creating a new QWeb report in Odoo

Like we learned in Chapter 13, *Customizing Odoo for Your Business*, you often are almost never better off creating a blank record and instead are better served by duplicating an existing record that is close to what you want. For example, we duplicated the Sales Order action and menu to create our custom Sales Order - Rush options.

Let's do the same thing for a new custom Odoo report. Simply go to the **Settings** menu and pull up the **Reports** option to list the available reports. Use the search filter to locate the sales order form and duplicate it. Now make any changes you'd like. You could then tie your new report to an action using the skills you learned in Chapter 13, *Customizing Odoo for Your Business*.

Learning more about the power of QWeb templates

Now that we have learned to make that small change, let's look a little closer at how Odoo is able to use the exact same template for both the quotation and the sales order. In fact you may have already figured out how Odoo does this from looking a little bit around the code we just modified.

One of the best things you can do to learn how to modify reports is looking at existing reports within Odoo and seeing how they accomplish what you may wish to accomplish. When trying to solve a problem, see if you can find another report in Odoo that is already doing something similar to what you want.

 Often it can make it a lot easier to copy and paste part of template you need and then change it rather than trying to get all the < . / ?> syntax all straight and just right. It's easier if you are working from a reference point.

Using a t-if to create a dynamic QWeb template report

Much of the power of QWeb allows for you to conditionally show information depending on various fields and information within the document. In this case, Odoo is looking at the status of the order to determine if the template should have a label for **Quote** or for **Sales Order**. Let's take a close look at the syntax, so we can understand exactly what it means.

If you don't understand at least some basic XML, now would be a good time to look at some of the available resources we have listed in the appendix, or do a simple Google search on an XML tutorial:

```
<span t-if="o.state not in ['draft','sent']">Sales Order # </span>
<span t-if="o.state in ['draft','sent']">Quotation #:</span>
```

You will notice that each section is wrapped in its own set of <span> tags. Then right after the first span tag starts we have the t-if= condition. Everything between the double quotes is the condition that will determine if what is included between the span tags will print.

In this specific case, o represents the order. We use the period or dot notation to specify which field we want to check. In this case, it is the State field. Even if you are not a programmer, if you read it out and ignore the confusing syntax and punctuation it should start to make sense. The only difference between each of these t-if statements is the word not, which follows o.state. When the state of the order is not in draft or sent, then it is an order. When the state of the order is in draft or sent, then we have a quote.

If XML and programming is very new to you, some of this could be a bit confusing. But if you take some time to look at existing reports and use some of the resources in the appendix to learn more, you will be customizing Odoo reports in no time.

Summary

In this chapter, we started by walking through how to change the templates on company reports through Odoo, to modify the header of your report. Next, we learned about Odoo's reporting system and how reports are organized within Odoo. Finally, we learned how to use the powerful QWeb template language, to make changes to reports.

In the next chapter, we will explore how to build our own custom applications in Odoo.

15
Discovering Custom Odoo Modules

In previous chapters, we covered how to install, configure, and even customize Odoo's standard modules. While Odoo has a lot of built-in and community modules, it is inevitable that there will be quite a few businesses that will have requirements that are difficult to achieve with the currently available modules. The Odoo framework offers developers the capability of extending Odoo to accomplish business objectives and (hopefully) make Odoo fit in better with the workflow of the company. It is important, however, before attempting to write custom Odoo modules that you completely understand the functionality of Odoo and the various modules that are already available in the community to ensure that you are not reinventing the wheel.

In this chapter, we will cover:

- Learning the basic structure of an Odoo module
- Using a module to add additional fields to your Odoo system
- Extending the views in your Odoo instance to include new fields
- Making changes to the available states to use in an Odoo workflow

Through careful configuration, many business objectives can be achieved without writing custom modules. It is important to make sure that before you go down the path of writing custom Odoo modules that you make absolutely sure that the business requirements are clear and you have thoroughly explored all the options available inside of Odoo. There are many settings that provide additional functionality to the Odoo system. You don't want to spend days, weeks, or even months building an Odoo module to then find out that much of that functionality was already available.

The goal of this chapter is to introduce you to custom module development in Odoo. Even if you are a beginning developer and don't know much about programming, you should be able to follow along and build a module in Odoo. If you don't know Python or XML, you will likely find some aspects of this chapter a little more challenging. Fortunately, there are many resources in the Odoo community that can help you along your path to Odoo development.

Exploring the Odoo application and module directory

In addition to the built-in Odoo modules and the various settings that can change the way Odoo functions, there is also a growing collection of custom Odoo modules written by the community. When you find a business requirement in which you believe you may need to do some custom module development, take the time to go to the Odoo application repository and search for modules that could perhaps fit the purpose. Even if the module is not exactly what you are looking for, there can often be a lot of valuable code in those modules that can help you with your own module development.

 You can find the Odoo application and module repository
at: https://www.odoo.com/apps

Even more importantly, these applications are invaluable for studying how to build and customize applications in Odoo. When you get stuck trying to solve a development problem, there is no better source of how to solve it than the Odoo source code and the available applications you can find in the Odoo application repository.

In Odoo development, we can sometimes refer to custom applications and modules interchangeably. For the most part, modules are customizations that extend Odoo applications with additional functionality. Odoo applications would typically add an entire new set of features that would be more substantial than a module. There is however, no real difference between them in how you approach development. Both are created in the same way.

Building our first Odoo module

One of the best features of the Odoo framework is that we can extend Odoo and write our own modules without having to modify any of the Odoo source code. Instead, the changes we make are all contained in their own directory and within their own files.

The primary advantage to this point is that when Odoo modifies their source code with patches or bug fixes, we do not have to worry about our changes getting overwritten. Also, while we may still need to modify our code if Odoo makes a dramatic change to their source code, there is a reasonable chance that the changes required will be minimal.

> **WARNING**:
> Like in other areas of Odoo development, make frequent backups of your databases. Some of the examples we will show make changes to the database that can be difficult to undo.

Each module in Odoo has basic requirements for it to be properly recognized by the Odoo framework and installed. Once we successfully install our module, then the framework will extend Odoo with the appropriate functionality.

Preparing your basic development environment

Before you can begin creating an application you must get yourself situated on the server that you wish to do your development. This includes having an installation of Odoo that you can use just for development. You should not be doing any development on a production server. For this example, we are going to assume that you have followed installing Odoo on an Ubuntu server as was outlined in Chapter 1, *Setting Up Odoo 10*.

Finding your Odoo configuration file and installation

During the installation of Odoo, a configuration file was created that contains the necessary parameters for starting your Odoo server.

> In the Ubuntu desktop, you can use the key combination *Ctrl + Shift + T* to bring up a terminal window.

We will now look at the Odoo configuration file so that we can find the directory for our Odoo installation and modify the `addons_path` to contain our new directory:

```
sudo nano /etc/odoo/odoo.conf
```

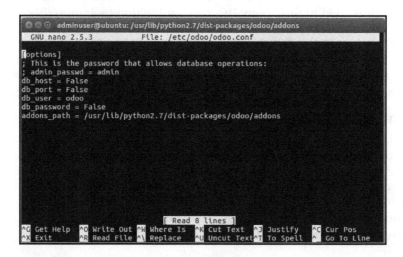

You will notice that the very last line in our configuration file contains the `addons_path` to where the source for the Odoo applications are located.

Nano is a relatively simple text editor. A few of the more important commands you will need to use include:

- *Ctrl + O* to write out any changes you may make. You will be prompted for a file name.
- *Ctrl + X* to exit Nano.
- *Ctrl + C* to cancel an action.

After exiting Nano, you could verify the location of the Odoo applications by using the following command in the terminal:

```
cd /usr/lib/python2.7/dist-packages/odoo/addons
```

If you use the `ls` command, you will then see the directories containing the source code for the Odoo applications.

Specifying a custom directory to hold our Odoo modules

We will begin by creating a directory to hold our Odoo module. We have two options of where we can create the directory to hold our module. With our first option, we could create our directory in the `addons` folder where all the rest of the add-ons for Odoo are stored. This method is easy and allows Odoo to see our module simply by restarting the Odoo server.

A more preferred method, and the one we will use for this example, is to create a separate folder to hold our add-ons. This method has an advantage that we keep our modules separate from the standard Odoo modules.

Create a new directory to hold our modules by typing the following command in the terminal:

```
sudo mkdir /home/mymodules
```

For Odoo to find this directory, we need to modify the Odoo configuration file we looked at previously:

```
sudo nano /etc/odoo/odoo.conf
```

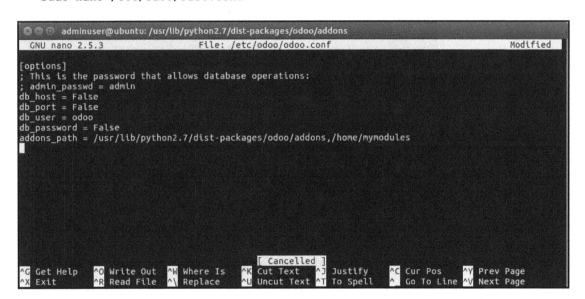

We have edited the `odoo.conf` file to have the `mymodules` directory within our `home` directory to store our custom Odoo modules.

Now we need to create a directory to hold the actual module itself:

```
sudo mkdir /home/mymodules/silkworm
```

When you are getting started it is important that you understand how to create these required files and how they work together. Depending on the build of Odoo you have installed, you can use scaffolding to more quickly create an Odoo application. While the templating can save time, how it is used has undergone a lot of volatility, and the syntax for using it changes frequently. It is therefore recommended that you always know how to create an Odoo application without relying on scaffolding.

Contents of your module directory

Within our module directory, `silkworm`, we will create two files that are required in every Odoo module.

To navigate to our module directory, use the following command:

```
cd /home/mymodules/silkworm
```

These two files must always be named the same:

- `__init__.py`
- `__manifest__.py`

Although it is difficult to tell, in both cases there are two underscores together at the beginning and then another two underscores just before the file extension. You must name these files exactly this way to have a valid Odoo module.

These are Python files and they can be edited with any text editor. We will begin by defining these two required files.

Creating and editing the files

Depending on your operating system of choice, there are a variety of editors you could use to create and edit the files for your module. In Windows, you could use something as simple as Notepad. In Ubuntu, there are also several choices including Nano, Vi, or Vim.

The __init__.py file

The purpose of the _init__.py file is to specify the Python files you wish to include in your module. At the very least you will usually have one Python file, but you could have more depending on the complexity of the module you are developing. If you were to have a Python file with your code and that file was named `codexample.py`, you would have to import `codexample` inside the __init__.py file. Notice you don't have to include the .py extension inside the __init__.py file.

To create the __init__.py file in Ubuntu, make sure you are in the module directory and use the following command:

```
sudo nano __init__.py
```

This will bring up the blank text editor.

For our example, the __init__.py file should contain one line that specifies the name of the file in which we will be placing the Python code for our module:

```
import silkworm
```

The __manifest__.py file

The __manifest__.py file is essentially a description of necessary attributes for your module. Sometimes this file is also called the module descriptor file.

To create the __manifest__.py file in Ubuntu, make sure you are in the module directory and use the following command:

```
sudo nano __manifest__.py
```

The structure in the file is what is called a **dictionary** in Python:

```
{
    'name': 'Screen Printing',
    'version': '1.0',
    'description': """
    This module adds functionality for screen printing companies
    """,
    'author': 'Greg Moss',
    'depends': ['base','sale'],
    'data': ['silkworm_view.xml'],
    'demo': [],
    'installable': True,
    'auto_install': False,
}
```

This is how the __manifest_.py file appears when edited in Nano.

The __manifest__.py file contains a single Python dictionary. Even if you don't know Python, the syntax is rather simple if you have had even a little experience in programming. When you install a module in Odoo, this file describes the details the framework needs to properly configure your module.

name:

The name entry is what will appear in the modules listing inside Odoo.

version:

This allows you to specify a version number for your module. This is valuable, as you extend the functionality of your module and need to keep track of the various releases.

description:

This description will appear when you prepare to install the module in Odoo. It should clearly describe the purpose of the module to someone who may be entirely unfamiliar with it. You should take the time to fill out this entry. Even this little bit of documentation can help someone who is trying to utilize the module in the future.

In this example, notice the triple double-quotes before and after the description value. Python uses this syntax to allow you to continue a string on multiple lines.

author:

Providing the name of the author of your module is also important, as it could help future users track down the main person who can provide assistance.

depends:

The preceding elements were pretty self-explanatory and are mostly for documentation purposes. This entry, however, tells the framework what other modules your module will build upon. At the very least, you will need to include base as one of your module dependencies. In our example, we will be extending the sales order system, so we have also included sale as one of the module dependencies.

data:

The `data` item specifies the XML view files you wish to include in your module. We will cover view files in depth later in this chapter. If you plan to change something in Odoo's forms or user interface, it will most likely involve creating a view file. Other types of data files can be specified here, such as files containing initial data or access rights, but for our example we have named only the `silkworm_view.xml` file.

demo:

Odoo provides a rather convenient method of including demonstration data with your module. When you create your database, you have the option to include demonstration data with that Odoo instance. We have left this blank for our example, but if we wished to make demonstration data available when the module is installed, we could fill in this entry.

installable:

This is an entry that you may use to temporarily disable a module for installation. Most often it will be `True` because you want the ability to install the module in an Odoo instance.

auto_install:

When this entry is set to `True`, Odoo will then automatically install this module when it finds that all the dependency modules are installed. If you have no dependencies, this means that it will be automatically installed when you create a new database. Given Odoo's modular application approach, you typically would not want to have the `auto_install` flag set to true for most module development.

Extending an Odoo model in silkworm.py

Next, we create another file named `silkworm.py`. We will begin by creating a module that performs the same customizations we performed through the developer mode in Chapter 13, *Customizing Odoo for Your Business*.

Why would we want to put our customization into a module rather than just using the developer mode?

First off, changes made through the developer mode are isolated within that instance of Odoo. If you decide you wish to create a new database, you will have to make all the developer changes again by hand. More importantly, when you make the changes in a module, you have much more control over the final results.

The developer mode is very powerful for quickly looking at views, analyzing fields on forms, and understanding more about the Odoo framework. However, it is typically far better to make any actual changes by creating a module rather than modifying the views or models in the developer mode.

Using a module to add custom fields to a model

In Chapter 10, *Creating Advanced Searches and Dashboards*, we added **Date Required** and **Rush Order** to our sales order model. Now let's see how we can do exactly the same thing in our module.

In our __init__.py file, we only had one line, the import silkworm command.

To add the **Date Required** and **Rush Order** fields to our sales order, we can place the following in the silkworm.py file:

```
from .import models, fields

class silkworm_sale_order(models.Model):
    _inherit = 'sale.order'

    daterequired = fields.Date('Date Required')
    rush = fields.Boolean('Rush Order')
```

In Python, the from command allows you to specify which libraries you wish to utilize in your custom classes. For our simple example, we are only pulling in models and fields.

Inheriting from the sales application in Odoo

In our class statement, we specify the silkworm_sale_order class, and it has the models.Model parameter. Remember that when learning the Odoo framework, it will take a bit of time to get familiar to the syntax. For the time being, you don't have to necessarily understand why you are specifying models.Model; just understand that it is required with most classes:

```
_inherit= 'sale.order'
```

For those new to object-oriented programming in general, the _inherit statement essentially makes the functionality of the Odoo sales application available to your class so you can extend it with your own fields and methods.

Next, we can extend the Odoo sales application with our two custom fields:

```
daterequired = fields.Date('Date Required', required=True)
rush = fields.Boolean('Rush Order')
```

You will notice in the syntax that we also specify the data types and provide the labels we want to display in the views inside Odoo. Notice that we have also set `required=True` for the `daterequired` field so that the user will be forced to provide this data when they create a sales order record.

Python conventions

Unlike many programming languages, Python takes white space very seriously. In fact, you must exactly indent your code or the Python compiler will generate an error. For example, the `_inherit` attribute is indented exactly four spaces over from the `class` command.

Adding the fields to our sales order view

Now that we have specified the fields we want added to our sales order model, we must now create our view file that will display the fields in the sales order header. We have specified the name of this file inside of `__manifest__.py` within the `data` entry. For our example, the file name is `silkworm_view.xml`.

Using your editor of choice, create the `silkworm_view.xml` file. In this file, place the following code:

```xml
<?xml version="1.0" encoding="utf-8"?>

<Odoo>
  <data>
    <record id="sale_view_order_form" model="ir.ui.view">
      <field name="model">sale.order</field>
      <field name="inherit_id" ref="sale.view_order_form"/>
      <field name="arch" type="xml">
        <field name="payment_term_id" position="after">
          <field name="daterequired"/>
          <field name="rush"/>
        </field>
      </field>
    </record>
  </data>
</Odoo>
```

Now let's walk through this code and describe what it does. Odoo specifies views using XML syntax. The first line in the file is the standard element you will find at the top of many XML files, specifying the version and type of encoding used.

Next, Odoo view files contain beginning and ending Odoo tags. Inside those tags there are matching opening and closing `data` tags. To modify or add views in your custom Odoo module, you add `record` tags.

Each record must have an `id`. In this case, we also have a `model` tag that is specified as `ir.ui.view`:

```
<record id="sale_view_order_form" model="ir.ui.view">
```

This is a framework convention, and you will learn about other models that are available as you continue to study Odoo development.

Next, we must specify the base `model` with which this view interacts. For our example, this is `sale.order`. This relates directly to the fact we have added the fields to the `sale.order` model in our Python file:

```
<field name="model">sale.order</field>
```

If instead you were adding additional fields to the purchase order header, you would specify `purchase.order`.

> Use the developer mode in Odoo to mouse over fields and determine to which models they relate. To find the view names you need to use, go into manage views in the developer mode. This can save you a great deal of time when developing in Odoo.

Next, let's look at the line that contains `inherit_id`:

```
<field name="inherit_id" ref="sale.view_order_form"/>
```

Much like we had to inherit from `sale.model` when we created our `silkworm_sale_order` class, we must inherit from the `sale.view_order_form` view so that we can add the additional fields.

How did we know that we had to inherit from `sale.view_order_form`? One big trick in finding the value you require is to use the edit form view while in the developer mode.

For this example, while on a sales order in Odoo, choose **Edit FormView** from the developer menu. You will then get taken to the form that shows you exactly the **External ID** you need to add fields to the form:

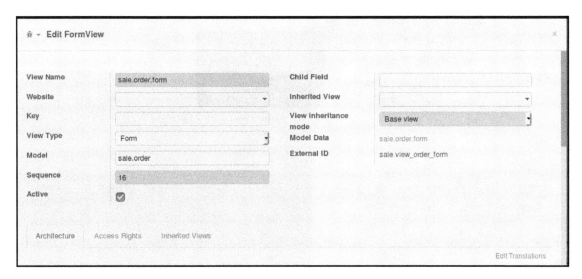

The **Edit FormView** screen shown here shows the **View Name** that has been assigned to the view we are currently looking at. Now we know that the **External ID** we need to use is **sale.view_order_form**.

When you are adding fields to a form, it is important for Odoo to have the information it requires to determine exactly where the fields should go. In this example, we are telling the Odoo framework that we want to first find the field named `payment_term_id`. Next we use `position="after"` to specify that we wish the fields to appear after `payment_term_id`.

 In addition to `after`, the position attribute can be specified as `position="before"` to place a field before that element or `position="replace"` to replace an element. So if instead of `after` you used `replace`, the `payment_term_id` field would be replaced by new fields that we add down below.

Once again, we can use the developer mode to visually find the field name we require. Here we have moved the mouse over the customer reference field to reveal details about that field:

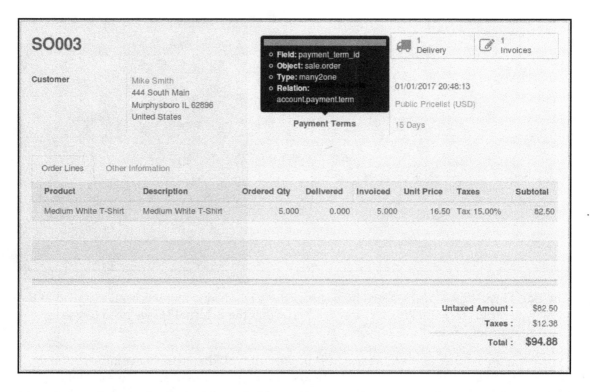

Now that we know where to add our fields, we can specify custom fields to display:

```
<field name="daterequired"/>
<field name="rush"/>
```

Getting ready to install our module

Right now our module is very simple and just adds two fields to our sales order form. We should still quickly review the files you should have in your module directory:

- __init__.py
- __Odoo__.py
- silkworm.py
- silkworm_view.py

When you run Odoo in Ubuntu, it is good practice to run the service under a special account that has limited permissions. This is set up automatically when you use the Debian install. Therefore we need to change the permissions on our module directory so that Odoo can properly access the files. Use this command to set the permissions:

```
sudo chown odoo:odoo /home/mymodules -R
```

To install the module, you must also restart the Odoo server. If you don't restart your server then Odoo will not see your module. The following command can be used to stop Odoo server:

```
sudo /etc/init.d/odoo stop
```

then to restart the Odoo server, use the following command:

```
sudo /etc/init.d/odoo start
```

In the top menu, click on **Settings** and choose **Update Modules List** from the menus on the left. You will then see the following screenshot:

On the **Module Update** screen, click on the **Update** button. Once you have clicked **Update**, Odoo will refresh the available list of add-ons.

Next we will install the module. Click on **Apps** from the menu on the left.

Remove the **Apps** filter from the search box. Yes, this entire process is somewhat counter-intuitive. Once you take off the **Apps** filter, you can search for silk to locate your module for installation.

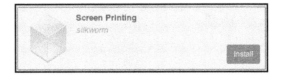

Click the **Install** button to begin the installation process.

After a few seconds, the screen will refresh. You can now pull up a sales order and see the fields added to your form:

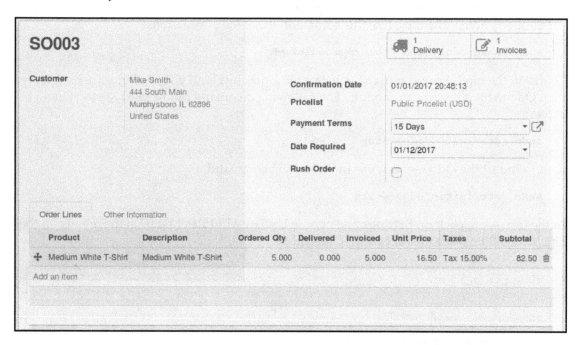

This screenshot of a sales order shows the custom fields added in our module.

When developing, it is inevitable that a module may not install correctly or after installing, you will have an error that will prevent you from logging into Odoo. If you find yourself unable to resolve the error, one workaround to get Odoo back up and running again is to rename the module directory. This prevents Odoo from locating the module to install.

Troubleshooting your module installation

You won't be the first Odoo developer who created a module from scratch to not have it show up in the list of apps. There are a few things you can check if you don't see your application in the list.

First of all, it is always good to know how to check the logfile for errors in your Odoo installation. This is particularly important while you are developing an Odoo module. If you followed the standard Ubuntu Debian install, you can open the logfile and view it with the following command:

```
sudo nano /var/log/odoo/odoo-server.log
```

To demonstrate how this can be useful, we have modified the `silkworm_view.xml` file to contain a small error. When we attempt to install the module, we get an error that we can then view in the `odoo-server.log`:

```
●●● adminuser@ubuntu: /home/mymodules/silkworm
 GNU nano 2.5.3              File: /var/log/odoo/odoo-server.log

    doc = etree.parse(xmlfile)
  File "src/lxml/lxml.etree.pyx", line 3427, in lxml.etree.parse (src/lxml/lxml.etree.c:85131)
  File "src/lxml/parser.pxi", line 1803, in lxml.etree._parseDocument (src/lxml/lxml.etree.c:124287)
  File "src/lxml/parser.pxi", line 1823, in lxml.etree._parseFilelikeDocument (src/lxml/lxml.etree.c:124599)
  File "src/lxml/parser.pxi", line 1718, in lxml.etree._parseDocFromFilelike (src/lxml/lxml.etree.c:123258)
  File "src/lxml/parser.pxi", line 1139, in lxml.etree._BaseParser._parseDocFromFilelike (src/lxml/lxml.etr$
  File "src/lxml/parser.pxi", line 573, in lxml.etree._ParserContext._handleParseResultDoc (src/lxml/lxml.e$
  File "src/lxml/parser.pxi", line 683, in lxml.etree._handleParseResult (src/lxml/lxml.etree.c:112276)
  File "src/lxml/parser.pxi", line 613, in lxml.etree._raiseParseError (src/lxml/lxml.etree.c:111124)
XMLSyntaxError: expected '>', line 13, column 10
2017-01-12 22:37:26,851 20943 ERROR SILKWORM-DEV odoo.http: Exception during JSON request handling.
Traceback (most recent call last):
  File "/usr/lib/python2.7/dist-packages/odoo/http.py", line 638, in _handle_exception
    return super(JsonRequest, self)._handle_exception(exception)
  File "/usr/lib/python2.7/dist-packages/odoo/http.py", line 675, in dispatch
    result = self._call_function(**self.params)
  File "/usr/lib/python2.7/dist-packages/odoo/http.py", line 331, in _call_function
    return checked_call(self.db, *args, **kwargs)
  File "/usr/lib/python2.7/dist-packages/odoo/service/model.py", line 119, in wrapper
    return f(dbname, *args, **kwargs)
  File "/usr/lib/python2.7/dist-packages/odoo/http.py", line 324, in checked_call

^G Get Help   ^O Write Out   ^W Where Is    ^K Cut Text    ^J Justify    ^C Cur Pos     ^Y Prev Page
^X Exit       ^R Read File   ^\ Replace     ^U Uncut Text  ^T To Spell   ^_ Go To Line  ^V Next Page
```

When we look at the error log, we can see the `XMLSyntaxError` that was introduced by the error we put into the `silkworm_view.xml` file. The error log is your first stop in attempting to solve problems.

Now that you know how to identify problems in an installation here are some typical things to check for that could be preventing your module from installing properly:

- Verify that the permissions are set correctly on your files. You can use `ls -l` to list out files with their permissions.
- Make sure that the addon path for your module directory is in the configuration file. You can verify that it is set by examining the log file.
- Stop and restart the Odoo server.

- Check if your __manifest__.py file is missing, is named incorrectly, or has a typo.
- Verify that you have no indentation problems within your Python files.
- Sometimes it can help to shift-refresh your browser when installing a new application.
- Always start simple. When in doubt test out your models first, then add in the view files once you have verified that the models have been modified as you expected.

Using a module to add a filter to a search view

One very nice feature of Odoo is the flexible but easy to use search functionality that is provided on every list view. With a module, you can add additional filter options that make it easier for users to find the information they are looking for. In our real-world example, we have placed an importance on rush orders. Therefore, it would be desirable to have a filter option on our sales order view that will limit our listing to only display rush orders.

Here is how the final search filter view will appear after we implement the module changes:

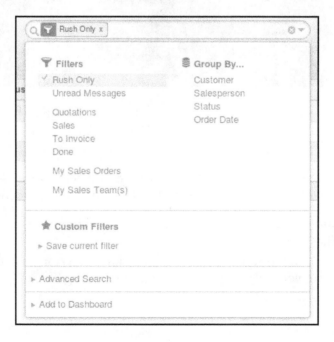

When **Rush Only** is checked, the sales order list view will limit the orders to only those orders that are specified as rush orders. Quickly users can now locate rush orders without creating custom filters. This is an example of how a small change can have significant real-world benefits to usability. Best of all, with Odoo you are making these changes without modifying any of the base Odoo source code.

Adding the code to create the rush order filter

The code segment will naturally be added to the `silkworm_view.xml` file. It will have the same record structure as our other modification. Adding this code segment and updating the module will implement the change we desire:

```
<record id="sale_view_sales_order_filter" model="ir.ui.view">
    <field name="name">sale.order.search</field>
    <field name="model">sale.order</field>
    <field name="inherit_id" ref="sale.view_sales_order_filter"/>
    <field name="arch" type="xml">
      <field name="name" position="after">
        <filter name="rush" string="Rush Only" domain="
        [('rush','=',True)]"/>
      </field>
    </field>
</record>
```

Let's look at some of the more important elements of this code segment. It follows a similar structure as the modification that added fields to our form. The most important thing to do, when looking at the code in any modules, is to identify the `inherit_id` field's `ref` value. This is what ties your view modifications to the view in the base module.

In this case, our `inherit_id` is `sale.view_sales_order_filter`.

Use the developer mode to look up the view name from inside Odoo. Navigate to the view you want to work with and in the developer menu you can choose the **Manage View** to see the **External ID** of the view. You can also use the developer mode to quickly look at the syntax of views and use them to help you determine how your filters should be structured.

Creating the filter

The filter is specified by one line of XML code:

```
<filter name="rush" string="Rush Only"  domain="
[('rush','=',True)]"/>
```

In this code, we specify the name of our filter and the string we wish to display in the search view. The filter is applied with the domain parameter. We specify the field from our sales order model and that it must equal true in order for this filter to be valid.

The technical name for this syntax in Python is a **tuple**. It is possible to include multiple filters in the domain. For example, we can also specify that we only want sales orders that are confirmed by specifying an additional condition in our filter:

```
<filter name="rush" string="Rush Only"  domain="[('rush','=',True),
('state','=','progress')]"/>
```

Odoo considers a confirmed sales order to be in a state specified as progress. With this change, our rush only filter will also limit the sales orders to only those that are confirmed.

Using Odoo to create websites and web services

In the previous examples, we have been extending the Odoo framework to include additional fields in the models and functionality in our views. Odoo also provides a powerful framework for creating your own websites and web services that can integrate easily with Odoo applications.

Let's see how we can create a simple web service that displays the rush orders on a page.

We begin by creating a controller that is tied to a URL. When we navigate to this URL in our browser, the controller will do whatever processing we require.

Create the controller file using the following command in your terminal window:

```
sudo nano controller.py
```

Add in the following code to create a simple output so we can test our controller and make sure it is functioning properly.

Place this code in the `controller.py` file:

```
from odoo import http

class Web_RushOrders(http.Controller):
    @http.route('/orders/rush/', auth='public')
    Def index(self, **kw):
        Return "Rush Orders"
```

You now must edit the `__init__.py` file to include the new controller file:

sudo nano __init__.py

This allows the `controller.py` file we have created to get picked up by the Odoo framework.

Now start and stop the Odoo server and navigate to the following URL: `http://localhost:8069/orders/rush`

You will then see the custom web page displayed:

Now that we have tested our controller and have a very simple page, let's see how we can hook into the Odoo sales application and display our rush orders.

Creating an XML template

For testing purposes, it was fine to output some text to our web page to verify that our controller is working. When you are designing a full website however, it can be very tedious and it is considered bad practice to mix your Python code and logic with your HTML code that you will use to display your website. Templates allow us to more easily separate the programming logic of our applications from the information we display.

Create a file to hold the template that we will use to display our rush orders:

```
sudo nano template.xml
```

Enter the following code into the editor:

```
<odoo>
  <data>
    <template id="index">
      <title>Rush Orders</title>
      <table>
        <t t-foreach="rushorders" t-as="rushorder">
          <tr>
            <td><t t-esc="rushorder.name"/></td>
            <td><t t-esc="rushorder.daterequired"/></td>
          </tr>
        </t>
      </table>
    </template>
  </data>
</odoo>
```

You will see that we are using XML much as we have become familiar with in earlier examples. The HTML code used is simple, and we have only included the name (sales order #) and the daterequired field.

Most significantly, you will see that we are using a foreach loop that will go through the orders and then display the name in one column and then the daterequired in another column.

Now we need to update our controller to pass along sales order data to the template.

Open up the controller.py file and change the contents to the following:

```
from odoo import http

class Webrushorders(http.Controller):
```

```
@http.route('/orders/rush/', auth='public')
def index(self, **kw):
    Orders = http.request.env['sale.order']
    return http.request.render('silkworm.index', {'rushorders':
    Orders.search([('rush','=',True)])})
```

Everything stayed the same until we got inside the `index` method. First we define `Orders` to give us access to the `sale.order` model.

In our final line, we use the `http.request.render` method to access the template and pass along our orders. The `Orders.search` method is passed the filter that limits the order to only those in which the rush flag is `True`.

When we save our `controller.py` file, stop and restart the server, and then update the module, we can see the results in the web browser:

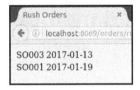

Make sure you flag a few orders in your system as `rush`, or you will get an empty page.

Integrating with the Odoo API

Often, when developing custom applications, you are going to need to create solutions that involve interoperability with other systems and platforms. For example, perhaps you need to integrate with a third-party CRM application to create records inside of Odoo. The API is also quite useful for data migration.

Connecting to the API

Accessing the API is relatively easy. We begin with the code that imports the required libraries and creates a connection to the Odoo server:

```
import xmlrpclib
url = 'http://localhost:8069'
db = 'SILK-DEV'
username = 'admin'
password = 'admin'
```

```
info =
xmlrpclib.ServerProxy('https://localhost:8089/start').start()
url, db, username, password = \
     info['host'], info['database'], info['user'], info['password']
```

Filtering and returning records through the API

We can use our same domain filters that we used to limit rush orders to use the API to return a list of sale order IDs that match:

```
models.execute_kw(db, uid, password,
    'sale.order', 'search',
    [["[('x_rush','=',True),('state','=','progress')]])
```

Using the search/read method

While the preceding code only returns the IDs of the records, the new Odoo API allows you to both search and read the actual fields from the model all with one single API call. Here, we return some fields from the sales order header:

```
models.execute_kw(db, uid, password,
    'sale.order', 'search_read',
    [[['x_rush, '=', True], ['state', '=', 'done']]],
    {'fields': ['name', 'country_id', 'comment'], 'limit': 5})
```

Summary

In this chapter, we learned about the basic Odoo structure for modules. Files must be named exactly the way the Odoo framework expects, and you must follow the structure for your module to properly load into Odoo. We explored how to extend Odoo with additional fields and display them on forms. Later we learned how to create a simple website that integrates with Odoo. Finally, we saw how we could use the Odoo API to create solutions for interoperability with Odoo.

Next we will take a look at the additional features available with the Enterprise edition of Odoo.

16
Comparative Analysis of Community vs Enterprise Edition

Beginning with Odoo 9 and continuing with Odoo 10, Odoo SA started offering a licensed version of Odoo known as **Odoo Enterprise Edition**. This edition offers a number of enhancements over the free Community Edition of Odoo, including an entirely re-designed user interface. In addition to actual enhancements to the software itself, Enterprise Edition also includes version upgrades and bug fix guarantees that require Odoo SA to respond and attempt to fix any known bugs you may come across in the core Odoo applications.

In this chapter we will cover:

- The primary differences between Odoo Community and Odoo Enterprise
- Improved accounting reports and external integration for Enterprise Edition
- Sales Management enhancements for VoIP integration and Subscriptions
- Enterprise shipping connectors
- Manufacturing applications PLM, Maintenance, and Quality

The primary goal of this chapter is to help provide information that will help you decide which version of Odoo, Community or Enterprise, is right for you.

 There are many features and options in Odoo Enterprise that we will not have the opportunity to cover within just one chapter in this book. It is recommended that if you are considering Odoo that you look at your specific requirements and research how Odoo Enterprise may be of benefit.

Getting an overview of Community and Enterprise Editions

While there are a lot of significant and not so significant differences between Odoo Community and Odoo Enterprise, Odoo SA does provide a quick reference sheet that summarizes at a very high-level view, the differences between the two versions. You can find this quick reference at link : `https://www.odoo.com/page/editions`:

Odoo Editions

	Online	Enterprise	Community
General			
Version Upgrades	√	√	×
Bugfix Guarantee	√	√	×
User Interface			
Desktop	√	√	√
Mobile version	√	√	×
New design	√	√	×
Accounting			
Basic accounting	√	√	√
Accounting Dashboard	√	√	×
Dynamic Accounting Reports	√	√	×
Bank Interfaces (U.S., NZ, Canada)	√	√	×
Statement Import: Coda, OFX, QIF	√	√	×
Check Printing & Deposit	√	√	×
Customer Follow-ups	√	√	×
Project Management			

While the checklist does give you a high-level view of what the differences between the various version of Odoo are, unfortunately there is no explanation or additional details as to what each of these features provides. In order to learn more, we have to take a look at the Odoo Community and Enterprise Editions side by side.

Using the Odoo runbot to compare Odoo versions

One consideration about comparing the Odoo Community Edition to the Odoo Enterprise Edition is that Odoo Enterprise requires that you pay license fees. At first you may think that makes it difficult to try Odoo Enterprise for yourself. Fortunately, there is a handy service called the Odoo runbot that will not only help you with comparing Community and Enterprise Edition but can also help you test out any version of Odoo.

You can access Odoo runbot by going to `runbot.odoo.com/runbot`:

When you first come to Odoo runbot, you are presented with a list of the Odoo Community builds starting with Odoo 10. You will notice that there are branches for 7.0, 8.0, 9.0, and the master branch, which is the current build that will eventually become Odoo 11. If you keep scrolling down, you will find many alternative builds that are for specific configurations or testing. For the purposes of this book we will be focusing on the 10.0 branch.

Launching Odoo Community Edition from Odoo runbot

Using Odoo runbot we can launch any of the Odoo instances by clicking on the small Quick Connect icon on the far left which looks like a fast-forward symbol:

After you click the button, a new window will open allowing you to select between two databases.

One of the database is just the base Odoo installation, while the other has all the Odoo applications. For our purposes, we are going to use the database that has all the applications already installed.

The password for all runbot installations is `admin`:

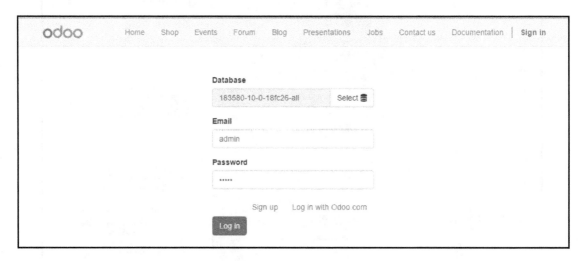

After you have selected the database and entered the password, you log in to the runbot instance just like you would any version of Odoo.

Remember, this is the Community Edition of Odoo 10. While we will be spending most of this chapter discussing Odoo Enterprise and the features that make it unique, it is still very valuable to have the Community Edition open to make it easier to see the differences between the two.

Now we will go back to the Odoo runbot page and open up the Enterprise Edition of Odoo in a separate window.

Launching Odoo 10 Enterprise from Odoo runbot

Now that you have Odoo 10 Community up and running in a window, let's go ahead and start up Odoo 10 Enterprise in a separate window.

First, begin with opening up a new browser window, or at least a new tab in the same browser. Then simply navigate to the Odoo runbot just like we did earlier in the chapter. This time however, instead of launching the Community branch, use the link at the very top labeled **odoo/enterprise**.

After you click the link, the runbot page will refresh and show the branches for the Enterprise version of Odoo.

Now just click on the connect button and login to the Odoo Enterprise Edition the same way you did the Community version.

You should now have both Odoo Community and Odoo 10 Enterprise running in separate windows on your computer, making it easy to switch back and forth and compare features. Best of all you didn't have to provide an email, install any software, or pay any license fees.

 WARNING:
Unlike a standard Odoo installation, runbot installations are only temporary and anything you put into them can be wiped out any time. The runbot is great for situations like this when you just need to check some specific Odoo functionality.

Finally, take the time to arrange the windows in a way that works best for your current workspace and monitor configuration. For example, if you have two monitors you could put the Community Edition on one monitor and the Enterprise Edition on the other monitor, so you easily compare the functionality of the two versions.

Examining the Odoo Enterprise interface

Without a doubt, the most noticeable difference between Odoo Community and Odoo Enterprise is the interface. In fact the entire set of application menus is gone and replaced with a page of icons that allow you to launch any of the installed applications:

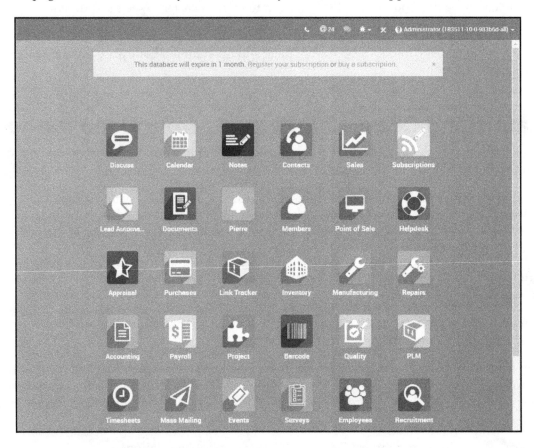

As we are only using this Odoo 10 Enterprise installation to check out the features, you can ignore the database expiration notice at the top.

Examining Odoo 10 Enterprise Accounting

While the interface enhancements are easily the most obvious different between Odoo Community and Odoo Enterprise, the reports in the **Accounting** application are the most valuable functional improvements over their Community version equivalents.

Let's look at the dynamic Enterprise reports by clicking on the **Accounting** icon to launch the **Accounting** application:

Once the **Accounting** application opens, notice that the menu that would have typically been on the side in Odoo Community is now along the top. This design allows for a lot more usable screen real estate for your applications:

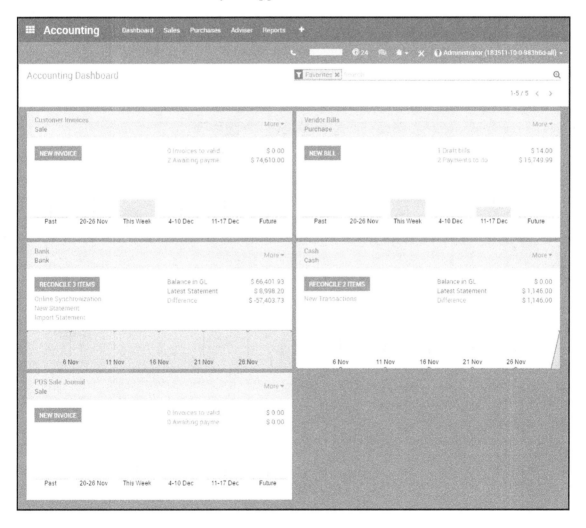

Aside from the **Accounting** menu appearing across the top and the buttons looking slightly different, there is not much difference on this screen between Odoo Community and Odoo Enterprise. One of the primary differences we will look at in this chapter is the set of Accounting reports that comes with Odoo Enterprise.

Looking at Odoo 10's dynamic Accounting reports

In Odoo Community, **Accounting** reports are launched with a wizard that allows you to specify the filters and then create a PDF document that you can open in any PDF viewer. Odoo Enterprise completely does away with that more clunky approach and allows you to bring up a report immediately within Odoo without having to create a PDF file.

Let's take a look at the Odoo Enteprise profit and loss statement, by choosing **Profit and Loss** from the **Reports** menu:

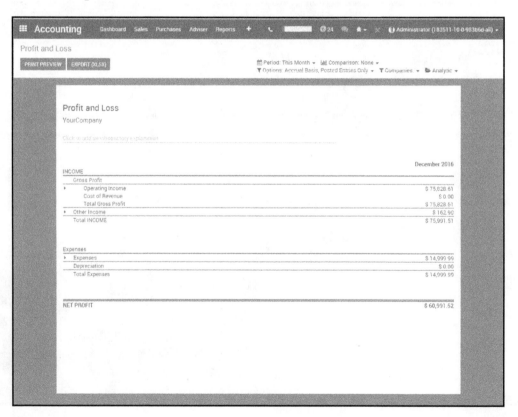

If you take the time to switch over to Odoo Community and attempt to produce the same profit and loss report, you can quickly appreciate the improvement in Odoo Enterprise. Even better, the reports are dynamic. There are a variety of options at the top to change the filters used on the report and to perform comparisons between different periods:

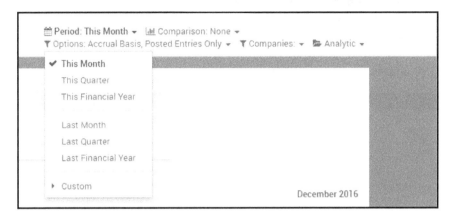

Another nice feature is that the reports have drill down capabilities. For example, you can open up the **Operating Income** and click on the **Product Sales** account to bring up a menu that will take you to the **General Ledger** for the account or allow you to add a note to the item on the report:

Even though the reports show up immediately, it does not mean however that you give up the option to have them in PDF. At the top left of the reports you have buttons that allow you to export the report to PDF or Excel format.

Using the bank integration features of Enterprise Edition

While the dynamic reports may be the most flashy part of the Enterprise **Accounting** application, the Enterprise version also offers more robust import options as well. To get a better idea of what options are available in the Enterprise Edition you can open up the **Settings** in the Community Edition. You will see a small **Enterprise** tag next to the options that are only available in the Enterprise Edition of Odoo:

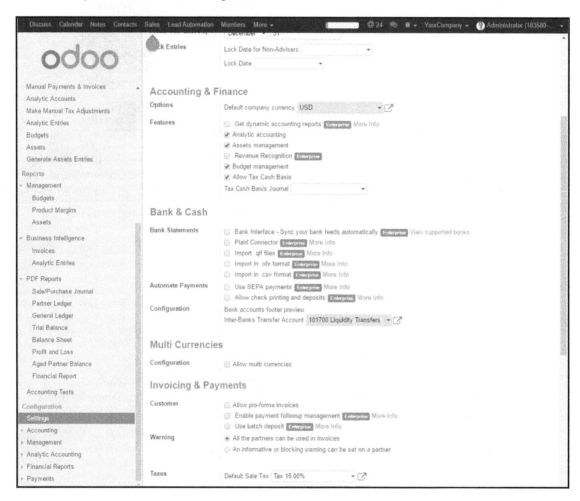

While the **More Info** links look quite hopeful that they will give you the specifics on a given feature, at the time of this writing they all take you to the generic accounting features page that is the same for both Enterprise and Community. Hopefully in the future this will change and users will be able to get direct access to the documentation on a given feature.

Though it is far beyond the scope of this chapter to go down each of these options, you will notice that one at the very top is an option to **Get dynamic accounting reports**. This in fact refers to the reports that we were looking at early in the chapter. Further down the screen under **Bank & Cash**, you will see that there is an option to integrate your Odoo system with banks, along with six Enterprise options for importing data from other accounting systems and auditing payments.

Depending on your own requirements, you may find these options very important in integrating Odoo into your business.

Sales Management enhancements

As **Sales Management** is a very popular Odoo application, it is not surprising that the Enterprise Edition of Odoo contains several options that are not in the Community Edition. While not as significant as the dynamic reports or enhanced interface, the Enterprise options in **Sales Management** can be quite useful depending on your business requirements.

Automating calls with VoIP integration

If you have a sales team that must make or take frequent calls, the built in VoIP integration in Odoo Enterprise can be a real time-saver. Instead of your sales team having to look up incoming calls within Odoo manually, Odoo's VoIP integration will automatically locate the contact within Odoo when the call comes in.

Unlike other Enterprise options, if you are installing VoIP in an Enterprise installation yourself, you will need to add the **Odoo VOIP** application:

Using the VoIP module to place calls is easy. Just add any call you need to make to your phone calls list. You can bring up the dialing panel by clicking on the small phone icon in the top center of the screen. All the calls that you need to place will be listed, along with several other buttons that let you handle how you manage the call, as shown in the following screenshot:

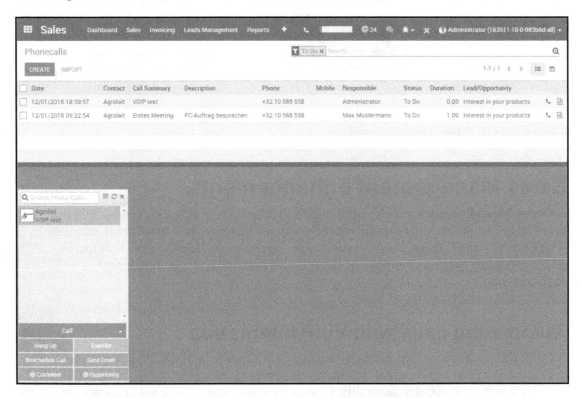

Naturally, to configure and set up the VoIP application, it will require some technical expertise to properly integrate with your phone system.

Understanding the Subscriptions application

Like the VoIP module, the **Subscriptions** application is also installed separately. When you open the **Subscriptions** application, you are presented with a rather full-featured KPI dashboard that lets you track your subscriptions:

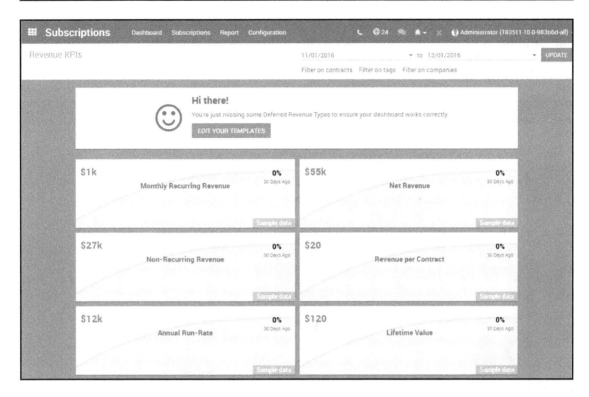

Subscriptions are configured as templates that allow you to easily see critical information such as the number of subscribers. Click **EDIT YOUR TEMPLATES** to see the current templates that are setup in the system. The following screen appears after clicking:

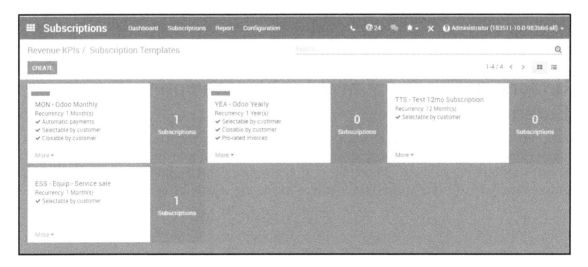

As you can see, the Subscriptions template displays the important information about the subscription in a kanban format. Clicking on a **Subscriptions** template will display the details of the subscription. As you can see, there are many options, as shown in the following screenshot:

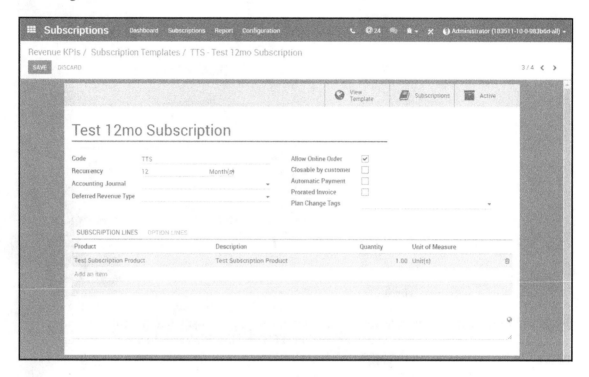

If you are running a business that has subscription-based sales, the **Subscriptions** application is a strong reason to consider Odoo Enterprise.

Understanding the available shipping connectors in Enterprise

As many companies are involved with shipping products, the availability of shipping connectors in Odoo Enterprise could be a major consideration for some companies. These Enterprise shipping connectors hook into Odoo inventory and e-commerce allowing you to automatically create the required transactions inside the selected shipping system.

TIP

If you only need Odoo Enterprise for shipping connectors or another feature or two, check the Odoo App store. There are many third-party Odoo applications that work with Odoo Community that offer similar functionality to Odoo Enterprise.

To configure your Odoo shipping connectors, go into the **Inventory** application and click **Settings**:

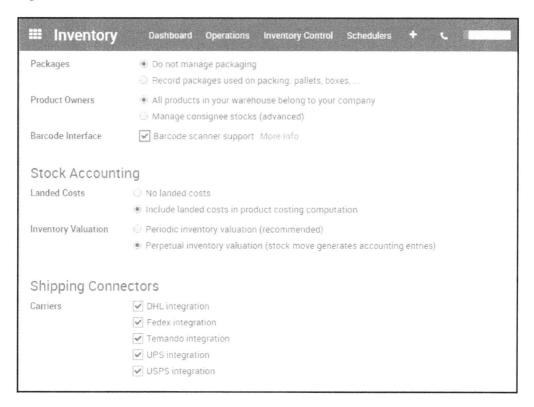

After you have checked which shipping connectors you would like available, you can use the **Delivery Methods** option under the settings menu, to see all the connectors and configure them as required:

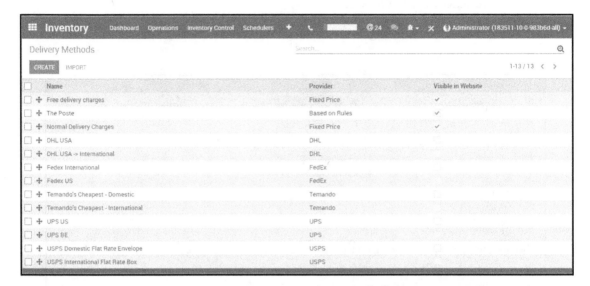

As you can see from the list, Odoo Enterprise offers quite a few connectors. Like with the VoIP integration, you will need some technical expertise and all the configuration information from your shipping system to properly configure the connector.

Understanding the available manufacturing applications in Odoo

Of all the applications the Enterprise Edition offers, the new manufacturing applications may provide some of the strongest incentives to consider the Enterprise Edition, if they fit your business requirements. These applications include **Product Lifecycle Management (PLM)**, **Maintenance**, and **Quality**.

Product Lifecycle Management (PLM)

When you are working in a production environment, it is inevitable that there will be changes to the build process of various items. Perhaps you get a new vendor for a part, or a small design change requires you to add or remove parts from a bill of materials. Managing these changes can be very time-consuming. That is where the **PLM** application comes into play. You can access it by the **PLM** icon from the main Enterprise menu:

Clicking on the **PLM** application icon will take you to the **PLM** Dashboard, which in this demo version is lacking any real data. Click on the **Engineering Changes** button to bring up the kanban view that displays the stages that are currently defined for the product lifecycle:

Here we can see the stages **New, In Progress,** and **Validated** are all expanded. The stages Effective and Refused are the two ways in which the cycle is complete. Either the product change is accepted and becomes effective, or it is refused.

Let's see what an **Engineering Change Order** looks like in the **PLM** application by clicking the **Create** button:

We have filled in a little bit of information on the form so you can see an example of how it may be used. You will notice that we have a **Short Summary** that will describe the change that must be managed.

The **Type** defaults to New Product Introduction. The **PLM** application is designed to work for a new product for which you wish to manage the cycle, or you can create a change order for an existing product.

One nice thing about the **PLM** application is, in addition to managing changes on your **Bill of Materials**, it also will let you manage changes on the **Routing** or on both the **BoM and Routing**. This gives you a great deal of flexibility when managing changes in the production process.

Naturally, to complete our change order, we must know what **Product** the order is for and the associated **Bill of Materials**. Each of these fields you can add on-the-fly, making it easy to configure a new product and the associated change order right from this screen.

Finally, the **PLM** application provides an effective date, so you can decide exactly when you want the change order to go into effect. This makes it easy to manage complex changes that are coming up in future product builds. One example, would be a model year changeover where you want to have all of the bill of materials changes become effective on a specific date, but it could require many weeks of configuration ahead of time.

Handling maintenance requests

Another common requirement in manufacturing operations is the handling of maintenance requests. This can be a machine that is malfunctioning or even a work environment that needs attention to be more productive. The Odoo **Maintenance** application integrates the handling of maintenance requests directly into the manufacturing process. Click the **Maintenance** icon on the main Enterprise menu:

You will then be taken to the **Maintenance** dashboard as shown:

You will see that the Odoo **Maintenance** application divides our maintenance requests by teams. In this case, we have three teams configured to handle the requests. Under the **Internal Maintenance** team, we can click the button that says **3 TO DO** and pull up the requests:

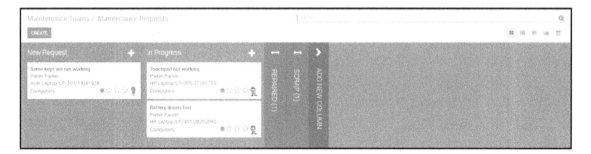

Here we can see that one of the requests is new and the other two requests are **In Progress**. Click on the **Battery drains fast** maintenance request to view the details:

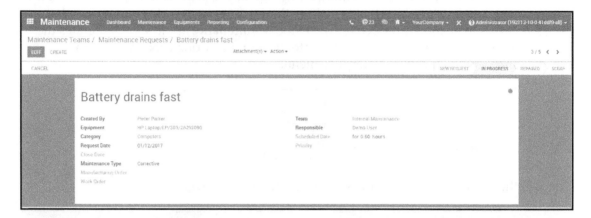

As you can see, there are a lot of details on this request that help us identify exactly what needs to be done to address the problem. In our example, we know who the request was **Created By**, what **Equipment** was involved, and the **Request Date** among other important items.

In addition, Odoo will automatically fill in the **Manufacturing Order** or the **Work Order** if a maintenance request is made during one of those processes. When you are ready, you can set a scheduled date for the repair as well as a priority level to help you manage on which items your maintenance team should be focused.

You can also quickly look at your equipment and see which items have outstanding maintenance requests. Click on the **Equipments** menu to see your equipment in kanban view:

Using this view you can quickly see what equipment needs the attention of your maintenance team.

Managing production quality in Odoo

As your team is manufacturing items, it is inevitable that there will be situations in which you will need to address the quality of the product. This could be because you received raw materials that were not adequate, it could be because there is a problem in the process, or it could be something that needs more investigation to determine why a product is not meeting your quality expectations. Regardless of the reason why, Odoo's **Quality** application can help you better manage quality in your manufacturing operations. Click the **Quality** icon from the main Enterprise menu to view the **Quality** dashboard:

Like the **Maintenance** application, the **Quality** application breaks quality alerts down into different teams. In the dashboard you can see there is currently one quality team defined. The **Main Quality Team**:

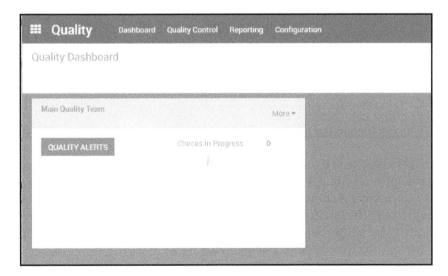

While we don't have any active **Quality Alerts**, let's go ahead and click on the button so we can see the stages that have been setup by default to manage our **Quality Alerts**:

As you can see that **PLM**, **Maintenance**, and **Quality** are all designed in a similar way. Like always we can click Create to enter a **Quality Alert**:

Here you can describe the product, and any of its variants, and which lot the product was in. Knowing the lot is useful in a case that the quality issue is with a specific lot. Items that you specify in **Corrective Actions** are automatically presented when someone begins a manufacturing order. This makes it easy to quickly alert someone in manufacturing when there is a quality issue and provide them with clear instructions on what they need to do to verify or fix the product quality if necessary.

Summary

In this chapter, we learned about some of the more important features that are part of Odoo Enterprise. We learned a bit about the new interface and how Odoo Enterprise restructures the menus to better use screen real estate. We took a look at the powerful dynamic accounting reports, as well as the bank account integration. Next, we examined the sales application and studied how Odoo Enterprise offers VoIP integration, as well as a Subscriptions application. We examined Odoo enterprises shipping connectors and how they could be used to connect with external shipping systems. Finally, we took a look at Odoo's new manufacturing applications that are only available in the Enterprise Edition.

In this book, we have covered a wide range of topics in an attempt to give you a solid foundation. We started, with trying out the online version of Odoo and performing an install of Odoo on Window or Ubuntu. As we moved through the book, you learned about the major applications that make up the Odoo business platform and some real-world examples of how they may be used. Later in the book, you learned how to administer and customize Odoo, as well as using Odoo as CMS for your website. Finally, we finished by exploring the basics of customizing Odoo and even building your own Odoo applications.

Like any ERP system, becoming an expert in Odoo will require many hundreds of hours of research, experimentation, and hard work.

Locating additional Odoo resources

Odoo is built using a variety of open source technologies and components. This Appendix includes a list of resources that can extend your knowledge in supporting an Odoo installation.

Locating essential Odoo documentation

If you are looking for the official Odoo documentation, you can visit the following link:

```
https://www.odoo.com/documentation
```

This documentation currently automatically directs you to the latest Odoo version and provides direct access to the primary technical documentation. The quality and scope of the documentation has increased greatly over the past several years. This is where you will want to look first when learning more about Odoo development.

Visiting the official Odoo help forum

When you run into issues with your Odoo installation or you have questions about specific features, one of the best resources available is the official Odoo help forum. On that site you can search for questions and if your specific question has not been addressed, you can then ask your own question. This has become a very active forum and is worth a visit if you need help with a problem.

```
http://help.Odoo.com
```

The Odoo Community Association (OCA)

The **Odoo Community Association** (OCA) is a nonprofit organization whose mission is to support the collaborative development of Odoo features and promote its widespread use. The OCA is committed to providing resources and legal support to the Odoo community and insuring that Odoo remains both open source and maintained for the public benefit.

```
https://odoo-community.org/
```

Finding Odoo applications and modules

Odoo 10.0 is typically downloaded in a format that already comes with many applications and modules available for installation. However, there are many more modules in the online repository. If you are thinking about making any customizations in Odoo, check this link to make sure someone else has not already done the work for you:

```
https://apps.Odoo.com/
```

Here you can browse for modules by the application they are associated with and even filter out applications by the version number of Odoo you require. Starting with Odoo 9, there are now paid applications in the library as well as free offerings.

Getting the latest Odoo 10 release notes

This link will take you directly to the Odoo 10 release notes:

```
https://www.odoo.com/page/odoo-10-release-notes
```

Downloading Odoo from GitHub

Odoo branches are maintained on GitHub. The primary Odoo project is located at:

```
https://github.com/odoo/odoo
```

Locating resources on Ubuntu

While you can certainly work with Odoo under the Windows environment, most of the community agrees that it is better to run your Odoo server under Ubuntu. At the time of publication, the stable release version is 16.04. Here are some resources that can help you get started with Ubuntu.

Official Ubuntu website

If you are planning on working with Odoo and Ubuntu you will want to begin by getting familiar with the official Ubuntu website:

```
http://www.ubuntu.com/
```

Direct download of the Ubuntu server or desktop

Resources for downloading Ubuntu in various formats and configurations can be found at the following URL:

```
http://www.ubuntu.com/download
```

Official Ubuntu documentation

The official Ubuntu website has a comprehensive set of documentation that is a great reference for troubleshooting your Odoo installation:

```
https://help.ubuntu.com/
```

Getting access to additional developer documentation

The Odoo framework provides a lot of power but also comes with a fairly steep learning curve. While `Chapter 16`, *Comparative Analysis of Community and Enterprise Edititon* of this book will help you get started, if you are serious about developing for Odoo, you will find you the following resources valuable in your pursuit.

Getting quick access to Odoo installations using Odoo Runbot

Wouldn't it be great if you could try out a variety of Odoo builds and installations quickly and easily without going through all the time and complexity of an Odoo installation? Well fortunately the Odoo Runbot provides you with many different Odoo branches that you can connect to and actually review the build for yourself.

This resource divides the installations by version, build, and age of the version. Even better, you can get immediate access to the branches right on GitHub.

```
http://runbot.Odoo.com/
```

Finding Postgres resources

With supporting any ERP system, it is important to understand the underlying database architecture. Odoo 10.0 requires Postgres 9.3 or later as the backend database. Here is a list of resources that can help you maintain your Postgres server:

Official Postgres website

While Odoo handles many of the complex database management tasks you would have with other ERP systems, there will be times when the official Postgres website will be useful in maintaining your Odoo installation:

```
http://www.postgresql.org/
```

Downloading Postgres

The following links are for downloading Postgres in various configurations:

```
http://www.postgresql.org/download/
```

```
http://www.postgresql.org/download/linux/ubuntu/
```

Postgres documentation

The standard Postgres documentation will be useful when you need to perform operations on your Odoo database.

```
http://www.postgresql.org/docs/9.3
```

Locating Python resources

Odoo modules are created in Python, a free and powerful programming language. Most module development will require you to at least become familiar with the basics of Python. Odoo requires Python version 2.7. Python version 3.x and above are not supported by the current builds of Odoo.

Official Python website

The following is the link to the official website for Python:

```
http://www.python.org/
```

Downloading Python

Depending on the platform on which you plan to install Odoo, you may need to download Python before you can install Odoo:

```
http://www.python.org/download/
```

Python documentation

Writing modules or applications in Odoo requires a basic knowledge of Python. The official Python documentation can be located here:

```
http://docs.python.org/2/
```

Finding XML resources

Odoo views are designed and maintained in **Extensible Markup Language** (**XML**). A basic understanding of XML will help you in customizing views, modifying search criteria, and managing workflows. Here is a list of XML resources.

World Wide Web Consortium XML resource page

This is the official page for the XML specification:

```
http://www.w3.org/XML/
```

XML tutorials and documentation

If you are just beginning to learn XML, make sure and visit this excellent collection of tutorials and documentation:

```
http://www.w3schools.com/xml/
```

Alternative Reporting solutions

Many companies will want more reporting options that are currently not available in Odoo. Like many other ERP systems, companies will typically utilize and integrate alternative reporting platforms. With the improved reporting in Odoo 10 there is less interest in some of these reporting solutions. Still there are a few that are popular in the Odoo community

OCA Alternative Reporting Engine

The OCA alternative reporting engine is the result of a project by the OCA and is hosted on GitHub. There is a 10.0 branch although it does not appear to be undergoing any major development:

```
https://github.com/OCA/reporting-engine
```

Aeroo Reports

Aeroo Reports is a reporting engine for Odoo that is based on the Aeroo Library. Report templates are created in **Open Document Format** (**ODF**) and were considered a very popular alternative to RML reports in Odoo 7. This reporting solution seems to have dropped off significantly with QWeb now the primary method for delivering reports in Odoo. There is a version for the master branch that still may be useful depending on your reporting requirements:

```
https://apps.openerp.com/apps/modules/master/report_aeroo/
```

Jaspersoft reports

Jaspersoft offers a variety of both open source and licensed reporting solutions. There is a report server as well as a very nice graphical report editor available.

Community edition of JasperReports Server

The community edition JasperReports Server can be found at:
```
http://community.jaspersoft.com/project/jasperreports-server
```

Community edition of iReport Designer

The server software provides report access and processing. To design reports graphically you will need to download the iReport designer for the operating system of your choice. Jaspersoft now has a product called Jaspersoft Studio that replaces their previous report editor:

```
http://community.jaspersoft.com/project/jaspersoft-studio
```

Pentaho/Kettle

Pentaho, also known as Kettle, is a very useful tool for data translations and for reporting out to Excel or other formats. It doesn't provide the extensive reporting tools of Jasper but is very robust integrating Odoo with other systems and creating automated data exports. Depending on your needs, Pentaho may fit your needs.

```
http://kettle.pentaho.com/
```

Index

__manifest__.py file 349

A

Accounting and Finance application
  chart of accounts, viewing 145
  installing 144
  specific account information, obtaining 146
  transactions, posting to accounts 147, 148, 149
actions
  about 303, 318, 319
Aeroo Reports
  about 395
  URL 395
architecture, Odoo
  about 17, 302
  actions 303
  coding, with Python 17
  Model-View-Controller (MVC) design 18
  models 302
  PostgreSQL database 17
  URL 17
  views 302

B

bill of materials (BOM)
  about 123
  availability, checking 126, 127
  building 123, 124
  production, confirming 125, 126

C

calls
  scheduling 87
chart of accounts
  defining 144

company information
  saving 49
  setting 48, 49
company report, configuration
  internal report header, modifying with QWeb 329, 330
  paper format, specifying 328
  setting up 324, 325
  Wktohtmlpdf installation, issues 325, 326, 327
content management system (CMS)
  about 255
  DotNetNuke (DNN) 256
  Drupal 256
  Evoq 256
  Joomla 256
  website builder, using 257
  WordPress 256
Coordinated Universal Time (UTC) 22
CRM application
  Access Rights tab 65
  account manager, assigning 63
  CRM Dashboard 63
  e-mail address, specifying 65
  installing 62
  sales representative, assigning 63
  salesperson, assigning to customer 68
  setting up, for sales 65
  user name, specifying 65
CRM system
  case study 61, 62
  designing, with company goals 61
  designing, with mission statement 61
  personalized customer experience, creating 60, 61
  used, for managing customer experience 60
  using, as business strategy 60
custom accounts

journal entries, creating 162, 163
legal reports, examining 161
setting up 157, 158, 159
specifying, for product category 159, 160
custom dashboards
creating 249, 250, 251, 252, 253
custom directory
contents, adding 346
files, creating 346
files, editing 346
specifying, for custom module 345, 346
custom field
adding 307
creating, in sale order model 310, 311, 312
form view, editing 312, 313, 314
models, viewing 308, 309
custom module
building 343
configuration file, searching 343, 344
custom directory, specifying 345, 346
development environment, preparing 343
fields, adding to sales order view 351, 352, 353, 354
installation, troubleshooting 356, 357, 358
installing 354, 356
model, extending in silkworm.py file 349
model, inheriting from sales application 350, 351
Python, conventions 351
used, for adding custom fields to model 350
custom report
creating 338
custom search
performing 246, 247
Customer Relationship Management (CRM) 43, 59
customer
Accounting, editing 43
Company option, selecting 40
creating 39, 40
data, entering into Odoo forms 41, 42
Sales & Purchases, editing 42

D

database manager
accessing 238, 240
database

backing up 168, 169, 305, 306
creating 33
default language, specifying 35
demonstration data, loading 34
e-mail, selecting 35
managing 35
name, selecting 34
password, selecting 35
restoring 170, 306
Debian repository 24
developer documentation
access, obtaining 391
Odoo runbot, using for quick access to installation 392
developer mode
activating 303, 304
exiting 304
dictionary 347
DotNetNuke (DNN) 256
Drupal 256
dynamic QWeb template report
creating, with t-if statement 339

E

e-commerce 278
e-commerce platforms
about 278
Magento 278
Shopify 278
Volusion 278
Yahoo's Aabaco Small Business 279
Employee Directory
installing 204
employee, HR applications
coach, specifying 208
creating 205
department, creating 206
departments, managing 210
HR Settings page 209
job titles, managing 207
manager, specifying 208
personal information, adding 208, 209
events
scheduling 87, 88
Evoq 256

Extensible Markup Language (XML)
   resources 394

F

files, custom directory
   __init__.py file 347
   __manifest__.py file 347, 349
   creating 346
   editing 346
filter
   adding, to search view with module 358, 359
   creating 360
   rush order filter, creating 359
   saving 248, 249
   using, in list views 243, 244
form view
   editing 312, 313, 314

G

General Information, work center
   Capacity 133
   Efficiency Factor 133
   Overall Equipment Effectiveness (OEE) target 133
   time, setting 134

H

Human Resource (HR) applications
   Employee Directory, installing 204
   employee, creating 205
   Leave Management application, installing 213
   modular approach 203
   Recruitment Process application, installing 217, 218
   Timesheets application, installing 210, 211, 212

I

implementation strategy, Odoo administration
   business continuity, focusing 167
   development server 166
   documentation 166
   planning 166
   production server 166
   staging server 166
interface, Odoo
   about 37
   search box, using 38
   views, selecting 38
internal report header
   modifying, with QWeb 329, 330
internationalization
   about 183
   currency, selecting for purchase order 191
   international currencies, setting up 187, 188, 189, 190
   language translation, configuring 183, 184, 185
   supplier price lists, managing 192, 193, 194, 195
   translation features, using 186, 187
invoice
   creating 56, 57, 58
   options 57

J

Jaspersoft reports
   about 395
   resources 395
Joomla 256

K

Kanban view 38
Kettle 395

L

language translation
   configuring 183, 184, 185
Leads
   about 83, 84
   converting, into opportunity 86
   creating 84, 85
   turning on, in Odoo 10 84
Leave Management application
   department, setting for leave 215
   duration, modifying 215
   employee, setting for leaves 215
   installing 213
   leave request, creating 213
   leave request, saving 215
   leave requests, approving 216
   leave type, selecting 214

mode, using 215
line items, sales order
  delivery, processing 53
  description, obtaining 53
  entering 52
  invoice, creating 53
  product field, selecting 53
  quantity, specifying 53
  quotation sales order, saving 54
  taxes, adding 54
  unit price, populating 54
Linux kernel 19
Long Term Support (LTS) 21

M

Magento 278
manufacturing applications
  maintenance requests, handling 383, 384
  Product Lifecycle Management (PLM) 380, 381, 382
  production quality, managing 385, 386
manufacturing orders
  bill of materials (BOM), building 123, 124
  creating 117
  creating, with routing and work center 137, 139, 140
  delivering 118
  Manufacturing Resource Planning (MRP) application, installing 119
  product, producing 118, 128, 129
  production, managing by work orders 130, 131
  real-world example 118, 119
  routing orders, creating 134, 135, 136
  routing, assigning to bill of materials 136
  stock valuation, analyzing 129, 130
  work center, creating 132
  workflow, defining 118
Manufacturing Resource Planning (MRP) application
  final product, configuring 121, 122, 123
  installing 119
  manufacturing order, creating 119, 120
meetings
  additional options, specifying 91, 92
  attendees, adding 89

details, specifying 90
  reminders, setting up 91
  scheduling 87
  tags, specifying 90
menu
  adding, to website 267, 270
  creating 320, 321
  managing, on website 269, 270
Microsoft Windows Odoo installation
  selecting 19
  Ubuntu 19
  Ubuntu, optional requirement 19
mobile device
  website, previewing 266, 267
Model-View-Controller (MVC) design
  about 18
  controllers, authoring 18
  models, designing 18
  views, rendering 18
models
  about 302
  viewing 308, 309
module descriptor file 347
module directory
  exploring 342
  URL 342
module
  filter, creating 360
  rush order filter, creating 359
  URL 390
  used, for adding filter to search view 358, 359
multiple advanced searches
  specifying 248
multiple companies
  managing 197, 198
  multi-company solution, implementing 200
  second company, setting up 199, 200

O

Object Relational Database Management System (ORDMS) 17
OCA alternative reporting engine
  about 394
  URL 394
Odoo 10 Enterprise

Accounting, examining 370, 371
dynamic Accounting reports, viewing 372, 373
Odoo 10
  Leads, turning on 84
  URL 22, 390
Odoo administration, considerations
  about 165
  database, backing up 168, 169
  database, restoring 170
  implementation strategy, planning 166
Odoo API
  connecting to 363
  integrating 363
  read method, using 364
  records, filtering 364
  records, returning 364
  search method, using 364
Odoo application
  exploring 342
  URL 390
Odoo Community Association (OCA)
  about 390
  URL 390
Odoo Community Edition
  overview 366
Odoo e-commerce
  accessory products, displaying 294
  additional configuration options 287, 288
  advanced options 293
  alternative products, displaying 293
  basics 281, 282
  checking out 296, 297, 298
  draft sales order, viewing 295
  installing 279, 280
  PayPal, adding as payment processor 298, 299, 300
  picture, adding to product 283, 284
  product order, modifying on store 288, 289
  product price, setting 283
  product, describing 286
  product, publishing 286, 287
  shopping cart, adding 294
Odoo Enterprise Edition
  bank integration features, using 374, 375
  interface, examining 370

manufacturing applications 380
  overview 366
  Sales Management 375
Odoo implementation
  requirements, gathering 32
  Silkworm case study 32
  with modular approach 32
Odoo installation, on Ubuntu
  about 24
  sources.list file, modifying 24
  testing 25
Odoo installation, on Windows OS
  about 21
  all-in-one Odoo installation, performing 22
  PostgreSQL, configuring 23
Odoo Online Pricing
  URL 16
Odoo online
  about 10
  accessing 10
  browser requirements 11
  free trial, accessing 11, 12, 13, 14
  mobile phone support 11
  subscribing 15, 16
  tablet support 11
  trial version, using 15
  URL 11
  using, without subscription fees 17
Odoo runbot
  Odoo 10 Enterprise, launching 369
  Odoo Community Edition, launching 368
  URL 367, 392
  used, for accessing to Odoo installations 392
  used, for comparing Odoo version 367
Odoo SA 15
Odoo service
  additional resources, obtaining 29
  admin password, modifying 29
  configuration file, modifying 28
  database management tools, accessing 28
  execution, verifying 25
  in Ubuntu, checking 27
  in Windows, verifying 26
  port numbers, modifying 28
  primary Odoo log file, searching 27

starting, in Ubuntu 27
stopping, in Ubuntu 27
Odoo
  about 9
  and e-commerce 278
  as e-commerce platform 279
  Community Edition 9, 10
  downloading, from GitHub 390
  Enterprise Edition 9, 10
  OS option, selecting 20
  releases 20
  resources 389
  upgrading 21
  URL 21
  URL, for editions 366
  used, for creating web services 360, 361
  used, for creating websites 360, 361
Open Document Format (ODF) 395
opportunities
  about 83, 84
  Leads, converting into 86
Overall Equipment Effectiveness (OEE) 133

P

pages
  adding 268
  adding, to website 267
PayPal
  adding, as payment processor 298, 299, 300
Pentaho
  about 395
  URL 395
PostgreSQL
  about 17
  configuring, on Windows 23
  resources 392, 393
  URL 17
Product Lifecycle Management (PLM) 381, 382
product variants
  setting up 290, 291, 292
product
  Can be Purchased option, selecting 46
  Can be Sold option, selecting 46
  configuring, for procurement 100
  cost price, setting 47

creating 45
entering 44
goods, receiving 110, 111
internal reference 46
Invoicing page, entering 47
invoicing policy 48
naming 46
product type, selecting 102
receiving 109, 110
records, setting to active 102
sale price, setting 47
Sales page 47
saving 48
supply chain information, managing 101
supply chain information, managing with buy
  route 101
supply chain information, managing with Make To
  Order route 101
types 46
Project dashboard 225
Project Management application
  about 223, 224
  installing 224
  real-world project example 225, 226
purchase quotation
  creating 105, 106
  products, adding to request 107
  purchase order, confirming 107, 108
  RFQs, printing 107
  status, updating 107
purchasing process
  about 95
  cost price, setting of product 103
  invoice, settling 97
  product, configuring for procurement 100
  product, receiving 96, 109
  purchase orders, generating 96
  purchase quotation, creating 105, 106
  purchasing application, installing 97
  purchasing information, modifying 102
  quotations, generating 96
  vendor bills, paying 111, 112, 113, 115
  vendor companies versus individuals,
    designating 99, 100
  vendor, setting up 96, 98, 99

vendors, assigning to product 103
warehouse locations, setting up 96
Python
resources 393
URL 18
used, for writing code 17

Q

QWeb
about 323, 324
advantages 338
custom report, creating 338
dynamic QWeb template report, creating with t-if statement 339
used, for modifying internal report header 329, 330
used, for modifying sales order 333, 334, 335, 336, 337

R

Recruitment Process application
employees, hiring 221
employment application, creating 220, 221
installing 217, 218
recruitment, for new job position 218, 219
report modification
skills, developing 324
reporting solutions
about 394
Aeroo Reports 395
Jaspersoft reports 395
OCA alternative reporting engine 394
Pentaho/Kettle 395
reports
modifying 330, 331
organizing 331, 332
types 333
Request for Quotation (RFQ) 105

S

sale order model
custom field, creating 310, 311, 312
sales application settings, in CRM
about 65
Email Messages and Notifications option 67

language, selecting 67
Manager 66
Signature 68
timezone, selecting 67
user password, setting manually 68
User: All Documents 66
User: Own Documents Only 66
Sales Management
calls, automating with VoIP integration 375, 376
enhancements 375
installing 36
shipping connectors, configuring 378, 379, 380
Subscriptions application, using 376, 378
sales order, workflow
about 55
Cancel button 56
Confirm Sale button 55
Print button 55
Send by Email button 55
sales order
customer, selecting 51
entering 50, 51
expiration date, specifying 52
invoice, creating 56
line items, entering 52
modifying, with QWeb 333, 334, 335, 336, 337
payment terms, setting 52
search engine optimization (SEO) 274
search operations
additional fields, specifying 315, 316
customizing 315
search view, editing 316, 317
search view
filter, adding with module 358, 359
search
about 240, 241, 242
custom dashboards, creating 249, 250, 251, 252, 253
custom search, performing 246, 247
database manager, accessing 238, 240
database, creating with demonstration data 238
favorite filters, saving 248, 249
filters, using in list views 243, 244
information, grouping 244, 245
multiple advanced searches, specifying 248

requirements, determining 237, 238
sequences
  managing 195, 197
Shopify 278
Silkworm case study 32
Sunny Hill Lil League project
  additional tasks, creating 231, 232, 233
  creating 226, 227
  project costs, calculating 234
  project tacks, defining 229, 230, 231
  project tasks, completing 233
  project time, calculating 234
  stages, defining 228, 229

T

t-if statement
  used, for creating dynamic QWeb template report 339
themes
  modifying 271, 272
Timesheets application
  installing 210, 212
transactions
  following 150, 151, 152, 153
  posting 157
  results, tracking 157
  viewing 153, 155, 156
troubleshooting
  browser destination, checking 25
  Odoo service execution, verifying 25
  tips 25
tuple 360

U

Ubuntu
  about 19
  Odoo service, starting 27
  Odoo service, stopping 27
  Odoo, installing 24
  resources 391
  URL 19
  used, for Odoo installation 20
user administration
  about 170, 171
  Access Rights 179, 180, 181

group inheritance 177
groups, assigning 174, 175, 176
groups, rules 181, 182
internationalization 183
menus, defining for groups 178
multiple companies, managing 197, 198
sequences, managing 195
user preferences, managing 172, 173, 174
user, selecting 171, 172

V

vendors
  assigning, to product 103
  delivery time, calculating 104
  establishing 104
  minimum quantity, setting 104
  price, setting 104
  product code, designating 104
  product name, designating 104
  validity, setting 104
views 302
Volusion 278

W

web services
  creating, with Odoo 360, 361
Website Builder application
  about 277
Website Builder
  advantages 257
  determining 258
  frequently asked questions web page, creating 269
  installing 258, 259, 260, 261, 262, 263, 264
  limitations 257, 258
  menus, adding to website 267
  menus, managing to website 269, 270
  pages, adding to website 267
  using, for CMS 257
  web page, saving 264, 265
  website, backing up 258
  website, previewing on mobile device 266, 267
website
  creating, with Odoo 360, 361
  description, creating 274

keywords, specifying 274
menu, adding 270
promoting 272, 273
title, creating 274
XML template, creating 362
Windows OS
  Odoo, installing 21
  PostgreSQL, configuring 23
Wktohtmlpdf
  about 325
  installation issues 325, 326, 327
  URL 326

WordPress 256
work center
  creating 132
  General Information, setting 133

X

XML template
  creating 362

Y

Yahoo's Aabaco Small Business 279

www.ingramcontent.com/pod-product-compliance
Lightning Source LLC
Chambersburg PA
CBHW081502050326
40690CB00015B/2890